W9-BVD-091

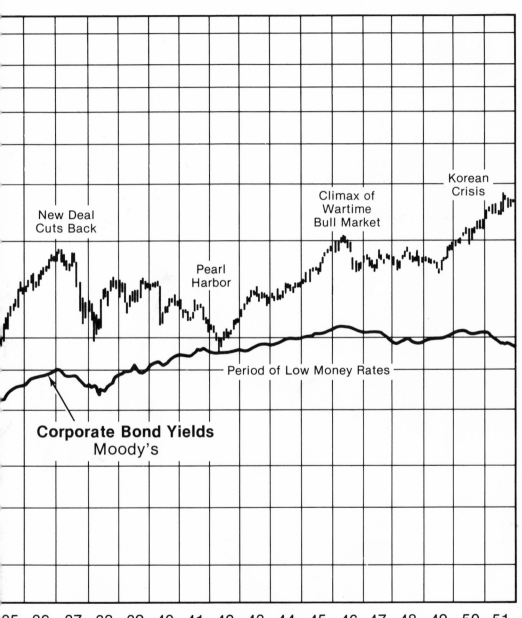

New Deal
Cuts Back

Climax of
Wartime
Bull Market

Korean
Crisis

Pearl
Harbor

Period of Low Money Rates

Corporate Bond Yields
Moody's

35 36 37 38 39 40 41 42 43 44 45 46 47 48 49 50 51

The Ωmega Strategy

How You Can Retire Rich by 1986

By the same author

AROUND THE WORLD ON THE QE2
With Alfred Montapert

The Ωmega Strategy

HOW YOU CAN RETIRE RICH BY 1986

William David Montapert

CAPRA PRESS
Santa Barbara

CAPRA PRESS
Post office box 2068
Santa Barbara, California 93120

Copyright © 1982 by William Montapert.
All rights reserved.
Printed in the United States of America.

12th Printing, June 1983

Library of Congress Cataloging in Publication Data

Montapert, William David, 1930-
   The omega strategy.

   1. Speculation—Handbooks, manuals, etc.
2. Investments—Handbooks, manuals, etc.
I. Title.
HG6021.M79   1982   332.6'78   82-12770
ISBN 0-88496-187-7

Dedicated to the person best suited to manage your money

Y O U !

Preface and Acknowledgments

As a young man I went to school in Switzerland. I quickly learned that there is no more serious, harder working, ambitious, clear thinking and—let's face it—money oriented people on the face of the globe than the Swiss. It seemed logical then that when I reached middle age and began wondering myself how to make enough money to get out of the economic rat race that I would remember my Swiss friends. I decided to play the reporter, asking a group of Swiss bankers how, when and where to make a lot of money fast. I already knew the *who* and why. I was asking for myself, and like everyone else, the *why* was because inflation had lowered my standard of living, making it increasingly difficult to pay my bills.

Arranging the interviews was no problem. I have an old relative in Europe to look after and so travel there frequently. Switzerland is just a hop, skip and jump from everywhere in Europe and as everyone knows in Switzerland there are banks on every corner with the money just oozing out the windows. Inside, naturally, are Swiss bankers. Well, maybe it wasn't quite so easy as I'm pretending but as an attorney having represented many foreign clients I was not completely unfamiliar with the inner sanctums of Swiss banks. What really made the interviews possible is that Swiss bankers are *people* first and foremost. They just happen to be people who live with money. Some even have ideas of their own that don't always reflect the policies or even advice of the institutions they work for. They see much with their own eyes that quickly educate them in the ways of the world and like all of us they sometimes feel a need to talk to someone other than their business associates, wives, mistresses and French poodles or dachshunds. When you know their language and the ritual of building the trust necessary to win their confidence, the rest is easy. It is easy providing your questions are objective, not slanted to pry into the private lives and numbered accounts of individuals. When all of the prerequisites are met, even a Swiss banker can be surprisingly talkative.

I began by making contact, explaining my purpose, then putting down our conversations on paper using a question and answer format. I noticed that when I had compiled a few dozen pages my notes read more like a legal deposition than a book. Still I persevered. After three or four interviews a definite pattern of uniformity in their answers and advice began to emerge and I began listing points under subject headings. It soon became apparent that the consensus felt that our economic world was sick, so I abandoned the straight question and answer approach of the reporter and set about structuring their thoughts as a good doctor analyzes a medical problem—diagnosing the disease (which in this case was inflation), determining its etiology or cause, the possible cure, and specific treatment necessary to effectuate the cure. An economy, like a complex biological organism, could not fully fit this simplistic approach, so I had to take into consideration the complications and previous history of the patient to make certain points meaningful.

I was obliged to return to the question and answer method only once, in Chapter 14, for clarity.

My Swiss contributors asked only two things of me: That my questions be brief and objective having nothing to do with the bank's clients and that their anonymity be protected so they could be perfectly candid. I began by such general questions as how did the peoples of the world get collectively into the economic mess in which they now find themselves? I ended with what specifically can an average American investor do to make money out of all the chaos? In between there were lengthy discussions of inflation, taxation, welfare payments, military spending, debt, deficits and all forms of intriguing and sophisticated ways to make money. I found myself with enough material for several books. So much so that I was forced to severely edit the manuscript. More than a few pearls of wisdom were given back to the sea, perhaps someday to make another book.

Also, as clear-thinking and entertaining as the average Swiss might be, no single interview possessed the necessary unity or interest, so I found myself organizing, and reorganizing again and again until anonymity was no longer assured, it was guaranteed.

What follows then is a distillation and compilation—a compendium organized as to subjects that occurred with the greatest frequency put together to extract the pertinent meaning expressed in words of the greatest clarity. It has been structured (as only a lawyer is wont to do) to prove the most salient points with more than a moderate amount of emphasis. Although I have tried to be apolitical, any political shadings or ideological preference that crept into the text are mine alone. We were attempting to talk money, not politics.

Thus the answers came to be set down with an intermixture of my own supportive material to prove their central points—especially the original one—that *speculative riches really can be won* by anyone—that theoretically even Americans unschooled in the ways of high finance can understand and use the world's economic turmoil to profitable advantage—even to the extent of retiring rich.

The year when this great event—my becoming rich—was to occur, 1986, wasn't chosen arbitrarily. A three year consensus emerged spontaneously, and needless to say, fit my purposes and desires to a tee. I figured I had at least three good years left in me. It seemed to put a meter on my dreams so that I can pace myself, knowing that no matter how bad things look today, tomorrow will be better, for tomorrow I shall be rich.

In preparing the material for publication I have convinced myself and decided to pursue the advice of this financial brain-trust. I thought perhaps you the reader might want to, if not participate quite as fully, at least know what those who live and breathe the rarefied air of a Swiss bank are thinking and *why* they believe it is possible for one to still perform the seeming miracle of getting rich in three short years.

I make no apologies for my ambition. If getting rich is a fantasy, it is at least a harmless one, somewhat like daydreaming of quarterbacking the Dallas Cowboys, running the four minute mile, pitching a perfect game, bowling 300, or knocking out the World's Heavyweight Champion and making several movies about it. Let me make it clear that *you* don't have to want to get rich. Even if you are untroubled by such weighty ambition, by reading the book you should learn something about why certain things are happening to you—such as why your job is threatened or why you have such difficulty paying your bills or why you might not collect your social security or company pension or why your IRA and Keogh plans could prove worthless and why your lifelong savings might be wiped out and your house mortgage foreclosed and why in the midst of these disasters everything will still cost so much—little things like that.

By being exposed to a compendium of eight sophisticated economic minds (not counting my own) you will, in any case, be able to pick from more sophisticated insights and ideas than could possibly have been extracted from one cranium no matter how voluminous.

The rest is up to you. You can believe the contents and conclusions or not as it suits you. Read the book for advice or amusement, fact or fantasy, as you please.

I thank all those anonymously and publicly who have contributed to this book and hasten to add, in closing, that any brilliant insights or happy phrases are usually (but not always) theirs and any omissions and/or errors are regretfully, invariably my own.

William Montapert
Newport Beach, California

Contents

Introduction

If only one-tenth of what the Swiss bankers told me is true, you could be holding in your hands a most valuable book. Why? Because it is information you can use—now. No matter how much or how little money you may have today, you need more. You need more because everything *costs* more. Without these added dollars you are experiencing and will continue to experience a decline in the quality of your existence. You are thus at a point in your life where you are ready for a change.

Perhaps it is no accident that you are reading this book. Perhaps it is fate. Perhaps it is your destiny to be rich and this book can help in some small way to get you started, be an instrument of favorable change in your life and it's exactly the right time for you to read it. There couldn't be a better time!

Why? Because there was a uniformity of feeling amongst the bankers on one central point, that is:

Once in a lifetime there is a period of economic change so disruptive that those with very little money who never speculated in their lives can become rich, while the very rich, seemingly well-entrenched and protected in the most conservative investments, can be reduced to poverty almost overnight. They feel the world is about to enter such a period. How much you know about this change and how well you prepare for it will determine your economic future for a long time to come.

They assured me that in every similar period of history there has been a group of winners—people who understood the secrets of when to speculate and how—who have turned the tables on adversity and prospered in spite of, and even sometimes because of it.

The economic and social problems facing the world today may persist and even be unsolvable *en masse,* but you as an individual can profit, live well, and retire rich even in hard times. How? By developing new ways of seeing and thinking; ideas and concepts more commensurate with our times.

None of the Swiss bankers said he could make one rich. All agreed *one can make oneself rich.* They just might be speaking to you when they say this. Today would be exactly the right time for you to listen to this chorus of voices as they chant the lessons of history, showing you how this remarkable phenomenon of acquiring wealth really works. They insist that at a given period in an inflationary cycle certain speculators win big and I assure you that all that's knowable about speculation can be learned if you're willing to apply yourself. This book doesn't pretend to contain a simple magic formula for riches but it can definitely put you on the right road—the road to knowledge and understanding. We'll begin by trying to remove the impediments—the things that have kept you from becoming rich in the past. Later, we'll concentrate on making you sophisticated—fast. Knowledge is power. Knowledge of how things *really* work will give you a competitive advantage as you advance toward your goal of a rich and fulfilled life, climaxed by a comfortable and dignified retirement.

CHAPTER 1

Whatever Happened to the Nice Old World We Used to Know?

It's still here, but it costs more to live in it. As Socrates said, the desire for things is unlimited, so there are two ways to approach your material life: decrease your wants, or increase your income.

Decreasing Your Wants

The best way to decrease your wants is to decide what you can live without and then stick by it. Many things cost more in time and money than the pleasure and benefits they provide. America's whole economy, including its multi-billion-dollar advertising business, is based on creating wants and needs where they never existed. You have only to turn your back on this game of artificial needs to discover that the first form of wealth is within you. Your attitude toward life at any age can be one of challenge, learning, exploring, and having fun. With the right attitudes you don't need the crutch of external objects and gadgets. It's important to have the quality of enjoying simple things. Without this characteristic, you're going to need a ton of money to compensate. There are millions of people who are rich without money and others who are poor with plenty. Swiss bankers see thousands of them. Only with the right attitudes you are well on the road to real wealth.

By being able to resist temptation and having the right attitudes, you take a giant step forward on the path toward the
realization of true riches.

Increasing Your Income

Having said all that, this book is really about increasing your
income. For most of us there is a limit to what we can do without. There are many things we would all like to have to expand
our potential as intelligent, sensitive human beings. A good
many of these things cost money. Having a certain amount of
money will even buy the most precious luxury of all—time.

"O.K.," you say. "I agree. Now tell me quick, how do the Swiss
bankers think I can make money?"

Unfortunately, there is no pill you can take that can make you
sophisticated, knowledgeable, experienced, wise, or rich. If you
are going to accomplish the objective of living well and retiring
rich, you are going to have to do it yourself with a lot of concentration, study, and hard work. Even then it won't be easy.

These are the appalling facts:

- Over 90% of all Americans are broke at age 65. Only 3%
  have $3,000 a year apart from their meager social
  security payments. Less than 1% are financially
  independent.
- Company pension plans are currently paying off only one
  in twelve employees. There are 50,000 of these such plans
  supposedly worth over $600 billion. Most are unfunded
  and depend on future earnings of the sponsoring
  companies.
- One out of every six senior citizens lives in poverty.
- The average income of those over 65 is one-third those
  under 65.
- It's even worse for women. Of all women over 65, 47% have
  incomes of less than $3,000 per year and only 12%
  receive $7,000 per year or more.

- Retired persons comprise the fastest growing poverty group in America.
- According to a former governor of California, 30% of the dog food sold in Los Angeles County is consumed by senior citizens.

Even if you are not personally facing this kind of hardship, it is easy to commiserate with others who are. In essence, they'd better do something or they're going to be damned poor. Being rich is not just a question of being able to spoil your grandchildren (although that's nice too); it's a question of esthetics and art, the art of living. It means adding a strong ending to a good story—the story of your life.

Positive Action

But you don't exist in a vacuum. You live in the world—an increasingly dangerous and depressing place. Many conditions seem to be beyond your control. The more you think about war, taxes, inflation, big government, crime, pollution, and politics, the worse you'll feel.

The Swiss would have you adopt another approach, one based on thinking and acting positively. There is no need to lament the modern world. The *today* it offers is the only one we have, and we must learn to make the most of it. If there are problems— and even absurdities—then we must learn to understand them, live with them, and use them first to make a good living and then to build a comfortable retirement fund for ourselves and our families. Hard work will make our optimism justified, and this kind of self-fulfilling optimism is the basic energy of civilization.

This is the positive thinker's approach. The dictionary defines optimism as a belief that reality is essentially good, that the good of life overbalances the pain and evil of it. Basically, optimists don't hide from difficulties but anticipate the best possible outcome and do their best to bring it about.

In addition to being optimistic, retiring successfully requires that, like good Swiss, you be *pragmatic*. This means dealing with separate events by recognizing their interconnection, using thought as a guide to action, testing ideas by their practical results, learning to love reality, and bending it to your will. These are the elements we shall stress.

Where shall we begin our pragmatic search for positive solutions to today's investment problems? By emphasizing this point:

WE ARE IN A PERIOD OF GREAT CHANGE. ALL PERIODS OF GREAT CHANGE ARE TIMES OF OP-PORTUNITY AS WELL AS DANGER. INHERENT IN CHANGE IS OPPORTUNITY: THE POTENTIAL FOR IMPROVING YOUR RELATIVE POSITION.

"That's all very nice," you say, "but can I really get rich?"

Yes, you can. Once every fifty years or so there is a period so dynamic, so disturbed, so crazy that those who learn to be risk-takers can get rich and those with vast fortunes to protect, seemingly ensconced in the most conservative investments, can lose it all, almost overnight. The Swiss bankers feel strongly that we are about to enter such a period and how well you prepare yourself now will determine how you will live for the next twenty years. This is a message of hope, not doom.

By viewing time as a constant succession of new opportunities, we can look forward to each day with good feelings and smile as we turn many of the doomsayers' negative laments into positive action for ourselves. So much that is negative is being written that many have become paralyzed with fear. Thinking everything is hopeless, they have come to view the world as a dark and dreary place both for themselves and their children. Fortunately this is not true. If we take a long view we see that materially the Western industrial world is getting richer, not poorer. Every new cyclical upswing takes us to new highs in improved comforts and standards of living. Most of the twentieth century's necessities were luxuries in the nineteenth

century. So it will undoubtedly continue to be in the twenty-
first century. This is not to say there aren't problems in the
world to be surmounted first. If there weren't great social problems we as individuals wouldn't be able to help solve them and
become rich in the process. So let's begin by having the right
attitude, the one that is more fun anyway—an attitude of benevolent (but realistic) optimism. This is the Swiss way.

Using Other People's Pessimism

However, an attitude of benevolent and realistic optimism does
not preclude our being cognizant of others' disenchantment in
order to profit by it.

No healthy, red-blooded Swiss ever had anything against
making money. The pessimism of others often provides the difference of opinion necessary for a good horse race, and horse
races can be wagered on, and wagers can be won.

What are the ingredients of making money today? The same
as they have always been: desire, hard work, intelligence, luck,
and above all, an ability to look ahead. After that it is an ongoing
process of listening to what your own eyes and ears (not the
newspapers and news announcers) tell you, then fitting the con-
fusing bits and pieces of information into a series of plans of
your own making—plans that are integrated and unified—blue-
prints for where you want to go and how you're going to get
there.

To see the value of looking ahead, let's start by looking back
and see what we could have done with knowledge of how the
world would be just two years in the future. Just suppose it is
the spring of 1927 (two years before the crash) and you see great
opportunities on Wall Street while others tremble in fear because, believe it or not, things looked bad then, especially in the
stock market. Ah, those were the days when elevator boys and
bootblacks could, and did, make enough from speculation to
retire in two years. Could it happen again? Yes, it could. There
are great, big, wonderful clouds of mass hysteria that come

along regularly to envelop investors, blind their judgment, and make them mumble phrases like "new era" or "this is it" in their sweet, dream-filled sleep.

"But those were the good old days. Now things are really terrible," you say.

Don't be so sure. Things change fast. Besides, things look better when you are personally thriving. For you, the "good old days" may be tomorrow.

And don't worry. There's room for cautious skepticism too— as long as it's a minority opinion. Just suppose you could be transported back to 1929 with a little cash and a great deal of foreknowledge. When everyone had turned bullish and was speculating wildly, what a time to stand back from the crowd. What a fortune you could have made selling stocks short.[1] In the following months, even though Americans were biting their fingernails and jumping out of buildings, many had reason for optimism. Today, the prophets of doom may be right in that it *is* a time of danger for our world. But this is the optimist's advantage: we know it is a time of opportunity for ourselves as well.

How do you see it? Are you willing to be open to something good happening, or do you view the world's problems as insolvable, yourself as a pawn being moved about by forces beyond your control? If you are flexible—ready to see that the golden age for you may just be starting—maybe you can help make it happen. Maybe you're destined to be one of the far-sighted individuals who historically have used hard times to retire rich.

If, in spite of gloom and pessimism all around, you still see yourself as master of your fate and if you don't think *your* world is going to end tomorrow, you are the rarest of God's creatures: a real, honest-to-goodness optimist. So join forces with the Swiss and get on with discovering some of the opportunities the future may hold for you.

---

1. Usually stocks are bought first then sold later. When you "sell short" the process is reversed. You sell first and buy later. Where does the stock come from that you sell in the first instance? You borrow it from your broker and replace it (pay it back) when you buy later. If you don't understand this, don't worry. The language of speculation will become clearer as we go on.

The pessimists tell us that modern man has tried to invent a new world, and it's not working; that our society has not only failed to find the right answers, it's even forgotten the pertinent questions. The pessimists are quick to point out what's wrong, but they're a little divided in their opinions as to what's causing the problems.

Some blame greedy corporations and labor unions; others point to the perennially present poor with their burden of welfare. Some say it's the criminal element; some say our ills are traceable to the oil companies, Madison Avenue, or the Pentagon. A number lay the blame on the doorstep of politicians, while some point to overpopulation; the moral majority are sure it's the crumbling of traditional values in our homes, schools, and government. A few even think the problem lies in our greedy and rapacious nature. In essence, what's wrong means different things to different people.

It's the optimist's role not to deny the problems but to believe that whatever they are, they are definable and, most importantly, solvable. The nation that can put a man on the moon or the space shuttle Columbia in orbit might just be able to solve its social and economic problems, too. First, though, its citizens must be able to get at the root of its trouble and analyze not only what is wrong, but the reasons *why.*

As we work through the problems, never forget that it's the pragmatist's job to turn problems to his or her advantage and profit by their solution, and this is not a bad thing. Rich is not a dirty four-letter word and never will be, either for a country or an individual. Wealth is no longer a sin, it is a miracle.

Inflation at the Root of Our Problems

Most of what's wrong with America—the anger, crime, violence, immorality, greed, political corruption, and economic problems—can be traced to the government creating money, and the government creating money *is* inflation. If you study history, you will see that these social problems have always accompanied the cheapening of a nation's money, and they always will.

This is not an oversimplification; according to the Swiss it is a fact.

In the whole universe, there are only two things: reality and those who resist it. Inflation continues only because people do not see the causal connection between inflation and all the rest of what they don't like in the world.

When there is inflation, people can't plan and they become frustrated. When there is inflation, there is an arbitrary division of the wealth and people become angry.

When there is inflation, people have to be dishonest to survive and immorality becomes a way of life.

When there is inflation, people can't pay their bills and crime and violence increase.

When there is inflation, governments have the perfect way to finance even bigger and bigger wars.

If you can start seeing inflation as the problem, you've already reduced most of the evils that bedevil others to just one. Now that we've isolated it, you can see it for what it really is—a way to finance the vote-buying tactics of politicians anxious to perpetuate their own power. What can you do about it? Plenty. You are the people, the ultimate source of all power. But that power only becomes meaningful when you are able to make intelligent economic decisions. The first thing you can do to make your power felt is to take some time to learn how inflation works and how it is undermining our America and making a mockery of your retirement future.

"But we're in a recession, experiencing deflation," you may say. You will learn that recessions are part of inflationary cycles. Deflations are merely the seldom-seen other side of the inflationary coin.

Before we're through, you are going to become an expert on the subject of inflation. This new knowledge will give you a competitive advantage in the fine art of speculation. Speculation, properly mixed with a fair amount of luck, will enable you to retire rich.

But first a word of warning.

Others have tried to explain inflation before. Some Swiss think you wouldn't make the effort to grasp complex concepts and ideas. They don't know how smart you can be when your survival depends on it. They don't understand that your back is to the wall and that you are ready to take desperate measures to protect yourself. They don't know how hard you will fight for your economic survival. They don't know how angry you really are and how tired you are of losing to inflation.

The reasons for your hard life, your struggles, the daily mortifications and embarassments of having too little money, of being priced out of one thing after another, lie within the heretofore-obscure subject of economics. Fortunately, so do the answers. But you must not begin your study of this subject timidly or with trepidation.

Someone is causing inflation which, as the gloom-and-doomsters so eloquently point out, is destroying our society. Let's find out who and why, and be optimistic enough to believe it's not too late to find pragmatic solutions for ourselves, our families, and perhaps even our country.

What about inflation's who and why for the last fifty years?

It's been simple. If you like reruns of old movies, this script is based on one of the oldest scams in the history books. Let's take a quick look as seen through the eyes of a Swiss banker.

ACT I, SCENE I:

Camera pulls back to reveal a shot of dull granite buildings in Washington, then moves in close to reveal gangs of hirelings at the U.S. Treasury and Federal Reserve Board, running the presses, turning sheets of newly printed paper into supposed wealth to make sure business gets its fix and the unruly mob is kept quiet. Camera tracks to Capitol Hill, then moves in on a tight shot of a fat, bald-headed politician sitting in his office contentedly smoking a cigar, overseeing the whole thing and enjoying his reward: POWER.

Got the picture? Inflation is a government monopoly, and none of it just happens by accident. *Someone* benefits.

That's it. End of scene. An oversimplification? Sure, why not? That's as good a place to start as any.

Oh, by the way, pragmatically, we've already learned our first lesson from our Swiss banker friends:

EVIL IS THE ROOT OF ALL (FUNNY) MONEY.

CHAPTER 2

Becoming a Pragmatic Optimist

Benjamin Franklin was a pragmatic optimist. Yet if Benjamin Franklin had lived in the twentieth century, he probably would have said, "A penny saved is a waste of time."

So how are you going to make a lot of money while you're still young enough to enjoy it? A good beginning would be to become sophisticated—fast. Not cynical—cynics don't do anything because they think everything is hopeless—but sophisticated, which means knowledgeable. Sophisticated pragmatic optimists accomplish all that's worthwhile in the world. It's time you joined them.

Reality Is Inflation

Reality has many manifestations, but the one that concerns us most immediately is the phenomenon of government printing money, commonly referred to as *inflation.* Inflation has been a very bad, even terrible, thing for the country in general but has allowed a few crafty citizens—members of strong unions, real estate speculators, politicians, and those that have a good racket going—to profit handsomely. These special interest groups account for the myth abroad in the land that inflation really isn't so bad. Those of us who have no rackets do not believe this myth. We are tired of losing and we are ready to finally acknowledge the existence of inflation, its evils and injustices, and start doing something about it—something more than throwing a few of the rascals out of their bastions of power and installing a new set in their place.

Seeing some new faces in Washington, D.C. in 1981 initially ushered in a period of euphoria which was quickly downgraded to mere hope, which in turn became harsh reality. In the future there's sure to be more disappointment and despair, during which all pragmatic optimists can become truly rich. This is as it should be, because the good things in life should belong to optimists in all circumstances, good and bad, for they have a secret. Their secret is that what they are optimistic about is essentially just one thing—themselves (and their grandchildren). This bit of Swiss wisdom is easy for all you pragmatic optimists with the dream of becoming millionaires to accept.

Stop Surviving, Start Winning

However, what concerns us more immediately is that when it comes to seriously preparing for your retirement you have just been fooling around. You have been so busy earning a living that you haven't given enough time or effort to making any real money. If you continue your "survival" attitudes, you face the unpleasant prospect of being poor in your old age.

Just to achieve the minimum goal of retiring in dignity with only the basic comforts will require enormous efforts on your part, efforts that in the past you have not made. About 60% of the human brain has not even been developed. Of the part that *is* developed, the average person rarely uses more than a third. Isn't it time to give substance to your optimism by using that brain and making the effort to become a winner?

Retiring Rich

At this point someone says, "But the only place I make any money is at my job and I'm working as hard as I can there now."

Working hard at your job isn't the way to retire rich. It's merely the way to get enough money to use to get rich by skillful placement of the money. Successful speculation is a whole new job requiring new skills and, as in your first job, you'll have to remember that all worthwhile goals require great effort. Yet, perhaps the effort is less than you would have expended just getting along. It is also true that successful speculators make more money than any employer could possibly pay them.

You only have to get rich once. After that, the money sustains and perpetuates itself like a living thing, pulsing out a profusion of interest, rents, and dividends. It is easier to make a few sustained and well-thought-out speculative efforts to achieve wealth than it is to face the daily hardships of genteel poverty with a permanently stiff upper lip. Be optimistic. If 500,000 people have already become millionaires in America, it just might be your turn.

How should you begin? *By learning what to eliminate.*

Today, one of the problems of the modern world is that we are confronted with thousands of choices; millions of bits and pieces of information bombarding our senses. Unfortunately, this is conducive to neither knowledge nor wisdom. Knowledge can help us make a lot of money. If we had enough wisdom, we might not even need the money, but what happens in our daily lives is that the plethora of minutiae that we call "information" keeps us from getting either.

To win, you will have to learn how to be selective, how to discard and eliminate all that is unconnected with achieving your goal. If your goal is financial independence you need to understand not a million subjects superficially, but just *one* very well. That one subject is *pragmatic economics with special emphasis on inflation.* If you think this sounds difficult, you're right. It is. Did you think retiring rich would be easy? Trust in your ability to change your life. These studies and your good common sense and intelligence can help you be one of the few to understand the anatomy of an economic cycle and when you do, you can use your own special talents to make some real money out of such knowledge.

So far, we have considered the YOU factor in making money— the criteria of optimism, desire, sophistication, and hard work necessary for you to live rich and retire richer. Unfortunately, we can't stop there. We function in and interact with a world beyond ourselves that is full of traps, snares, and people diametrically opposed to our achieving wealth. This isn't because people are no damned good, but because they are naturally interested in their own success, not ours. In the chapters to follow, we will examine these pitfalls and discover how to rise above them.

The first prerequisite for making a lot of money—wanting to and knowing you can do it—is easy. The second part—understanding inflation, thoroughly and technically—is not so easy.

What Is Inflation?

The Swiss bankers believe that economics can often be a very dry and boring subject, but *money* is invariably interesting to everyone. They suggested we concentrate on that, assuming that the more we know about money, the more we'll make for ourselves. Let's begin our study of inflation by seeing first what it is *not:*

Americans are always being told to fight inflation by not spending. Claiming that rising prices are a result of people spending money is to confuse cause with effect. It is the falling value of money that causes people to try to convert it to real goods while they can.

Nor does inflation consist merely in the phenomenon of rising prices. That is something that a bunch of government statisticians and economic scribblers have told us so often that by now almost everyone believes it. Inflation is *not* rising prices. Pick up a dictionary and you will see that by definition,

INFLATION IS AN INCREASE IN THE MONEY SUPPLY.

Now, who increases the money supply in America, or any-where else? The government!

What is the result when governments start manufacturing money that is not backed by something real? Inflation.

The Anatomy Of An Inflationary Cycle

There is a common pattern, for all inflations, that has reoc-curred throughout history. The steps are as follows:

1. Government begins intervening in a nation's economy by performing more and more functions.
2. These added undertakings cost money, which increases taxes.
3. Taxes quickly reach a limit that is difficult to surpass.
4. At that point the government abandons gold and silver coins and issues either base metal coins or unbacked pa-per money to pay for the added expenditures.
5. As the additional money works its way through the econ-omy it first stimulates business as wage and material costs lag behind (rise slower than) prices received for goods produced.
6. As the price increases become general, costs and wages catch up and business activity declines.
7. To counteract the decline in business, the government issues still more paper money.
8. Business turns up as costs and wages lag again.
9. When production costs and wages catch up business slumps again.
10. People begin anticipating the effect of increased money creation_and factor advancing prices into their business decisions.
11. As inflation continues, people hoard gold, spend freely, and contract debt.

12. Inflation gets so bad people start complaining. Government accuses the ones who are hoarding, spending, and borrowing to protect themselves of causing the inflation, passes laws against gold, and institutes price controls.

13. Price control leads to rationing.

14. These government regulations cause such distortions and the resulting rationing becomes so unpopular the controls are finally lifted.

15. Prices rise even more steeply as they catch up.

16. Production is interfered with as no one wants to lend.

17. Markets are so disrupted that only speculators are able to profit.

18. People lose their incentive to work, the thrifty lose their savings to inflation, speculation becomes more and more widespread, savings more rare, until lack of money to borrow suddenly puts a premium on savings.

19. Cash is king as business declines.

20. Production falls and inflation lowers the standard of living of the elderly and marginal producers to a poverty level. Unemployment increases. More and more people go on relief.

21. All the unemployment causes bigger and bigger welfare payments, the burden of which is passed on to the few remaining producers.

22. The producers decide they can make more with their capital by loaning it out at the very high prevailing interest rates than by buying new machines and capital goods.

23. The stock markets move wildly up and down, destroying what capital is invested in it.

24. Bonds decline, causing large losses.

25. Bankruptcies increase.

26. Credit markets break down and money is not available for borrowers at any price.

27. There is a financial panic followed by a period of economic stagnation and high unemployment.

28. The politicians become frightened and turn on the printing presses for one last burst of artificial stimulation.
29. There is a flight from cash to anything real. The commodities markets soar. The new money is spread arbitrarily throughout the economy and does not stimulate business enough to prevent more bankruptcies and chaos. Speculation replaces production. Speculators flourish.
30. Prices begin to drop, and the money is finally repudiated, first by the public and then by the government, which responds by devaluating it, creating a new currency as old debts are extinguished and business returns to normal. Life begins again, all without teaching the leaders or the people anything that will keep it from happening again.

If an American tries to create money, the government will put him in jail. The only entities that can legally create money are the Federal Reserve (through creation of cash) and the bankers (through creation of credit). The Federal Reserve determines how much the banks can lend, then, after a structured and predictable shortfall in government borrowing, creates the rest by buying government bonds and crediting bond dealers' accounts with new funds (cash creation). Why are their acts so circumscribed? Why don't they just print the money directly? To hide what is happening, of course. Why are these subterfuges and absurdities tolerated? Because they have become ritualized over time and because so many distinguished, white-haired, pipe-smoking, sober-looking, and otherwise intelligent men are involved in the charade that everyone just assumes there must be something to it.

Beyond the ritual, what is the intellectual foundation for the absurdity of inflation? Inflation is first tolerated because it is the antithesis of deflation. Deflation conjures up visions of closed factories, bread lines, soup kitchens, men on street corners selling apples, shanty towns, and dust bowls. In other words, "hard times." This brings us to another circle of truth:

THE FEAR OF HARD TIMES LEADS TO INFLATING
THE MONEY SUPPLY AND INFLATING THE MONEY
SUPPLY EVENTUALLY LEADS BACK TO HARD
TIMES.

The process is as circuitous as a doughnut and the average
citizen is destined to receive only the hole.

Up until now, you, like so many others, have been inflation's
fool. You thought that because your salary had gone up substantially over the last ten years, you'd been climbing the ladder
of success. Wrong. Every time you took a step up, someone
shoved the ladder deeper and deeper into the ground. It takes

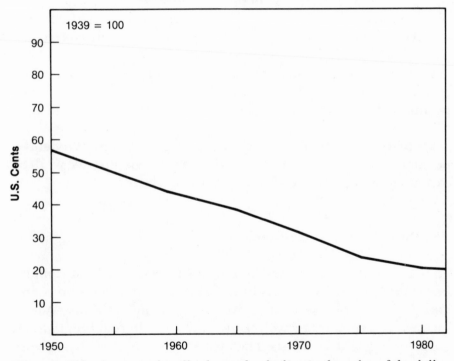

Figure 1. This chart graphically shows the decline in the value of the dollar
since 1950.

a $70,000 salary to equal what $25,000 bought in 1970. That's right; you are now close to six feet under.

Nor was your paycheck the only victim. Even when you managed to save a little and invest it, you still lost. This is because you had (after taxes and loss to inflation) a *negative yield* on your money.

How did this work? Let's say you put your money in Treasury Bills and received 12% on $10,000.

12% of $10,000 =	$1,200
Assuming you were in a 40% tax bracket,	
you paid $480 in income taxes	(480)
which left	$ 720
After a 10% inflation rate	
(10% of $10,000 = $1,000)	
you lost	(1,000)
For a net loss of	($ 280)

We are now in a period of temporary respite; but, if you aren't careful, a few years from now they are going to bury you—permanently—under an avalanche of negative yields and negative salaries and wages.

Who are *they?* Is there a conspiracy against you? Why call a politician's acts a conspiracy, when they can just as well be explained as ignorance, stupidity, and greed?

The Danger Of The Do-Gooders

To begin your climb up the ladder of success, you must remember what you learned as a child—that there are good guys and bad guys. If you were brought up on a diet of John Wayne movies, you remember well. But sometimes in real life, the bad guys don't wear black hats. They wear impeccably shiny, velvety white hats and they are clean-shaven and dress well and have nice smiles and speak softly. You can usually identify them because they are always promising to do something *for* you, but they have a little trouble with prepositions and they really mean *to* you. They are called several things, the most polite and deceptively simplistic being "a nation's leaders."

These men are regular guys. They probably even start out like decent human beings, loving the whole human race. The problem is that they have trouble loving anyone in particular and that is why they are so desperate to do good to a lot of people all at once. They are inexorably drawn to politics and, being sincere, they send out the right vibrations and remind us of our parents and get themselves elected.

That is where the trouble begins. If they just wanted to steal a little for themselves and leave us alone that wouldn't be so bad, but the problem is: *They sincerely want to help us.* They want to help us because helping people makes them popular, and being popular makes them get elected and getting elected gives them power over others, which makes them feel needed.

Why should you be so afraid of the do-gooders? Simply because most of the world's problems have been caused by do-gooders, and whatever motivates them—whether it is power, greed, stupidity or even misguided idealism—they constitute a formidable challenge even for the greatest optimist. The only way to protect yourself from all the good they are trying to do you is to be sure of yourself and sharpen your ability to solve the problems they are constantly causing so that you can stay ahead of them.

How can you become sufficiently sure of yourself so that you intuitively and instinctively trust your judgment and reject theirs? This can best be done by realizing your true worth and appreciating the fact that you and your ancestors have been pretty good at solving your own problems for a long time. You have a lot to be proud of. You are a very special person. In point of fact, you are unique—the end product of a million years of fantastic struggle, hardship, and triumph over difficulties. Did you ever think how intelligent, energetic, and successful all your ancestors must have been just for you to have had the chance to be born? Your ancestors proved they were the fittest by surviving. Surviving is the ultimate measure of success.

Your brain can outperform any computer ever built. What science coldly describes as three-quarter-inch glutinous globes

made of fat and protein molecules are really your eyes—eyes
that can see and encompass all the world, its beauties and its
lies. Imagine being able to encompass the whole world, even
the stars, within your brain. As a human being, *you* are the
most important thing in the universe. *You* give the universe
meaning. Hadn't you better decide right now that you owe it
to yourself, your family, and your ancestors to survive?

The significance of your uniqueness is tremendous. First, it
means that looking after your interests and living your life successfully are the highest tributes you can pay to yourself and
your creator.

The reason for acknowledging your uniqueness is that if you
realize how important you are, you will handle your money,
your freedom, and your life accordingly and stop looking to
others for solutions. The do-gooders prey on those who think
they are insignificant, those who see themselves as helpless victims that powerful leaders, in their great benevolence, might
save. Your weakness makes them strong.

What does it take to keep you physically, mentally and financially stronger than they are? As an optimist, believing in
yourself and your own uniqueness. As a pragmatist, making up
your own mind and deciding things for yourself; placing a high
value on your own independent judgments. Once you're there,
the do-gooders are in real trouble and you are on your way to
freedom and riches.

A recent study was made of executives from top corporations
all over America to determine what personal characteristics
were necessary to achieve success. The successful executives
that were interviewed and tested displayed little uniformity.
There were tall ones, short ones, thin ones, fat ones, educated
ones, and uneducated ones—every kind of man and woman
imaginable. The only characteristic they shared in common is
also the point of this chapter:

THESE SUCCESSFUL INDIVIDUALS ALL HAD A
HEALTHY SENSE OF SKEPTICISM ABOUT EVERY-
THING BUT THEIR OWN VALUE. THIS PROTECTED
AND FOSTERED THEIR OPTIMISM AND ENABLED
THEM TO SUCCEED.

CHAPTER 3

Taxes, Taxes, and Very Little Protection

Having read the previous chapter, you now have a true perspective on your uniqueness, powers, and potential.

Now that you feel good about yourself, you may wonder what that has to do with attaining financial independence. The Swiss say EVERYTHING! According to them, people fail because they don't know they can succeed, because they don't realize their true worth, their uniqueness, their power.

Your Power

Because of forces that up to now were beyond your control, you have been prevented from reaching your potential. The bad guys, the soft-spoken ones in the white hats with the nice smiles, have had the drop on you. They have been stealing your power by stealing your money. Your are now about to learn enough to be able to kick that gun out of their hands. But before you can do this, you're going to have to be motivated. It just might help motivate you if you're forced to face up to just how bad things are, to just how far your indifference, timidity and, yes, even optimism have brought you on the road to your own destruction.

The truth is that you have been and are presently a *slave*. This may come as a nasty shock, especially since you felt so

good about yourself a minute ago, but it is just one of the unpleasant truths to be digested if you are ever going to obtain
your freedom, let alone become rich.

Tax Slavery

Even if you never took a civil service examination, you work
for the government. The average taxpayer works from January
1st to June 12th just to pay his or her taxes. For an average
family of four that's about $8,000—45% of all the money they
earned last year! Cumulatively, this represents a chunk of about
twenty working years out of your life!

The reason why you can't make ends meet and don't ever
seem to have enough time is simple: You are only working part-
time and *they* have been working *all* the time Spending *Your*
Money!

But how does that make you a slave? Just because, in our
society, your money *is* your power. Economic and political freedom are synonymous. It is a mistake to think you are politically
free if you are economically enslaved. And the American taxpayer is a *valuable* slave—one that isn't going to be let go of
without a fight. It is apparent just how valuable a slave he or
she really is when you consider that the return on slaves in the
pre-Civil War South was only 12%. Today, you (as an average
American) are paying total taxes of 45%. So it's simple—*you
are over three-and-a-half times as valuable as any slave this
country has ever known.*

Let's get back to those taxes. You may say, "Well, that's for
the ones in high tax brackets and before the tax cut. Certainly
I don't pay 45%." But you do—and more. Every day!

Most of you realize by now that inflation has been taxing
away 10% of your income for years, but did you know how many
taxes levied on businesses are really hidden charges passed on
to *you?* Did you know, for example, that there are thousands of
regulations that the McDonald's fast food chain has to comply
with and pay for just to make a hamburger? It's not their fault

that it costs more to make the Big Mac® you buy. Did you know that these regulations alone cost the average citizen thousands of dollars a year?

- Did you know that when you buy a quart of milk or a loaf of bread, you are reimbursing the makers and distributors for hundreds of taxes that have already been levied and that amounts to many times the actual cost of the product?
- Did you know that when you pay $8,500 for a new car, a full $4,500 of that sum represents taxes paid and passed on to you, the consumer?
- Did you know that in 1980 the various levels of government managed to spend 45% of the total national income? For an average family of four that amounts to $7,928. This is an amount that equates with the total income of the country every day of the year up to June 12th.

So really, the poorer you are, the more you've been paying in proportion to your income. But all that is past. In the future, the politicians are laying plans to institute a value added tax to really give you the *coup de grâce*. This juicy little tax bite makes a bureaucrat's mouth water at the very thought of it.[1]

Government has a positive genius for doing things poorly and none of them are free. The government's gifts to us are paid for in two ways: (1) taxes and (2) inflation (another name for a subtle tax).

Besides making everything cost more, taxes and inflation take jobs away, too: jobs that would exist without the government's many protection rackets.

"But the government dispenses so much to so many needy people," someone says in rebuttal.

Does it? How? Where? Give one example.

"Social Security," someone else says.

---

1. This would add a given amount of tax (in Europe it's around 15%) to the value of all wealth as it is created. It would, in other words, tax each step of the production process.

Not true. The government doesn't give *anything* away. The people covered under the Social Security plan contributed the money. In fact, they are currently contributing a lot more than they will ever get. Social Security taxes have risen from $45 a year in 1940 to $1,975 a year today. They'll be pegged at $3,000 soon. Then why not $30,000 or $120,000 later on? The government acts as an insurance company—as a mere collector and distributor—and even there it isn't doing a good job. It's actuarily unsound and is currently paying out $12,000 a minute more than it takes in.

"What about welfare?" another asks. In the decade prior to 1976, welfare spending went from $77 billion to over $330 billion *annually*—an increase of a quarter of a *trillion* dollars. Government statistics show there are 25 million people eligible for welfare, Assuming the increases took place in equal increments over the ten year period the average annual per person payment should have been $5,000. This means that during the ten year period each one should have received $50,000, or $200,000 for each family of four. Just go to Harlem or Watts and ask any family if they got their $200,000. After you pick yourself up off the street, you can tell them why:

THERE ARE SO DAMNED MANY BUREAUCRATS THAT EACH NEW PIECE OF SOCIAL LEGISLATION IS A WELFARE PROGRAM FOR THEM, NOT YOU.

This is important:

No Government Has Anything—Not One Thing—Of Its Own To Give Out That It Doesn't Take From The People *One Way Or Another,* and like sand in a sieve an awful lot is lost in the transfer.

The do-gooders have made a *big business of allocating income*—deciding who will get what. And it is a big business—the biggest the world has ever known. Did you know that each second it is in session, Congress spends over $200,000 of our money? But its wastefulness and profligacy are such that even the recipients lose.

Just in the time that it takes the average reader to read this page, the money Congress has spent could have created eight new millionaires.

Nor is one's slavery a personal thing. Even Children Are Slaves. Each baby born in the United States is saddled with a debt of over a hundred thousand dollars—his or her share of the unfunded future obligations of the United States.

The Great Protection Racket

On discovering that he or she is a slave, a true optimist looks forward to freedom. In order to do this, you must know how your enslavement came about so you can throw off the chains of your oppressors.

Slavery can't exist without docile slaves who have let someone else obtain power over them. Why would you give up so much control over your life? The answer, from the feudalism of the Middle Ages to America's federal bureaucracy in the 1980s, is always the same. We allow someone to control us because they convince us they are protecting us.

Who is the government protecting us from? This is not an easy question to answer. In the 1940s it was the Germans and Japanese, but now they're our best friends. Now we drive German cars and look at Japanese T-V sets; and since they are usually cheaper, everybody but Chrysler and Zenith is very happy.

Then there were the Chinese. They too were friends until they read the book that Mao wrote, and since he wrote beautifully and had plenty of submachine guns, they saw it was true and that made them mean and they threw Chiang Kai-shek out. But then our leaders figured out that if the Chinese hated the Russians and we hated the Russians, we could use that to build a lasting friendship because we had so much in common.

Hating the Russians has a long history (since 1946, and maybe even since 1917) so we will probably continue to hate them until we hate the Chinese or the Libyans or someone else even more sometime in the future and decide the Russians weren't so bad after all. These then are the enemies the government is protecting us from.

Some of you may detect a certain cynicism about all this protection and wonder if it's because of the fact that the U.S. has essentially lost every war since 1946. No. That isn't it. But something is wrong. Someone is preying on our fears not to protect us but for their own purposes. It is not unpatriotic to point this out. It is easy to get one's fears mixed up with loving a country, but patriotism is more than our gazing in awe at the Statue of Liberty or standing at attention when the flag goes by. It's more than feeling wonderment when contemplating the hardships endured by Washington and his men at Valley Forge, thrilling to reading the fiery speeches of Patrick Henry, or taking pride in the Constitution. Real patriotism is an act of the head as well as the heart. It is realizing why the Founding Fathers rebelled in 1776—why free men always rebel. They had the temerity to want to keep what they had produced. Specifically, they were fighting the oppression of taxes without representation. If England had won the Revolutionary War, history would have spoken of these heroes as renegades. In the eyes of George III, head of the established government of the time, they were a bunch of rogues, cutthroats, and tax evaders. Old George III was, in the best tradition of government, protecting the people from the Founding Fathers! The government is still doing the same thing today. It's even found ways to protect us from the Constitution our founders gave us.

It is a strange world! It seems that there's always someone—from the Mafia to Congress—who is sure that others need protection and, if necessary, will take their last ounce of blood to prove it. The feeling is perhaps best summed up in the immortal words of one of the U.S. field commanders testifying before a Senate committee on Vietnam: "It was necesary to destroy the village to save it."

Now we have seen that governments get power over their people by protecting them. This is not a subject to be treated lightly. To be slaves ruled over by one's own leaders is bad, but to be conquered militarily by a foreign power would be far worse. No one would deny we need to be strong militarily—that eternal vigilance is the price of freedom—but the point is that all governments use the role of defender against foreign aggression in order to slip into another role, that of protecting us against *everything*, especially ourselves. Unfortunately, that costs so much there isn't enough left over for real defense.

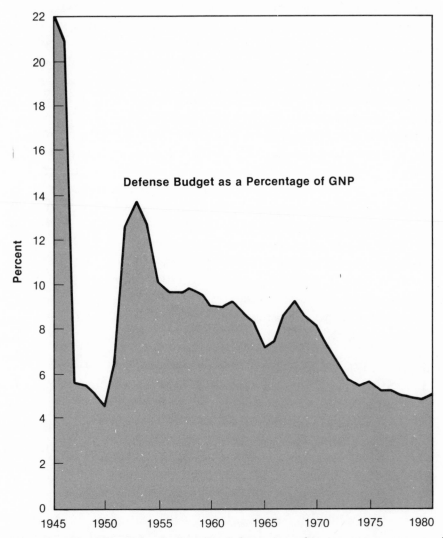

Figure 1. The alarming decline in defense spending as a percentage of gross national product indicates that the U.S. is not getting the protection it's paying for.

It took 198 years (until 1974) for America's spending to reach $250 billion, but only four (to 1978) to double it to $500 billion. Social welfare programs alone now cost $350 billion compared to only $90 billion in 1971.

In Jimmy Carter's presidency alone, federal spending *increased* more than the government's total budget as recently as 1974. Since 1946, federal expenditures have increased more than 20 times (2,000%); since 1929, more than 130 times (13,000%). Yet only a small part of this increase has been for actual defense spending as the Swiss know it. In spite of the trillions of dollars spent since World War II, U.S. defenses are woefully inadequate and spare parts are not even available to keep its current military equipment running.

Something is definitely wrong. You should become familiar with the protection issue and have an answer that satisfies you as to whether you are still victims of the great protection racket. A Swiss would be cynical enough to ask, "If you're going broke paying for all this protection, how come you can't even walk down your neighborhood street at night?" It is not for a Swiss to poke his nose into a problem that does not concern him, but America is not getting the military (or even police) protection its citizens are paying for. This offends the Swiss sense of economy.

If you have read this chapter carefully, you already know:

1. You are a slave to taxation.
2. Taxes are tolerated because someone has to protect you.
3. A Swiss view of whom you have been protected against in the past.
4. You are being protected against so many things that cost so much that there might not be enough money to pay for the protection you originally required.
5. You can love your country without loving everything its politicians do.
6. Until Cornwallis surrendered, the founders of America were just a bunch of common tax evaders and would have been hung as such if England had won the war.

7. When politicians tell you something is in the national interest, it usually means in the interest of the national association of bureaucrats, not in the people's interest.

The point of this chapter might be summarized as follows:

HISTORY IS WRITTEN BY WINNERS. YOU MUST SEE THAT YOUR NATION IS A WINNER OR NOTHING ELSE WILL MEAN ANYTHING (INCLUDING YOUR WEALTH)!

CHAPTER 4

Learning to Play the Game,
Plus the First of a Series of Useful Tools
to Help You Win

We've seen that the necessity for American taxpayers to pay protection money, first to be saved from the threat of foreign aggressors, then lately from themselves, removes enough from their collective paychecks to make them end up feeling awfully poor individually—so poor that the natural wealth of the country no longer allows them to live well.

At this point you are justified in asking a basic question.

IS THERE MORE?

Yes, there is more. More than living in fear of aggression from criminals or Russians, more than paying some politician to tell you what to do. More than supporting welfare and knowing the needy aren't getting it, more than knowing the Federal Reserve is printing money and your bankers are loaning it to some undeveloped nation that isn't going to repay it. More than knowing government needs so much money it's bankrupting the company you work for and threatening your job. In spite of all these very real horrors, there is still such a thing as "the good life" and though it has become more elusive and theoretical than ever before for most people, *you can still attain it.*

You may not be able to obtain food as wholesome or as delicious as that which your great-grandparents ate, or buy cars made like those your parents drove, or dress yourself in the same high-quality clothing or fish in a lake quite so clear or breathe air so clean or send your children to quite as good a school with the kind of devoted (and protected) teachers you had, but you can obtain many of the good things that still remain as well as enjoy a lot of the world's wonderments and modern miracles that your parents never knew. You can even retire rich.

Never forget that the makings of a good life are still around and will be as long as you have freedom of choice.

FREEDOM.

You are free to ask for more money (until wage controls), sell your product for more (until price controls), even send your money abroad (until exchange controls). You can work even harder, make more money, decrease your expenses, hit your boss up for a raise, avoid (not evade) taxes, borrow money, live it up—any one of a dozen things to take some of the sting out of inflation. Failing to increase your income, you can become stoical and decrease your wants—even use your prerogative as a consumer to inflict the ultimate punishment—by choosing not to buy. But when you have done all these things, you are still a long way from the good life or from becoming rich.

What can you do to fight back in a meaningful way? It is unreasonable to think the world is going to get rid of wasteful politicians, so why don't we seek a solution based on making enough money to support both them and ourselves in style? This solution has the merit of being simple. In order to get rich you have to have peace of mind, and fighting the IRS is not the easiest thing on your nerves. By making a lot of money and giving the devil his due, you'll not only have peace of mind, but you might even end up being a hero to the Internal Revenue Service and be able to influence a few hungry politicians on your own account. Are these strange ideas from a Swiss banker? No. Tax evaders are not welcome in Switzerland. When they do get in, they make them pay dearly for their cheating ways.

How then can one make enough to support both the politicians and oneself in style? History tells us that in a period of chaotic inflation a small group manages to make enormous profits. Who are these people? They are speculators who *understand* inflation. How do they make these enormous profits? How can you become one of them?

The word "speculate" derives from the Latin *speculari,* which means to spy out, observe, or look ahead. At the end of every inflationary supercycle, there arises a speculator class—the only ones who really profit by the chaos. These are the ones who understand how to constantly shift their investments in order to profit from rapidly changing times.

What It Takes To Be A Speculator

Before we get down to investment specifics, let's analyze how speculation differs from investment.

Speculators try to gain by a change in prices. Sometimes they are even gamblers. They are honest enough to admit this, but they only gamble when they feel the odds are strongly in their favor. Investors, on the other hand, attempt to preserve purchasing power and do not take any unnecessary chances. This sounds good in theory, but in practice they put a lot of money at risk, usually with little chance of making anything but small profits.

What characterizes the really successful speculators and makes them different from the average person? Do you have some of their winning personality traits already? Are you willing to try to develop the ones you don't have so that you can profit in the future? What follows is a checklist of characteristics of successful speculators.

1. Speculators are not perturbed by losses. They quickly forget them, retaining only the lessons learned to help them in the future. Speculators do not take losses personally. This separates them from compulsive gamblers who almost always take losses personally.

enemy and how he operates is half the battle, for we will soon turn this knowledge into a battle plan that will give you a good chance to win.

The real problem is the third requirement—guts. When we are young, we have it. As we get older, we may get more money and more knowledge, but almost in direct proportion, there is a waning of our adventuresomeness, an abhorrence of danger and risk. Most of this lack of guts is based not on indifference, but on fear. It isn't that we don't want to make a lot of money. What we fear is losing what we have. Old people's conversations are full of stories of someone who did such-and-such and failed, which is a quiet justification of their own prudent course of doing nothing.

In the past, inaction usually meant maintenance of the *status quo.* That is, if your neighbor was playing the stock market with his savings and you were too frightened and just left your money in the bank, he could lose his and your inaction might have protected you. Sometimes inaction works very well. Deliberately doing nothing at certain times can indeed be a virtue.

The concept has often worked in the past. It is still working beautifully today with smug investors cosily ensconsed in Treasury Bills and savings accounts at a time when cash is temporarily king. But some day doing nothing will not work any more. The greatest danger you will face (if you have anything to protect) will be from inactivity. Why? Because the essence of inflation is this: Those that have something real that increases in value will prosper; those that don't fall by the wayside.

As the Bible says, "Those who have, will get more until they grow rich, while those who have not, will lose even the little they have."[1] Doing nothing will no longer suffice because someone will be working very hard doing something. An army of bureaucrats much more powerful than any president will be once again tightening the screws on the economy so much that they'll bring severe pressure on all interest-sensitive businesses.

1. Matthew 25:29

In the process of reducing inflation, they'll threaten the value of your inflation hedges, including your home and make it so hard on business your job will be in jeopardy. Having almost killed you by a recession, they will next try to revive you by throwing a bucket of funny money water in your face.

The bureaucrats will call it "stimulation" but it really means printing so much "legal tender" they will not only make a mockery of your retirement, they will impoverish you.

How can you fight back? The same and only way the sophisticated have always fought back—by speculating. You can become a successful speculator by mastering certain principles.

First, a successful speculator must remember that

The World is Constantly Changing

Every action brings a concomitant reaction. One day everyone may be talking about high interest rates and soaring inflation; a few months later, you're hearing about recession, unemployment, declining interest, and no one wanting to borrow. The prime rate in April of 1980 was 20%, in July it was 10%, in November it was back up to 18%, then over 21% a few months later, then down again.

Dips and ascensions are currently being crowded together and the economy is foundering. There is one simple rule to guide you through the rocky shoals of change. In spite of all rhetoric to the contrary, if you would know the future keep one test firmly fixed in your mind: Determine what is best for the government (not your country or you) and know that is what the powers that be are working to make happen.

What is best for someone who, like a government, owes an enormous debt? More inflation.

What is best for those who, like politicians, increase their power every time there is chaos? More chaos.

Put the two together and expect inflationary chaos.

Sometimes it might look like the ship of state has changed course and is following the path of fiscal restraint, but be patient and you will see it is just taking in sail. Keep your eye on that inflationary north star as you steadfastly ride out the waves of conservatism and restraint and you will prosper. Beyond the horizon is ever more spending, ever more fiscal irresponsibility. The only survivors will be flexible, forward-looking young thinkers. Now this doesn't mean you have to *be* young, but you must *think* young. Thinking young means getting rid of old ways of seeing and being open to new perceptions. This is important because all the old, prudent principles of investment can be quickly rendered obsolete by severe or hyper inflation.

Before we try to formulate new principles of investment more compatible with the lessons of history that apply *now,* let's talk about timing.

Timing *Is* The Inflationary Game

Not complaining about inflation or explaining it but using it to win (make money) is the only worthwhile, meaningful objective of this game. If you know when inflation is going to accelerate, you can win. If you know when inflation is going to decelerate, you can win.

One principle on which winning depends is: realizing that the total price of many financial assets today is largely determined by the expected rate of future inflation discounted back to the present. Therefore, a substantial amount of money can be made when majority opinion wrongly assesses the future inflation rate. If you could ascertain coming changes in that rate that were not anticipated by the majority you could win big.

How can you do this? By studying history. History gives us several clues, one of which is as follows:

THE FUTURE INFLATION RATE IS LARGELY DE-TERMINED BY PAST MONEY GROWTH RATE PRE-VAILING EIGHTEEN TO TWENTY-FOUR MONTHS PREVIOUSLY (MINUS 1%).

If inflation is caused by the government printing money, it is easy to understand why this should be so.

Why look to the rate of money creation that existed eighteen to twenty-four months ago? Because it takes that long for the newly created money to filter through our financial system and make its effects felt.

What about the minus 1% part of the rule? Because historically part (1%) of the increased money gets lost (like energy is consumed) in the filtering-down process.

This formula thus becomes a tool that, when put together with others, can help you to win. Changes in the inflation rate are telegraphed like a boxer's punch by the increase (or decrease) of past money supply. As inflation speeds up the lead time contracts.

Stated as an equation this becomes:

$$x - 1\% = y$$

where x equals money growth rates as shown by changes in the M_1 supply (expressed as a percentage) and 1% equals the amount lost in the filtering down process and y equals the inflation rate eighteen to twenty-four months later.

How do you know what these rates are? Money growth rates can be ascertained by writing the Federal Reserve Bank of St. Louis, P.O. Box 442, St. Louis, Missouri 63166, for a monthly publication called *Monetary Trends*. This will contain money growth rates for the last few years and keep you posted on what to expect in the future.

The current rate of inflation to measure against it can be determined by consulting the consumer price index, which is obtainable from your local office of the U.S. Government's Bureau of Labor Statistics.[2]

Proper application of this equation will give you periodic clues to movements in future inflation rates. By comparing the figures of past money creation with present inflation you have a starting point for the exercise of your own judgment to as-

---

2. Both these government agencies will put you on their mailing list and the service for both is free. Letting you keep track of their latest monetary crimes may indeed prove the only thing the government ever did for you for free.

certain the future. If past monetary creation is substantially out of line with what inflation is running currently you can project unexpected changes. By weighing these figures against prevailing sentiment as to future inflation you can pinpoint important bulges and declines that have not yet affected the current inflation rate. To understand why this rule should work think of the analogy of a full moon affecting the tides.

MONEY CREATION IS THE MOON THAT CAUSES THE EBB AND FLOW OF THE INFLATIONARY TIDE.

Determining when the full moon of past money creation will appear in the form of higher inflationary tides can be a very profitable pastime.

You have an infinite variety of ways to use this information, from buying a house to determining your own levels of inventory in your business, to trading in stocks, commodities, and especially in financial futures. This subject will be covered in more detail later.

If you can master timing you can win big. Nothing is impossible for one who understands this subject well and who in addition develops the instinct to know when to act. Timing has always been the most important thing in speculation and is what separates the winners from the losers. To be right *too soon* has always been the equivalent of being wrong, and to be right too late is just another way of saying you didn't act at all. The point you must grasp to prosper and survive is

TIMING WON'T BE THE MOST IMPORTANT THING IN THE 1980s, IT WILL BE THE **ONLY** THING.

What about timing that big future inflation? History teaches us that all inflationary bonfires require the tinder wood of previous economic slowdowns to feed them. Politicians don't dare run the printing press unless they have the justification of trying to cure the high unemployment present in an economic recession.

Hence another rule,

ALL BIG INFLATIONS COME OUT OF PERIODS OF SEVERE RECESSION.

This historical point can give you a clue to look for a more severe recession than others are looking for presently and, in the midst of that paralysis, a more virulent inflation to follow than others expect. Remember that no big money can be made with majority opinions.

Be willing to see the good side of everything, but keep in mind the truths that it is easier to be optimistic when you are right than when you are wrong, and it is easier to be optimistic when you are making money.

To summarize briefly:

1. The leaders of the last few decades have been politicians, not statesmen: expedient men carefully chosen by cheap money special interests; and they have represented them, not you. Even well-meaning conservative leaders cannot solve our long-accumulated problems quickly, and people may not be willing to suffer the deprivations, austerity, and discipline necessary to reform an economic system. Consequently inflation will continue.

2. In spite of the problem, the good life will exist as long as you have freedom to pursue it and later to enjoy its fruits in retirement.

3. In the future you won't be able to prosper economically except by speculation.

4. There is a certain group of characteristics common to speculators that allow them to win. You can acquire these characteristics, too.

5. Speculation requires money, knowledge, and the ability to act (really God's Undeniable Terrific Secret, but known in the workaday world as GUTS).

6. Before, you could stand pat and when life passed the deck say, "I pass." In the future, inflation will force everyone to choose between being gamblers or paupers.

7. All the old prudent investment principles become anti-quated as inflation progresses, so you have to think young and be open to new speculative ideas.

8. No matter how busy you are, you're either going to tend to your investments yourself or be wiped out financially.

9. Timing in the future won't be the most important thing—it will be the *only* thing.

10. Since future inflation is determined by the quantity of money that has been created eighteen to twenty-four months before, and these figures are available to you, this equation can act as a tool to help you forecast future rates of inflation.

11. Your flexibility and foresight in meeting the problems head on will not only help you make money, it will also keep you optimistic, because there is a wonderful satis-faction in fighting back.

Successful speculation requires a fortuitous mixture of academic analysis of abstract concepts and practical knowledge of how these concepts can be applied in the real world.

So far, we have covered the problem of excessive taxation and what it is doing to the producers of the country—the ones that create the wealth. Politicians believe they can continually re-distribute wealth from the producers to the non-productive by the use of taxes and direct transfer payments. The producers, however, hold the ultimate weapon—they can choose not to produce. This is the problem ostensibly being addressed by the Supply-Side economists that have the ear of the Reagan ad-ministration. But what is wrong with the U.S. economy doesn't stop with high taxation. There is also the problem of excess debt to contend with. As more and more producers decide to leave the game, governments are forced to run bigger and bigger deficits to make up the difference. These deficits inevitably re-sult in more inflation. In a complex world there are no easy solutions. The Supply Siders are learning that cutting taxes itself raises deficits. Later we shall see that tax cuts, however desirable, must take into account the weaknesses in credit markets that have already been caused by excess debt. Later on we will consider the enormous implications of this weakness in our credit markets—how shaky the whole debt structure really is. Before we do, however, for a change of pace let us examine just what categories of investment and speculation are available to you—what vehicles can be used to take advantage of our insights.

Abstract economic principles are important but their practical application in specific situations is what is going to enable you to win big in the years ahead.

In the following chapters we will delineate the areas of potential profit and consider the pros, cons and techniques of each area in turn. Later we will return to the problem of excess debt and with the specific investment vehicles already in mind, plot a detailed road map of how you might just possibly retire rich by 1986.

CHAPTER 5

The Paper Pyramid—
Banks, Bonds, Insurance,
and Short Term IOUs

Bank Accounts

According to Thomas Jefferson, banks are more dangerous than standing armies. If he were alive today, he would not only refuse to trust your banks with his money, he probably wouldn't even park his car near one.

To put your money in a bank is no investment at all; it's a guaranteed loss plan. Banks look so sturdy, safe, and conservative that they lull you into a false sense of security. The marble the best ones are built of gives an aura of permanence, and the guard who stands around with a gun makes you believe he is protecting something. The only trouble is, American banks don't have anything behind those marble facades to protect. There is no real money, just computerized accounting transactions. To prove it, consider this: Losses from bank robberies amount to only $45 million a year. That's just about one quarter of 1% of stores' losses from shoplifting. When the robber says, "Put all your cash in this bag," he doesn't usually end up with enough to buy a decent meal in the restaurant next door.

Do you know where bankers keep the money that's supposed to be sitting in your savings account? Your savings exist only as computerized journal entries—tiny blips on a memory drum stuck away in a basement of a building somewhere. If anybody ever came along and pulled the electric plug on the computer, your savings would go "phew," your money would no longer exist, and the bank could prove it because the computer is always right. If you don't believe me, try arguing with a teller about your balance some day, and remember, the real crisis hasn't even come yet.

Unsafe Loans

Bankers, being great humanitarians, have already loaned (given?) a few hundred billion dollars of your money to the less-developed nations. A default by any one of the debtor nations could produce an international banking panic overnight. Nor have the bankers confined their loaning frenzy to international loans. In the last thirty-five years, commercial banks have increased the total of their loan portfolios thirty-five times! All these dubious loans have brought banks dangerously close to the limits of the functional reserves required for safety.[1] This is not a proper subject for titillation and amusement, even for an optimist.

Modern credit practices have added some interesting twists to the stodgy old principles of banking and credit that are printed in business school textbooks. In the past, the lender determined the ability of the borrower to contract debt. This is no longer true internationally, where banks are forced to make loans to less-developed countries in order to enable these countries to pay the interest on their previously contracted debt. Lenders don't even control borrowing domestically. Borrowers make their own loans by the use of their credit cards. Nor are these loans insignificant. The public is in debt to the banks for well over $300 billion of consumer loans, and the volume of loans to underdeveloped countries is even greater. The total capital of the nine largest American banks is only about half the amount loaned out to underdeveloped countries. Think about that next time you fill out your deposit slip. And please

---

1. When loan reserves drop below 15%, watch out. This happened in 1873 and 1929 and is at that danger point again now.

don't come to Switzerland with your money. Swiss banks are no better off.

What profit banks make comes from financial services. Even this source is threatened. The whole field is being invaded by everyone from retailers to stock brokers, insurance, and even steel companies. How long can U.S. banks compete with money market funds for the saver's dollar when their fixed overheads are so much higher than those of the funds? Like the savings and loans, banks can only offer risky and non-competitive alternatives for the saver's dollar.

Eurodollars

Even more disturbing is the activity of foreign banks. About $1 trillion or so in Eurodollar loans are subject to no credit restrictions and have been made without *any* reserves. What are Eurodollars? They aren't even paper. They are simply created electronically and exist in the memory discs of giant computers around the world.

Like many of the good things in the modern world the Russians claim to have invented Eurodollars. For once they're right. In the early 1950s Russian bankers thought up a way to use a trade dollar without the risk of having it seized in case of war. Eurodollars were so well-received that American banks learned to love them too. From a handful of branch offices with a couple of billion Eurodollars in the late 1950s, American banks have now built over 1,500 outposts to defend this $1 trillion Eurodollar empire. This growth was not necessary to facilitate America's foreign trade, since foreign trade amounts to only 8% U.S. gross national product. Eurodollar deposits grew for only two reasons: bank profits and to escape domestic regulations.

How do Eurodollars function? These IOUs represent claims of foreigners on future American production. In the meantime, an alarming portion are loaned out to underdeveloped countries.

The philosophy of these less-developed nations is as timeless as their promises to pay are worthless. It can all be summed up in the words of Celso Ming, the Brazilian economist who served as architect for much of his country's magnificent $57 billion edifice of debt. He said, candidly enough, "If one owes a million dollars *he* is lost. If he owes billions *the bankers* are lost."

The abuses behind these absurd loans are covered up—hidden by government-sanctioned accounting legerdemain that enables U.S. banks to write bad debts off over the entire term of the loan rather than immediately. The Federal Reserve euphemistically calls this "maturity transformation," making it sound like another fountain of youth which it is. Instead of going old-fashionedly bankrupt for past mistakes, a careless bank is given a new lease on life to go out and make new bad loans. In the past, incompetent bankers were forced out of the system. Now, they are not only kept in the system, they are encouraged to exercise the same bad judgment that got them in trouble in the first place on a whole new series of transactions so that they can bankrupt everyone they do business with.

Another fascinating accounting rule lets financial institutions continue to carry bonds and mortgages on their books at par[2] even though the real worth of these financial instruments may have declined as much as 40% to 50%. Today, if the assets of savings institutions were figured the way customers have to figure assets—at current market value—a growing number of banks (and savings and loans) actually have a *negative net worth.*

A whole arsenal of these accounting tricks has created a credit structure that is rotten to the core. The tricks seem to work as long as the bank's depositors do not demand their money from domestic banks, or, the dollar does not weaken as foreigners convert their dollar holdings abroad. One or both of these things is inevitable if the government's spending is not curtailed. Continued government deficits will so affect America's credit markets as to eventually force liquidation of the depreciated bonds and other assets the banks are currently holding. This in turn will cause real, unhideable losses, and result in plain, old-fash-

---

2. Par means 100, the original offering price of a bond. Where it goes from there is determined by having to compete with future interest rates. If future interest rates rise the bond's price will decline.

ioned domestic bank runs in the U.S. and/or plummeting exchange rates abroad.

"But I'm Protected"

Even if you are an incurable optimist about other things, please don't be misled into thinking that the government will be able to do anything to stop your losses then. The safeguards set up to protect America from the type of recession the country experienced in 1907 proved totally ineffective in 1929. A few more agencies or a lot more bureaucrats won't stop the next one. A financial crisis of the magnitude experienced in 1929 is an economic force bigger than any government, and just as a lifeguard can't do anything to stop a tidal wave, no president, no matter how well-meaning, will be able to stop what is shaping up for the 1980s.

I can just hear the murmur of depositors saying, "But *I'm* protected. The little bronze plaque says my funds are insured up to $100,000 by the FDIC (Federal Deposit Insurance Corporation)."

Oh, you'll get a stack of dollars all right, but they'll be worth a lot less than the dollars you deposited. These are the facts: The Federal Deposit Insurance Corporation has only $7 billion in reserves to insure over $600 billion in deposits. That's a little over 1% of the money now on deposit in its member institutions. In 1980 alone, the FDIC had to put out $1.3 billion of its limited funds for rescue operations; and if it hadn't handled the problem with clever mergers in 1981, bank runs would have been front-page news. In 1982, losses were the highest in history. Furthermore, the government agencies that do the rescuing are separate corporations with no liability beyond their assets. Small savers think they are insured, but they are not and cannot be. The amounts at risk have become too great to respond to the next liquidity crisis and must invariably be paid off in so much printing-press money. This money will of necessity be relatively worthless compared to the dollars originally deposited. When the government makes good depositors' losses in batches of freshly printed new currency, it will destroy what little is left of the dollar's purchasing power. In other words, what depositors collect individually in insurance they will lose collectively in taxes and inflation. This is true because *the more dollars the government prints, the less each one is worth.* Banking is the only business in which liabilities (incurred by creating money) are assets. When you hear a bank say that it is so many billion dollars strong, it is talking ultimately about your money, not the bank's, and all its calculations are based on your never needing it. The only cash banks have they use to build and lease new bank properties just as quickly as they can, because bankers know better than anyone else that they need desperately to suck in new deposits just to keep the game going.

Banks (even Swiss ones), have a creative kind of accounting that allows their little mistakes to be covered over while they are given the time to make some real lulus. Their basic mistakes are:

1. Buying long-term bonds that (by the nature of inflation over the term of the bond) are likely to decline in price. The decline destroys the bank's real book value and overstates its current earnings so that no one knows the real situation until it is too late.

2. Making bad loans. Loans to non-OPEC, less-developed countries (LDCs) comprise a significant portion of the loan portfolio of the largest multinational banks. The nine largest American banks had $39 billion in loans to less-developed countries (LDCs) at the end of 1979. The total capital of these same banks totaled only $22 billion, so they could all be forced into insolvency if only a little over half of their loans proved uncollectable and had to be written off.

All of this becomes ominously significant when you realize that the loan-to-deposit ratios have now deteriorated to levels that haven't existed since 1929. For every dollar on deposit in U.S. commercial banks, there is only 20 cents in cash and investments to answer demands for withdrawals. Of that, over one-half is not liquid. To show how tight money has become, demand deposits at certain New York City banks were recently being turned over at an annual rate of 800 times. The total checking account money was shifting owners more than twice daily!

The next time you are comforted by the idea of your bank or any bank's safety, remember

- A banker's decision to extend credit depends more on the Federal Reserve current loan policy than on the safety of the funds belonging to you, the depositor. This has far-reaching implications in determining how prudent bankers are in making loans.
- Your savings aren't really insured at all. The money would have to be rendered practically worthless in order to discharge a 1932-style bank run.
- Banks borrow short and lend long, which means their assets are not liquid. Consider this: A lot of U.S. banks have taken 90-day Arab money and lent it for ten years to less-developed countries. Why don't the Arabs loan their money directly? Because they want our bank's *guarantees* and our bankers are greedy enough to risk their depositor's funds to make extra profits. Think about the bankers' stupidity. Their loans are for months (and usually years), and what they borrow is largely payable on demand. This is known as lending long and borrowing short—the classic formula for bankruptcy!
- Why does all this happen? Bankers at first expand their loans in order to maximize profits, then later they do it in order to survive. Being oriented toward profit, not safety, leads inexorably to a very small equity base supporting a very large number of questionable loans. This is somewhat like a Japanese wrestler balancing on the head of a pin in his bare feet or an Egyptian king deciding to build his pyramid upside down.

Why do bankers get themselves into this absurd position? For three reasons:

- *The government forces them to* because it needs the cooperation of the banks to buy its bonds and finance its profligate spending.
- Because *the money that the bankers are busy lending isn't even remotely theirs.* In fact, a large portion of it isn't anybody's—they create it. You can see how one might be

very detached and unemotional about losses in this type of situation.

- Because *all this is temporarily very profitable.* The smaller the equity base, the larger the profits on that base. A lot of banks don't earn 10% or 20%—they earn 25% or even 30%! Profits, not sound balance sheets, become the prime consideration of growth-oriented management.

Now what holds this whole magnificent house of cards together? Just one thing: Confidence. When that is gone and the depositors find out one-tenth of what you now know, kiss the whole thing goodbye.

This is not to say you shouldn't have some money in a bank.[3] We all need some ready cash to pay our bills, but beyond this regard money in the bank the way you think of Moscow.

It may be a nice place to visit in summer, but you wouldn't want to live there permanently.

How About S & Ls?

Everything that has been said about banks applies equally to savings and loans except the loan portfolios that constitute their assets consist largely of real property loans that are made for even longer periods. This makes them *even more illiquid* than banks. For over twenty years S & L managers have heaved sighs of relief every time inflation bailed them out of dubious loans on over-valued properties. What they didn't realize is that the same inflation that made their loans secure was raising interest rates and making the salable value of their portfolio of mortgages plummet to dangerous levels. David Stockman, Director of the budget under President Reagan, summed it up when he declared that the savings and loan industry is "on the brink of insolvency." Nothing has changed since then.

3. Only those banks that have the most broadly based domestic business and the lowest loan-to-deposit ratios should be considered when you deposit your money. You prefer to do your gambling elsewhere.

Losses for 1981 totaled in excess of $2 billion, but this pales in significance when you consider that savings and loan mortgage portfolios now have a paper loss of close to $100 billion. In other words, instead of having the reported net worth of $32 billion, the industry is really bankrupt to the extent of over $60 billion! This is ten times the Federal Savings and Loan Insurance Corporation's reserves for insuring depositors' accounts.

If all of this sounds frightening, it is. The government can create Money Market accounts and buy old mortgages so that the taxpayers are stuck with the loss, or it can merge ailing S&Ls into stronger ones. But this type of bailout doesn't cure the problems, it only postpones them. The more expedient the solutions the bigger will be the financial disaster when the defaults and withdrawals take place, and the more likely the avalanche of paper money that will bury everyone to save them. It is just another manifestation of the absurd things that happen when people use paper money to create the illusion of real wealth.

If you are going to win your battle to retire rich, or even just aspire to live in quiet dignity, there is no room in your portfolio for illusions, and bank (and Savings and Loan) safety and liquidity might prove to be an illusion of the first magnitude.

Bonds

What are bonds? The famous currency expert Dr. Franz Pick has called them "guaranteed certificates of confiscation," but that is a conclusion and, before jumping to it, let us take them in our hands the way the Federal Reserve intended and look at bonds through the eyes of the innocent.

Bonds are printed on heavy, white parchment paper of a good quality, usually with green and black printing like big pieces of money, which they have become. They have these seductive little coupons attached that tell your banker just how much to pay you on a given date. All you need is a pair of scissors to cut them with and you're in business. This happy activity is called "clipping coupons."

Some of these little pieces of paper are called tax-free bonds, which means that the politician promises the saver not to steal his or her money twice as an inducement to take even less interest.

Bonds As Wealth

Since bonds represent by far the biggest proportion of America's financial wealth, it behooves us to examine them carefully, even though it goes without saying that no sane person would put ten cents of his or her money into a long-term bond while there is any possibility of renewed inflation.

TO BE A LENDER OF ANY SORT IN A PERIOD OF DOUBLE-DIGIT INFLATION HAS HISTORICALLY PROVED TO BE NOT ONLY A LOSING BUT A DISASTROUS PROPOSITION.

A look at the chart below will make this clear.

Holding long-term bonds is one of the things that makes banks unsafe. Bonds themselves are basically unsound during a period of inflation because their current market value is inversely related to the current interest rate obtainable on new similar bond issues. This means that as interest rates rise existing bonds are worth less.

When the government borrows money, it does so by selling these pieces of paper. These bonds, together with newly created currency (more paper), is how government debt manifests itself. It is this mass of heavily engraved paper that becomes as oppressive as gold was before it—the new barbarous relic that must be destroyed if the government is going to start over again and get on with its business of protecting us from each other.

Middle-Class Patsies

The whole thing can perhaps best be understood by paraphrasing John Maynard Keynes, the English economist, who at the depth of the depression had the ear of the president: "There's too much saving going on. We've got to get people to

Figure 1. In a recent forty-eight-month period, a 7.5% treasury bond lost half the dollar amount of its principal. This means that if you paid $1,000 four years ago you now have $500.

spend, and the rich have a propensity to save. The only way to help a country with an unemployment problem—like yours, FDR—is to either shoot the bondholder class or destroy their wealth through inflation."

By the most charitable interpretation possible, this meant that the government can either eliminate the creditor class by taking its property all at once or expropriate it gradually through inflation. It has taken fifty years for bondholders to finally get the point that *this Keynes fellow meant exactly what he said.*

When Keynes shared his profound ideas with FDR, he was looking back to a time in England when the creditor class was the lazy, landed aristocracy holding the IOUs of the industrious bourgeois industrialists. Back then, no poor little old coal miner even knew what color a bond was.

Over the years, all this has changed. Who owns these bonds now? Who are the real lenders today? Sure, there are still a few unemployed millionaires who do nothing but clip coupons, but who *really* owns them—like a trillion dollars worth?

Is it the government? No. We have seen that government is a net borrower not lender. As a rule governments issue bonds, they don't *own* them.

Is it the rich? No. The rich are also large net borrowers. Not being stupid, they put their money in equities—real things leveraged with borrowed money—so that they can benefit from inflation. If they have bonds, it is just to brighten up their safe deposit boxes with a little bouquet of *flower bonds*[4].

Is it the banks? No, they hold them only in a representative capacity for depositors.

Is it big business that owns bonds? No. Business traditionally borrows the money, it doesn't lend it. Like government, businesses are issuers, not holders of bonds.

That puts us right back to the middle class, the only significant source of savings. These average workers save through their pension funds, union dues, insurance companies, banks, and savings and loans. But these institutions are just holding bonds for them. The poor good-natured savers probably don't even know they own bonds. They just plan on retiring on the money they deposited with the institutions that appear to own the bonds.

Thus, the government, the rich, business, and the banks are not the bondholders, and it is really the middle class that has this dubious distinction. That means what John Keynes really was whispering in Roosevelt's ear was, "We can either kill the middle class or destroy them financially through inflation."

Who comprises the middle class that is being destroyed by having its bonds and cash depreciated and its taxes raised

4. Government bonds selling for a discount (say 80) that can be used at par (100) to pay off American estate taxes.

through the graduated income tax? Unfortunately, the middle class happens to be the people who do the work, pay the taxes, save the money, send their children to college, go to church, and generally hold the country together. If any of you wonder what has been happening to you and our country, it is simple.

YOU ARE BEING EXTERMINATED ACCORDING TO PLAN.

But take consolation in the fact that you are being exterminated to save your country.

From what? Why, unemployment, of course. All of Keynes's ideas on increasing the money supply to punish savers and bondholders was directed at curing unemployment among the poor. This made some sense in the 1930s when unemployment was a catastrophic problem. Today many of the America's army of welfare recipients make more than the employed workers. The fact is that Keynes's economic ideas have not only made it more profitable not to work, they are further adding to unemployment by destroying the savings necessary to provide jobs. The subject today is completely clouded in emotion. The very word "unemployment" has become such a fantastic bugaboo that any red-blooded, nonthinking politician would gladly trade off the well-being of 90% of the working population to save the other 10% out of work. He is, in his own mind, convinced of the justice of providing one nation with stagnation and inflation for all.

Why Hold Bonds?

Projecting present trends into the future would indicate an eventual *zero* value for bonds. Yet people continue to buy them. Why would anyone buy bonds? They are tempting, even seductive. They offer a high interest rate (currently 5% to 10% higher than stocks) that in most cases will certainly be paid. At present, these interest rates are historically high and bond prices are historically low. The prospect of lower taxes make their returns even more attractive. And, as inflationary expectations periodically abate, bonds can even temporarily increase in price. If you aren't careful, it seems like you have struck pay dirt and found your El Dorado.

And there's more. You can sleep as well with a bond as you can with a time bomb—one night at a time. What you can't do is sleep for too long, because the bond you paid $1,000 for ends up being worth only around $500; although the return is the same as when you bought it, you have an uneasiness in the pit of your stomach and you can't help feeling that you've been had. And you're right. Bond values go down, just at a time when the cost of everything else goes up.

In each inflationary cycle, it is theoretically possible to make money *trading* bonds. You can do this profitably by buying them when interest rates are about to decline and selling them a few months later when interest rates level off. But as far as holding bonds is concerned, a better guaranteed loss plan has not been invented. One reason bonds bomb out is a simple matter of supply and demand. The demand is limited by a nation's savings, but the supply is virtually limitless. This is because no one ever seems to pay them off! When a bond reaches maturity, there's the government agency or corporation with its hand out again, offering a bigger bond issue (and usually a higher interest rate). The only way bonds' ever seem to be retired is by bankruptcy.

Lately the rumor of their imminent demise has finally reached the hearing aids of the bond dealers of Wall Street, convincing them to carry smaller and smaller inventories. For the speculator, this means markets for bonds are getting thinner and thinner.

Thus, the price you read in the paper may not be obtainable without a concession—*your concession,* and in any kind of credit crunch, you may obtain an actual sales price several points under the price quoted.

When all of the present financial madness finally plays itself out and congressional investigations are held to determine what happened to the horse that used to inhabit the barn, we suggest a star villain will be nominated for horse thief—your friendly bond broker. The bond broker should and probably will be publicly pilloried, stoned, and whipped. (The politicians will need all the whipping boys they can get to divert attention from themselves.)

All this is not without relevance to your using inflation to retire in comfort and dignity. The money managers—those future martyrs—are *already frightened to death.* The smartest among them are already pulling at their collars and hemming and hawing and beating their wives and kicking their dogs. They understand that they are on the spot. They aren't stupid or they wouldn't have been able to convince investors to buy all that overpriced parchment in the first place. Being scared, they are going to *want out in the next cycle.* This means unload bonds on someone else—just who hasn't been decided yet.

How To Play It

All these managers with all this money tied up in bonds might try to extricate themselves from the trap they're in without abandoning an absurd concept known as the Prudent Man Rule. This rule provides that if a money manager does the safest thing anyone can think of, after the money's been lost to inflation he or she won't be sued. Money managers have bought bonds for fifty years because that way they couldn't be criticized for not being prudent (and they could have three martinis at lunch because with a rule like that, they never had to worry about thinking). The very reason for bonds' inclusion in a money manager's portfolio is threatened. With bonds no longer providing a shelter from criticism, money managers will be inclined to shift to stocks and only the highest-quality blue chip stocks will match their conservative unspotted neckties and thought-free minds.

Blue chip stocks haven't done well over the last fifteen years or so because their capitalizations are so large that it takes enormous amounts of money to move them up.

SPECULATIVE POINT:
Blue Chip stocks could finally go up, this time to new highs, because the amount of money to push them there could come from bonds in the next cyclical upmove.

On the surface this sounds good but remember, large quantities of bonds can only be sold on an important rally. If they are sold on a decline, it could break our credit markets so badly that interest rates would skyrocket and there couldn't be a stock market rise. Look for a credit crunch first, then a bond rally of substantial proportions as loan demand finally abates. This will eventually be followed by a stock rally of substantial proportions as new government spending works its nefarious inflationary magic.

How to play it:

1. In order to get out, the bond dealers are going to need higher prices. In spite of all the negatives enunciated so far you should (as a speculator) buy bonds when you *anticipate* the kind of lower interest rates that traditionally follow a credit crunch.

2. Afterward, sell out your bonds and put your money first where these money managers are going to be putting theirs—in blue chip stocks. (But only as a speculation betting on a price increase, not as a semipermanent investment based on their dividend yield.)

In summary, you would short bonds through the time of a credit crunch, then buy bonds for a post-crunch recovery, then sell them and put the money in blue chip stocks. As stated previously, it is vital to time your purchases and sales to conform to a well-thought-out plan.

So you see, even if you never intend to buy bonds our little discussion wasn't wasted after all. It is one thing to just know you're going to make your retirement fund grow. It is another to know how and why you're going to make it grow.

Insurance

A few words will suffice to show why insurance isn't a proper investment or speculation. If you were rich enough, you could afford to insure yourself and come out ahead. Many Swiss do.

As for whole life or investment type policies they are not suitable for anyone, because one seeking insurance can buy term insurance and invest the difference in much higher yielding and safer Treasury bill type loans.

Insurance companies aren't really in the insurance business at all. That is just a sideline. They're really in the loan business. They take the policy holder's premium money that costs them very little and loan it out for much more. This is where they make their money.

Still, the business cannot be described as a good one since during periods of high interest rates holders of whole life policies can borrow at will, thus causing great capital outflows and sending the companies themselves scurrying to their bankers or into the financial markets to unload their bonds and mortages.

Much of what has been said about life insurance also applies to annuities. In a period of rapidly rising inflation who wants to give hard earned chunks of cash for the promise to receive it back when it's worth less? (Or worthless?)

Commercial Paper, Money Market Funds, Certificates of Deposit, Treasury Bills, All-Saver Certificates, and Other Interesting Pieces Of Paper

What is all this paper? Basically, it represents IOUs, preferably issued for a short term—usually thirty days to three years—by the biggest American corporations, banks, savings and loans, or the Treasury of the United States. Money market funds hold a combination of this paper and issue their own shares against it. All of these items may be purchased through your bank or stockbroker without any—or only a nominal—charge.

Just as all borrowers are not created equal, and the little guy pays more for consumer loans than General Motors does for its business borrowing, so historically small savers have received a lot less interest than large savers.

Why should the poor people—the ones that need it—have received so much less interest on their small savings accounts than the rich ones got by buying Treasury bills or commercial paper? No one has ever satisfactorily explained this. It is just the way the great humanitarians—the politicians—decreed that it should work.

The rates may have varied, but in the past large savers usually got anywhere from 5% to 15% more than banks and savings and loans were legally allowed to pay for a small saver's pass-book account. To qualify for the high rates, a person or organization had to have at least $25,000 (usually $100,000 or more) to invest.

A Safe Harbor?

For the rich, these short-term instruments were an attractive place to park their money while they were looking for something really exciting to do with it. Now, through the workings of the free market and the pressure to attract more savings, lending has become so dangerous and unprofitable that the Federal Reserve has decided to allow small investors (amounts as low as $1,000) to get in on the risk by pooling their assets together in money market funds. Most of the funds even allow share-holders to write checks against their balances.

From the standpoint of safety and maximum return, the money funds' portfolio of Treasury bills, bank certificates of deposit, and commercial paper issued by major corporations constitutes an apparently safe temporary harbor while waiting to take to sea in a really exciting venture. These money market funds now total an amazing $200 billion and, if nothing is done to limit their growth, they could again cause problems for bankers as money is disintermediated from sleepy bank ac-counts to work harder in these collective funds.

All Saver Certificates

To help the bank and ailing savings and loan industry attract needed funds, the government has instituted All Saver Certificates that pay up to $1,000 of tax-free income based on an interest rate of 70% of the current treasury bill rate.

Is there no end to the invention of ingeniously-shaped bandages to cover the poor financial institutions' bruised and battered bodies? If the government really wants to help the banks and savings and loans, let it stop wasting money and incurring giant deficits so that the bonds that constitute the reserves of financial institutions are worth something again and the solvency of these institutions is restored.

The latest gimmick is that the banks can now have Money Market accounts of their own that are insured by the FDIC. So short-term, at least, things are looking up for paper money and the savers are being wooed before they are tattooed with greenbacks.

Although currently a "hot item" all these new ways to buy IOUs provide no more of a solution to the average saver's long-term problem of inflation than a parking lot does to a person who needs a house. If anything, they give a sense of well-being that can lead to the kind of contented complacency that prepares you to do nothing in the next inflationary cycle. After all, parking places are hard to find and there is a natural reluctance to give one up. In a real financial crisis or panic, you want your assets *now,* and what can happen even to short-term paper of a year or two maturity is something you don't want to have to learn about the hard way.

After the government showed it could restrict the flow of cash *into* money market funds in the spring of 1980 by imposing penalty taxes, it became possible that in time of crisis a desperate administration could impose penalties for taking money *out* of such funds. A lot of the debt paper the money funds hold is issued by banks, and we've seen what can happen to them. A seemingly unsatisfiable demand for funds has driven corporate borrowers to issue commercial paper—a staggering $165 billion worth. These IOUs are held largely by the money funds and many are less than prime investments. Holding this dubious paper could cause major problems for money funds in the future.

Like anything that looks too good the speculator knows that money market funds or rates are not a permanent solution. When interest rates stop declining and new battles are waged for the saver's dollar it is even possible that some now unknowable default by a major corporation will embarrass, if not break, a few funds and send the true believers in this financial panacea scurrying for the exit of the temple.

CHAPTER 6

Stocks

If only bureaucrats and congressmen didn't exist, buying American common stocks would be a way of owning a part of the greatest industrial complex the world has ever known. Remember that the companies with listed stocks are not just numbers in the financial pages but the principal employers of America's workers and, along with land and natural resources, the source of almost all wealth. Still, as great as the companies themselves may be, what they have done for their stockholders over the last decade has left something to be desired.

If you had put $1,000 into such glamorous names as IBM, Avon, Xerox, and Polaroid in 1970, you would have had an inglorious $500 a decade later. That amount would have bought just about what $250 did when you purchased the stocks that your broker promised would put you on easy street. The average stock fell 42% in *real* terms (after inflation) in the 1970s, compared with a decline of only 32% in the 1930s, a decline which the leading gurus of Wall Street assured us would never happen again.

Graveyard In The Sky

Since 1965, the 1000 mark on the Dow Jones average has stopped the market on so many occasions that it has been aptly dubbed "the graveyard in the sky."

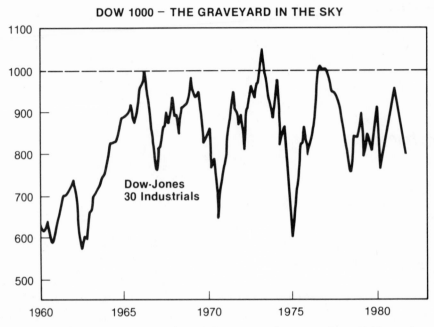

DOW 1000 – THE GRAVEYARD IN THE SKY

Figure 1. The Dow Jones Industrial Average from 1960 to 1982. It shows the invisible barrier of 1000 that has kept a lid on stock prices. When it is finally broken will it become a floor, just as tenaciously resisting declines?

After fifteen years of vacillation, meandering and downright disappointment, it's a wonder that stocks have any friends left.[1]

Why have stocks performed so badly for so long? For many reasons, but mostly because the investment consensus was that a little inflation was a good thing for stocks, but too much inflation hurt them. Translating this dubious bit of wisdom into

1. The Dow should now be above 2500 just to have kept up with fourteen years of the worst inflation in our history, even without allowing for any real growth. If you project a 10% annual inflation rate through 1990 (and assume no growth at all), just to catch up with inflation you'd have to see Dow figures above 3800 by 1985, and 5000 by 1988. At 1980's actual rate of over 14% inflation, the figures would be much higher; at 1981's 9%, a little lower.

something more substantial, we can say: Even though business profits increased from $73 billion in 1975 to $159 billion a few years later, after correcting all those earnings to constant dollars and taking into consideration the inadequacy of depreciation during a period of accelerating inflation, companies have been overstating earnings, if not actually losing money. So stocks haven't really been cheap at all.

In other words, stock prices have not been held down by profit figures, but by the fact that no one believed the figures.

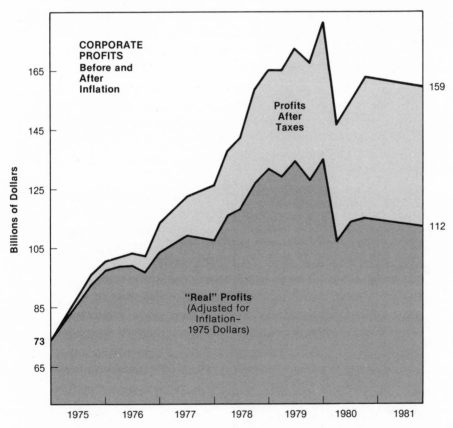

Figure 2. This shows 1980 profits to be overstated by 46% in terms of constant 1975 dollars.

Effects Of Inflation

How could a company with large earnings actually be losing money? As an example, assume a factory was built ten years ago at a cost of $10 million. After its completion, the company set aside $1 million a year to rebuild it. Now the factory is worn out, but it will cost $20 million to replace. Over the last ten years, the company reported earnings of $1 million a year, or $10 million total. In reality, the firm earned nothing during the last ten years because inflation made a mockery of its profits. Not only that, the company was forced to pay taxes on these paper profits. So it must now go out and borrow $5 million (the amount it paid in taxes), plus find another $5 million just to get back to where it was ten years ago with a new factory. This is why America has not been rebuilding its industrial plants and can no longer compete with countries like Japan.

What could eventually bring about a change that would justify placing a higher valuation on equities? Simply this: In a later stage of inflation, there is a recession during which the rate of inflation declines, and this happens just at the time that stock prices are so low they are finally recognized as bargains.

Why does a stock upmove finally occur? First, because the stock's real price (corrected for inflation) is also lower than its nominal price (the one you read on the financial pages), and, corrected for inflation, the Dow Jones Average looks something like what is shown in Figure 3. It can be seen that the Dow Jones is really under 400 in terms of 1970 dollars and this is *cheap*. Just how cheap becomes apparent when we realize that a lot of U.S. stocks are selling below what they sold for in 1968. This, theoretically makes stocks one of the best bargains around.

Second, stocks are finally seen as bargains because some ingenious securities analyst comes up with another idea:

"Those stock certificates aren't *just* pieces of paper," he says, "They're claims on brick and mortar, land, machines, a whole, valuable, *real* ball of wax."

"Really?" the stock buyer asks. "I'd forgotten that."

"And there's more. Inflation may have reduced earnings but

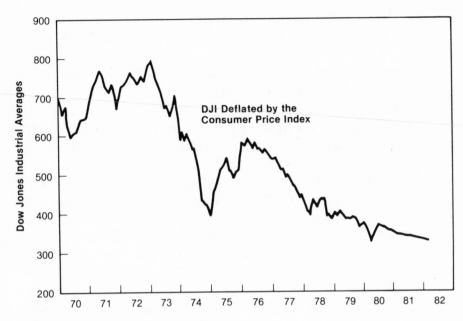

Figure 3.

it also reduced debt. The bankers have been passing out free money to those companies. The only way to get in on the deal is to buy the stock of the ones that borrow enough (but not so much that they can't repay)."

So sometime in the not too distant future the securities analyst will get the partners in his firm to begin buying and others will hear of it and they will buy too. Since no market is as attractive as one that is rising, everyone will start buying and the Federal Reserve will have created so much money by this time that it will be coming out of everyone's ears, and that's when investors will be easily persuaded that *anything* is better than money and buy some more.

Will this buying finally be justified? As a speculator in the stock market, you must learn to forget truth and instead pay attention to the latest piece of theory in vogue at any particular time because

THE ONLY THING THAT'S TRUE IN THE STOCK MARKET IS WHAT THE NUMBERS SAY IS TRUE

If you fight the tape, you may be right over the long term but go broke over the short term.

What happens to stocks during a money crunch? They decline as both the companies and investors scramble to rebuild their liquidity. Stocks bottom as the credit markets go through a panic stage. What happens next as government intervenes, pumps money into the economy and inflation accelerates? That depends on your frame of reference. If you are an American investing abroad or a foreigner buying American stocks you soon learn there are two variables—the price of the stock *and* the price of the money that the stock is traded in. As inflation heats up share prices come to be more and more influenced by currency exchange rates. Stocks can actually go up and you can lose money because the currency in which they are denominated may decline faster. Later, in an advanced stage of inflation, stocks perform amazingly well because paper money is trying to get into anything even remotely real and business itself is stimulated by renewed attempts to convert its cash into new plants and equipment. These two phenomena working together produced a 1,000% rise (100% a month for ten months) in the blow-off or final stage of the German inflation of the 1920s.[2]

Taking just a small fraction of the rise in the German market, the Dow Jones has the potential to move quickly to new highs once inflation begins again in earnest. This would not be so extraordinary—most of it would represent a catching-up process to reflect what had already happened to other prices and what would be continuing to happen to prices of anything even remotely real. Still, the question naturally presents itself: Where will the money come from to fuel a market move to a Dow Jones several times its present price?

Is there such money around? The best evidence of all for a

2. To cite a recent example, in 1980, even with a 22% inflation rate, the Italian stock market was able to make a new high.

real move in the stock market is that there are still plenty of speculative funds available.

1. There is the $200 billion (a figure that is growing daily) in money market instruments alone, waiting on the sidelines for investment opportunities versus only $4 billion at the end of the 1974 recession.

2. There are trillions of dollars in the bond market, whose owners are wondering for the first time if there isn't something more prudent than a guaranteed loss of part of their principal every year. At the end of a panic stage loan demand finally drys up and bonds advance smartly. As bond yields decline stock dividends look more appealing. But Keynesian oriented governments soon act to cure the economic paralysis and stimulate business. This frightens money back out of bonds but stocks continue to advance. When bond money starts coming into the stock market, the sky is the limit for stock prices.

3. Add to this several hundred billions in Eurodollar funds waiting to join the end of the credit boom party, and you have a potentially explosive situation for stock prices.

Making It Work For You

Do we have any way of determining when this move will start in earnest? First, it is well to remember that the stock market is strengthened, not weakened, by a decline. The lower stocks sink in price the sounder is the base for a sustained rise.

Second, prices move on surprises. The short-term surprise for causing stocks to go lower has been that the forces of deflation are in the ascendancy and hard times are biting deeper than was generally believed possible. But stocks could bottom out and begin to move up even in this environment. As soon as some kind of financial panic wrings the excesses out of the credit market the stage will be set for the biggest stock advance in decades. A slow economic recovery with diminished inflation would provide the best possible background for a sustainable rise. The basic economic problem facing America today, excessive debt formation, will not be solved, but it could temporarily appear to be solved if a saner tax policy finally coaxes some of the underground economy's hoarded funds out of hiding and the money panic dulls the attraction of borrowing for awhile. Over the long term, the problems of unemployment and stagnation will remain and be dealt with as always by government stimulating the economy. Printing additional money will have the effect of driving newly created cash into equities.

Having ascertained where the money can come from and that a new sustainable bull market is possible, let us consider what type of stocks you should be watching.

Traditional bond buyers and foreign bankers, being prudent men, will naturally want the biggest companies, the ones with the best sounding names. Interestingly enough, these are also the stocks that have performed the worst over the past fifteen years and are historically the cheapest. If there is an inflationary blowoff in the future, keep in mind that at market tops, the blue chip stocks that comprise the Dow Jones Average usually perform very well. This leads us to conclude that

WHEN THE MOVE STARTS, THE GREATEST DANGER WILL BE NOT BEING IN STOCKS.

This doesn't mean that even then your stock investments should be made for the long pull. Today, in our topsy-turvy world, changes that used to take years can happen in weeks and months. Today, it is a mistake to view anything on the economic horizon as permanent. The speculator knows that there are no "one-decision" stocks in this crazy world.

How can you avoid the fundamental mistake of thinking long-term about investments? By compressing your time frame and learning to be a trader. When we examine past influences, we see that as inflation progresses, the violence of price movements becomes more severe and produces spike-shaped market graphs.

Spike markets can produce huge profits for the speculator, especially the technically-oriented trader who is willing and able to sell in an atmosphere of euphoria and buy when others panic.

Why have markets become so volatile? Today there are many many billions of Eurodollars that are ready to move in or out of Swiss banks on a moment's notice. These capital flows can cause violent moves. All capital has become flight capital, ready to cross national boundaries to take advantage of opportunities. This instability must be factored into your investment decisions so that you learn to take advantage of these rapid changes.

Stock Selection

How do you go about choosing exactly the right stocks? Sophisticated stock buyers use many methods. Let's consider a composite that demands so much by the very structure of its stringent requirements that your chances of success are greatly enhanced.

First, look at future earnings. Big profits can be obtained from picking stocks with big projected earnings gains for the coming year. If the present price does not reflect these future earnings gains, time alone will put the odds in your favor. Standard and Poor's has a future earnings service that summarizes earnings estimates from various sources, and writers in *Barron's* and *Forbes* are always estimating earnings one to four years out. Next, look for stocks in this group that have small capitalizations (a small number of shares). The reason these stocks will advance is that the earnings increase (lightning) creates a bias to the upside, and the small number of shares makes the stock easy to move (greased). Together they add up to greased lightning.

To further increase your chances of success, consider the following rules for stock purchases.

1. Look for stocks whose future indicated growth rates exceed current price earnings ratios *by a factor of two or*

more—for example, a stock whose earnings are reasonably projected to grow at 16% annually for the next few years and that is still selling for only eight times current earnings. (Consult a stock broker for such a list. You will be amazed how many there are.)

2. Look for stocks that have a good chart pattern. (Consult a stock broker that is a technician.)

3. Consider stocks that have a Value Line Advisory Service rating of 2 or better. This means they are outperforming the market and have good relative strength.

4. Find stocks that have an historic price earnings ratio significantly above the present. (This too can be ascertained from Value Line.)

5. Purchase stocks that are *underowned* by the institutions. This means you are more likely to benefit from the funds' enormous buying power than suffer from their massive selling pressure when and if they change their minds.

6. Since these stocks are to be purchased in a period of great potential inflation, pay particular attention to *resource stocks* and give preference to them. After all, getting as close as you can to something real is what inflation investing is all about. Be careful of big oil companies, however, because they are a natural and convenient whipping boy in good times and a convenient source of taxable revenue in bad.

7. Pick stocks with a story. Stock buyers, like children, love fairy tales.

8. Don't overtrade. By applying the high standards set forth above, you will find that very few investments fit all the requirements. This may not make your broker happy, but it will serve you better.

9. Trade with the trend and don't chase stocks. If the trend is up, buy on dips. If the trend is down, sell on rallies.

10. Cut your losses short. This is what separates a live speculator from a dead duck.

The second method of stock selection is the simplest of all. It consists of getting someone else to do it for you. Try to choose someone that is inflation-oriented, if possible. The basic rule here is: Look for hot advisors, not hot stocks. Even if you find such a person, you should make the final decisions yourself. When the magic wears off, say "thank you" and go in search of new advice. Don't be bound by false loyalty or gratitude for past favors. You owe him nothing. If you feel guilty send him a nice present at holiday time but don't give back your winnings.

Now that we have made a case for a potentially large stock advance starting in a deflationary environment and have given you a general idea of how to proceed in selecting stocks for an inflationary move, here is a summary of the general dos and don'ts of stock speculation.

1. Try to disregard totally Wall Street advice, or listen carefully and do the opposite.

2. You won't get rich acting on items you read in the papers. Wall Street "news" is usually disseminated by insiders, specialists, and other smart money interests who want you to believe one thing so that they can do something else. When you read something somewhere, that isn't news. The only real "news" factor is sudden news that hits the market by surprise. As a speculator, you should pay great attention to how a stock reacts to this kind of news. If it continually shrugs off bad news, that stock is going higher. If it refuses to advance on good news, the stock is topping out and should be sold.

3. The more money there is around, the more money will find its way into stocks. In deciding whether to buy any stock, if you have to look at just one thing, concentrate on liquidity in the financial markets (lots of money available in money market funds and margin accounts to buy stocks) and forget the rest. (You can find out how much potential investment money is available from your FRB of St. Louis letter on monetary trends mentioned earlier.)

4. The fundamental economic danger that should act as a sell signal will be when you see the government's borrowing needs becoming so great that it is crowding business out of the

capital markets again. This could occur sooner than most economists think if government deficits are not reduced drastically.

5. In deciding whether or not to use stocks as a vehicle to profit from inflation, remember *liquidity*. The thing that makes heavily traded stocks especially attractive to the speculator is how easily and cheaply they can be acquired and disposed of. You can decide to sell as you pour yourself a cup of coffee and have made the sale before you finish drinking it. In this way, neither the stocks nor the caffeine keeps you awake.[3]

6. In a third-stage inflation, things move fast. Don't wait too long to get aboard after the market starts up.

7. Try to stay liquid as much of the time as possible. View "home base" as cash, not stocks. If you are rich enough you can speculate heavily with only a small percentage of your capital. This allows you to make your money work hard and still not be wiped out if you are wrong.

8. Gold stocks became respectable a few years back, just before they started their precipitous decline. Even stodgy old mutual fund managers discovered them, which was a warning to be careful. Since mutual fund managers only talk to each other they display a positive genius for being wrong. Gold stocks are usually companies with small-capitalizations. This means they are characterized by dramatic volatility up or down. South African golds are politically vulnerable, but pay very high dividends (on the theory that the dividends are a return on capital). Canadian gold stocks could go through the roof if there is racial trouble in South Africa, but gold stocks in general are more linked to *real*, rather than financial or paper, assets. Consequently, they experience softness when inflation declines. There should be plenty of time to buy this kind of traditional inflation hedge later, but don't forget huge profits are to be made in them sometime in the future. To make sure you don't forget, start keeping a notebook of future stock ideas now. Add to your list

---

3. However, be ever alert to impaired liquidity for a whole market that happens when there is a money panic or a general desire to sell. Later on in this section there is a discussion of what happens to stocks at times of crisis. This is information any speculator must be aware of.

when you read of future earnings projections by stock analysts you respect, of stocks that appear especially attractive.

9. Remember, even with unemployment high and business in the doldrums, stocks can climb a wall of fear. A declining inflation rate could provide the long-awaited turnaround in stock prices, and a reheating of inflation later on could perversely provide the final blow-off advance.[4]

10. Be cynical enough to keep in mind that the reason for using any stock selection method is not its inherent logic but the fact that others, including the most sophisticated money managers and stock buyers, use it. Since stocks move in anticipation of events, they can be used to increase the amount of money you will have to invest in *real* things later on.

SPECULATIVE POINT:
Once in a lifetime there is an opportunity to buy stocks that can advance first on a rationale of lessening inflation and finally go much higher in an inflationary blow-off. Carefully chosen stocks will be one of the first vehicles to help you arrive at your retirement goals, but let the recession squeeze some of the air out of the tires first.

A Postscript Of Difficult But Important Material

All of the preceding was based on finding an empirical way to capitalize on movements in the stock market, given the assumption that there exists in the real world a market of stocks providing liquidity. Now you are sophisticated enough to be told still another truth. Not only is there no tooth fairy, there

---

4. During inflation's final frenetic move, stocks will appreciate the most although most of their rise is illusory in that it only looks like they are advancing because they are discounting the drop in the value of money. A speculator takes movement where he can find it and tries to profit from it so don't worry about illusions. Look how well banks and governments have done with them over the years.

isn't even *real* liquidity in the stock market. The liquidity that is so highly valued and talked about in the stock market is just another myth of the modern world. This doesn't mean that you as a speculator can't make money pretending it exists. You can buy. You can, as an individual, even sell. You can take profits out as an individual, but as a sophisticated speculator out to retire rich by 1986 you must be aware of the fact that if a substantial number of investors try to sell *en masse,* they are going to be in real trouble. In order to see why and how let us consider the following argument expressed in the form of a closed-system example. If the material seems too difficult don't be afraid to skip to page 82.

A Stock Market Model To Prove The Proposition That Paper Profits Are, And Must Remain, Just Paper

The point of this reasoned argument is that the financial page is a statement of mass opinion and not a statement of real worth; that paper stock prices are not realizable *en masse.*

The Argument

Changes in opinion can apparently create riches on the stock market. The average investor—indeed, even the sophisticated speculator—regards the market price as published in the financial pages of his or her daily newspaper as not only symbols of tangible wealth but actual realizable wealth. This idea is based on the assumption that he or she, as an individual, can easily convert these figures into purchasing power. The investor who buys stock and then witnesses a decline in the quotation assumes that he or she has lost money and even believes that someone else has gained that money. Conversely, as the stock goes up, the investor thinks he or she has made a profit—become richer. It would take a persuasive person indeed to convince the stockholder that he or she is not tangibly richer when they read that their stock has advanced three points the previous day. To understand the actual workings of the stock market, let us construct a simple model using only two investors, Mr. Jones and Mr. Smith.

The Mechanism

Mr. Jones has $1,000. Mr. Smith owns 100 shares of XYZ Oil. XYZ Oil is quoted at $10 a share and Smith decides to sell his 100 shares to Jones for $1,000. A month later, Smith believes he made a mistake and wants to repurchase the shares. Jones, however, is not willing to sell under $12.50 a share. Smith buys back 80 shares at $12.50, paying the full $1,000 that he had originally received. The price is now theoretically $12.50. After selling, Jones reads that a new oil find will mean future earnings of several cents a share more and an eventual worth per shares of $25, and he regrets having sold. Next day Jones buys back 50 of the shares for $20 apiece, paying the full $1,000 that he had previously received and increases his holdings to 70 shares.

At this point Jones owns 70 shares of XYZ Oil but since each share is now worth $20, his holdings as quoted in the daily newspaper are worth $1,400 instead of the original $1,000 he started with. Thus, Jones has realized an apparent profit of $400. Smith is also very happy because he has 30 of his original shares of XYZ stock with a total value of $600 and he also has $1,000 cash.

Jones is apparently richer by $400; Smith by $600. In fact, however, the riches of both are on paper; the rise in price having been caused by the operation of supply and demand. The amount of money available throughout the original series of transactions has always been the same, e.g. $1,000. The amount of XYZ shares in existence was always 100 shares. Real value reflecting the earnings of the stock may not have changed at all or may have even declined. The price, however, was moved up by improving investor opinion through the workings of the law of supply and demand. Seemingly both parties gained from each other. This process could be imagined to continue indefinitely until the shares are theoretically priced at $200 each. Starting with only $1,000 in money, a capital appreciation of $19,000 in new wealth has been seemingly added to the wealth of the community.

Recognizing that this is happening not only to the stock of XYZ Oil but to hundreds of other securities, you can easily understand what the headlines mean when they say "Stocks

Rise $4 Billion." It makes no real difference whether two investors are engaged in the process or a million. All that happens in the latter case is that Smith buys his shares from Brown, instead of from Jones, and Douglas buys from Smith.

The essence of the phenomenon we are observing is that a small amount of money (the amount will always be relatively small) has *flowed in the right direction* and caused a succession of increases in capital values (on paper) of many times the original amount invested.[5] All these stock price increases are based on changing investor opinions of the value assigned to the shares in question. And the figures used don't even take into consideration the shrinkage caused by broker commissions or Uncle Sam's transfer taxes. It is impossible to realize real profits faster than new savings have accumulated, but paper profits can grow to the sky.

Up to this point everybody's satisfied. The faster opinions have changed and the more paper values have been assigned to stocks, the more deliriously happy investors have become. But, let's return to Jones and Smith and assume they have both have a change in sentiment. Both now think the market is headed down and decide to take profits. To realize these profits, they'll have to sell their shares of XYZ Oil to each other to realize ready cash. Shares worth twenty thousand dollars (for that was their mathematical value in yesterday's financial quotation) are now offered for sale. But there is only $1,000 in real money or cash available to purchase them—and, incidentally, Smith has all the money. But Smith is not a buyer because he is a would-be seller. The market orders on this day would thus be from sellers only. So, unless new savers came in, there would be no possible way for both Smith and Jones to convert their paper profits into money. The only possible course, in the absence of new savers willing to exchange their new savings for the old shares, would be a drastic fall in market prices until the amount of cash ($1,000) could equal the paper value of the

5. This is analogous to the way a small deposit by an investor is used to pyramid loans by a bank in the credit-creating mechanism of the Federal Reserve Board.

shares. However, this would probably cause an additional drop in the shares because at the point XYZ Oil is $10 again all profits will have disappeared. Smith, the holder of the cash, bearishly influenced by the decline in price back to $10 has become too cynical to purchase Jones's holdings, even at the originally low price. At this point, paralysis ensues.

We have thus seen on a simplified basis what happens in the stock market every day. For example, IBM with 600 million shares outstanding rises 2 points on a volume of 200,000 shares, thus adding a theoretical worth of $1,200,000,000 to the paper wealth of over 99 and 9/10ths percent of the shareholders who were not trading their IBM shares that day. The theoretical value or weight of each share traded is hence $6,000, whereas the market value of IBM on that particular day in question is only $50. This demonstrates that a little confidence can go a long way—how a small amount of money can cause enormous increases in paper capital increases until attempts to convert these paper values to cash suddenly cause them to vanish.

By studying this example, you can see that with a very small amount of newly-saved money (or bank loans), the supply of dealers' stocks can be exhausted, and prices can, and usually do, rise to any extent that investor optimism dictates. Following this reasoning, even so relatively small a sum as $10 million can cause a capital appreciation of $100 million dollars in paper profits on the New York Stock Exchange. This is accomplished merely by exhausting brokers' or dealers' supply of stocks and causing investors to spend in *succession* the $10 million on a large number of securities. You might think that the process would end as soon as the price rise, caused by the injection of the original $10 million, had induced the public to sell, thus enabling dealers to replace their stocks at the new high prices. But the answer to this is that the money paid by the dealers in replenishing their stocks is received again by the investing public, who can once more spend it and force up the price of still more shares. As a practical matter (outside and exclusive of genuine panic selling) when the trend lines are firmly up, new money will come in to enable all available sellers to get out, even if a healthy slice of the quotations is knocked off in the process. In a *major top*, however, as new savings are in short supply[6] stock prices stagnate. Seeing this, more potential buyers stay on the sidelines. A few investors, believing their shares to be fully valued, try to take profits. Even if their shares represent only 5% of the total paper capital appreciation, it is not realizable. This is true because only the original amount of money is available and if this is under the 5%, the withdrawal of even this small amount of paper capital may lead to a collapse. Also, keep in mind that a good portion of the original money put into the market has disappeared in subscriptions to new issues, whose proceeds go directly to the new company, as well as in commissions and transfer taxes mentioned previously.

Conclusion

Although investors may enjoy their profit on paper, they must not and cannot (as a group) try to enjoy these profits by converting them to *anything,* even paper money. They must not try to cash them or spend them because the liquidity of stocks is essentially artificial. Wholesale attempts to convert paper values into tangible wealth tends to cause the paper values to disappear. The rule is as follows:

NO MORE MONEY CAN BE TAKEN OUT OF THE STOCK EX-CHANGE THAN WHAT IS SIMULTANEOUSLY MADE AVAILABLE BY NEW SAVINGS OR WHAT WAS PUT IN ORIGINALLY (AS RE-DUCED BY NEW ISSUES, COMMISSIONS, AND TRANSFER TAXES).

One of the principal arguments advanced to justify the thesis that another 1929 type liquidation could not occur is that the prevailing margin requirements are much higher (50% versus only 10% in 1929). Hence, it is argued the reckless speculation of 1929 that saw a relatively small drop in stock prices wipe out individual investors, is not present. The people who advance this theory are really talking about another facet of the liquidity problem. The companies, in their dubious ingenuity, have by

---

6. Usually savings are insignificant at this point anyway since paper profits are large relative to savings.

their collective actions, devised a new way to ensure their stock's vulnerability. They have done this by increasing the number of shares to a point where small fluctuations can produce wide swings in paper values. The actual increase in shares, accomplished by stock splits, in recent years constitutes not only a fantastic liquidity threat in realizing paper profits, but also serves as the drag, or brake, to increasing per-share earnings. When IBM tries to pull down another $1 per share in earnings, they actually have to increase total earnings by over $1 billion. Since federal income taxes take roughly 43%, in order to account for these earnings on such a wide-share base (if we use IBM's current pretax profit margin after depreciation of 31% on gross sales and an after-tax margin of 13%), IBM must increase its sales almost $5 billion to make an extra $1 per share. This requires pushing a lot of computers through the door.

The only difference between the real financial world and the model is that in the real world we are not dealing with a closed system. There can be money flows into (and out of) the stock exchange just as there are flows into and out of the watertight compartments of a submarine. But, if the submarine ever starts to sink, the separate compartments are closed off, and all of the model's limitations for simultaneous *en masse* withdrawals come into play. The same line of reasoning applied in the construction of this economic model can be applied to other things like real estate, commodities, or collectibles. From this discussion the reader can gain some insight into why new infusions of freshly printed money become increasingly necessary to sustain any boom not based on solid consumer demand for newly produced goods.

All this has been set forth to make you truly sophisticated, not to frighten you out of speculating in stocks. Being aware of the difficulties will keep you from counting too heavily on the supposed liquidity of any asset.

As the charts on the front and back endpapers show, the stock market has been, and will continue to be, around for a long time providing opportunities to take advantage of future booms and busts.

CHAPTER 7

Real Estate

Real estate today represents the backbone of America's financial holdings. Everyone aspiring to be a speculator should begin by owning his or her own home. Why? Because a speculator can think more clearly with the type of security that owning a home provides. Whether you're psychologically cut out for speculation or not, there is much to be said for home ownership. What can compare with owning a piece of one of the freest, most prosperous, stable, and beautiful nations on earth? What really makes homeowners wax poetic is that house prices have just about tripled since 1967. Assuming an average leverage (large debt relative to small equity) of about three to one, the increase in home prices has produced a (usually untaxed) gain of about ten times the money invested. High leverage with cheap money has made people feel good about their homes. Inflation has, in essence, allowed them to live in a better neighborhood without moving.

Another important plus for home ownership as an investment is that in periods of inflation everything costs so much that people's activities are reduced and their lives becomes centered in their home. This makes home ownership even more desirable, and home prices reflect this element of increased usage.

Over the years, buying and holding land has created more millionaires than any other type of investment. It is also the most subsidized tax shelter you can own. When you buy real estate, you are aligning yourself with the most powerful interests in America. Since this is where the presidents, congressmen, and senators who make the laws keep *their* money, you can be sure that their own special privileges (for example, deducting interest payments on speculative real estate purchases) will continue for a good long time.

One of real estate's principal attractions is its simplicity. People understand real estate. They can touch it, walk on it, live and work on it, and use it to grow their food. They can even be buried in it. It is also a great way to borrow money. Through some of the creative financing techniques available, property owners have been able to multiply their equity working capital as if by magic.

Insurance companies, savings and loans, and even banks have understood real estate and felt comfortable in making top-dollar loans on its security. Often investors have been able to borrow enough money to recoup what they had invested and still hold on to take advantage of the rise in the *total* value of the property, while paying off their mortgage in ever cheaper dollars.

The interest rate on real estate loans has traditionally been about half that of consumer loans.

Best of all, in a third-stage inflation, land always appreciates substantially because it is *real*—as real and as profoundly fundamental a manifestation of wealth as can be found.

All of you who know real estate and are oriented to dealing in it should definitely continue your winning ways. I'm sure that the specter of renewed inflation on the horizon will not discourage you in your endeavors.

A Time For Caution

However, real estate has a few potentially serious drawbacks at the present time that make a repeat of its orderly price advance over the last decade unlikely.

Many think real estate prices can only go up. Historically, this is not true. Farm real estate declined 50% in price from

1915 to 1942. House prices lagged behind consumer prices most of the time between 1910 and 1948.

Circus Financing

A great deal of the real estate sold in the late 1970s was sold with financing that called for "balloon" or lump sum payments in three to seven years. These balloon payments will produce a scramble for mortgage funds as they become due in the early 1980s.

The way ingenious speculators have attempted to solve the problem of high prices is by dividing or syndicating the properties up amongst a large number of buyers. Some of these "investments" have become so complicated that they amount to nothing more than structured insanity.

Because of high interest payments and the bizarre mortgages sellers are forced to take back, real estate prices have been experiencing an invisible crash for some time. As inflationary expectations have subsided, the inflation premium built into land prices has declined, acting as a depressant on sales prices.

As *the* prime real asset, land has benefitted from inflation. But as financial assets, bonds, and money funds get a temporary play, it's invariably at the expense of the hard-money asset type of investments like land and gold. As long as the recession continues, the greatest real estate opportunities will continue to be in dealing in foreclosed property; making money (if you have the stomach for it) out of someone else's misery. But even if the present looks bleak, successful real estate investors traditionally take a long-term approach; above all, they have *staying power* which is another way of saying they're not frightened easily.

Real Estate In The Period Ahead

Looking beyond the current recession to a more virulent inflation in the future, does real estate have any disadvantages that might impede its performance at that time? How would real estate fare in a period of extremely rapid inflation?

It would do very well because it is real, but it is not as easily saleable as some other hard-asset investment alternatives. The length of time it takes to sell property could result in many lost opportunities in an inflationary blow-off period that may itself last only a short time. More importantly, because real estate is illiquid, you could be trapped by inertia into holding it too long.

One of real estate's real advantages in the up phase of an inflationary cycle is that its value is not published daily in the newspapers like stocks, bonds, or commodities. Thus you don't get shaken out by temporary dips in real estate prices. It is easy to be cool when you don't have someone telling you your house is worth $5,000 less today. However, this lack of market information can be a real disadvantage when the top of the market is reached and prices start down. You don't know how much you've lost until it is too late. This may explain the fact that volume dries up, but property does not decline in price at major turning points. After the 1929 crash, asking prices held up remarkably well. The scarcity of bids caused sales to decline, but it wasn't until 1931 that prices finally started dropping. There is a bullish bias among landowners that dies very slowly, and they are among the last to throw in the towel and agree to accept lower prices.

After prices do start down, they unfortunately drop precipitously and sales volume does not seem to be greatly stimulated by the lower prices. In the economist's jargon, real estate is price inelastic. If you don't want it and don't need it, you don't want or need it at a lower price. In brief, *you can be forced to hold real property for a good long time if you overstay the game.* This means you had better have a personal use for the property you are holding late in an inflationary cycle. Although very high figures might be bandied about and temporarily dress up your balance sheet, it will not be easy to liquidate property anywhere near those figures.

Mortgage Rates

The purchase of real estate is closely linked to mortgage rates. In the decade of the 1970s, mortgage debt increased from $270 billion to $840 billion. Most of the increase took place in the latter half of the decade. Until 1973, mortgage credit expanded an average of $15 billion a year. Then, starting in 1977, it sky-rocketed to $100 billion annually. This explosion of mortgage credit had the inflationary effect of adding to the real money supply and now has the deflationary effect of requiring great payments by debtors.

The big reason for the tremendous rise in real estate prices in the late 1970s was this huge supply of mortgage money. In the 1980s, things have changed. Increased competition for investment funds comes from both government and business. Potential real estate buyers have discovered that the mortgage market is a residual market that is accommodated only *after* government and business have satisfied their needs first. Since the huge federal debt now requires practically all the new capital creation of the nation just to pay its interest, very little is left for business and practically none for mortgages.

Even if mortgage money is available, the rate a prospective buyer has to pay for mortgage money is significant in determining the profitability of any deal. For many years, real estate buyers have been able to finance their purchases with OPM (other people's money). Most of these loans were made at interest rates that made it cheap or even free money.

The government made all this possible through artificially holding down interest rates legally payable on savings to around 5%. The do-gooders have been so anxious to help the housing industry that they have now almost made a cripple out of it. Let all recipients of the government's bounty take note! Speculative builders and land speculators were shamefully subsidized at the expense of small savers. Imagine, if you will, the government subsidizing loans to other fields of investment. What if stock buyers, for example, in the 1950s could have borrowed $50,000 at 5% interest payable in 30 years to buy IBM stock? All these absurdities are finally being extinguished by the realities of the marketplace. Now that the concept of variable interest rates has replaced the traditional fixed-rate mortgage, buyers have been deprived of their free money racket and real estate in the next up cycle will be no easier to leverage than gold or any other real asset.

Like the businessmen, real estate buyers need to make more

money with their borrowed capital than it costs them. Hence a change in interest rate can be devastating. Keep in mind that as we move to the end of a fifty-year credit cycle, the government is forced to rely more and more on high interest rates to dampen inflationary expectations and attract new savings for its own needs. High interest rates raise havoc with land speculators, builders, and even ordinary home buyers. The desire to buy or build is still there, but more and more people are priced out of the market.

Rent Control

Another pitfall in speculating in real estate is that as inflationary pressures build there is always great public demand for rent controls. Caught in the crossfire with what owners can get being controlled, and what they have to pay being elastic, potential danger lurks for the unwary who have gotten used to thinking land is a bargain at any price. With rents fixed and costs spiraling higher, landlords can easily end up becoming victims of the very inflation they bought property to hedge against. Rent control is especially a danger in multiunit buildings. In France, for example, after the second world war many landlords of large luxurious apartment buildings not only were unable to make repairs, but were forced to live in poverty themselves.

Neighborhood Values

Over the long pull what determines real estate values is its proximity to a large job market. Still, there are other considerations. Historically, real estate values have always been spotty, varying greatly within an area. As inflation progresses and causes more slums and crime, the variation becomes even greater. The value of all property is based on the maintenance of social order. Today there is a great deal of civil strife in most cities. The crime and social disturbance characteristic of large metropolitan areas might keep a damper on city prices and make small-town property relatively more attractive for a time. Since the government is giving us so little for the "protection money" it extracts from us, we can assume that in a period of increased inflation there would be even more crime and violence to cope with. If you think land cannot go down or be appropriated, discuss the matter with the land owners in Angola, Mozambique, Iran, Cuba, Lebanon, or Palestine, to name just a few. These people believed in land, too, but they ended up trading giant farms and mansions for a few gold coins or even airplane tickets. Maybe it can't happen in America, but it is something a Swiss banker can't help thinking about.

Farmland, offering the ultimate crisis protection, tends to do the best of all in a third-stage inflation because it is connected with the production of the most basic of all necessities—food (assuming it can be harvested in peace).

To Buy Or Not To Buy?

Having listed all the negatives that have been injected into the present market, real estate is still attractive. A knowledgeable speculator can still make more in one or two good real estate deals than he can earn in years of hard work. There is much evidence to suggest that

> IN SPITE OF ALL THE NEW NEGATIVE FORCES AT WORK, WELL-CHOSEN LAND IN THE UNITED STATES WILL INCREASE IN PRICE IN THE FUTURE MORE THAN IT EVER HAS IN THE PAST. BUT IF IT DOES THIS IT WILL NOT BE BECAUSE OF FREE MONEY FINANCING AS IN THE PAST BUT FOR THE SIMPLE REASON THAT MONEY WILL DECLINE MORE THAN IT EVER HAS.

What strategy should a sophisticated real estate speculator be considering today? Short term, he should be looking for a *buy* point. Being definitely a minority opinion gives the idea merit. Carefully considered purchases made during the present period of financial uncertainty should work out extremely well over the medium to longer term. The speculative buyer might even consider the use of options which will appear to have little or no value by an eager owner willing to rent his property. Assuming the same old Keynesian economists trot out the same old Keynesian solution of more money the snap in real estate prices from up to down could be dramatic. Make sure anything you buy at that time is either sold on the next rise or is something you want to hold on to for a long time.

SPECULATIVE POINT:
The most advantageous sell point for real estate still lies in the future. This one, unfortunately, could be the last one for a long, long time so you had better be a knowledgeable speculator to play it.

Conclusion

In the past, a certain group of creative people has always overcome whatever difficulties they faced, so if real estate is your game and you are aware of and equipped to handle the new obstacles that have developed in real estate speculation, then by all means continue to do what you know best.

If not, you are probably better advised in the near future to limit your real estate holdings to those that fulfill your own immediate needs and concentrate on areas that offer greater investment potential coupled with a higher degree of liquidity.

What About Mortgages As Investments?

As for real estate mortgages, a few words will suffice. They are a hybrid piece of paper that depend on real estate prices to assure their value. What argues against conventional mortgages from the lender's point of view is that in inflationary periods the borrower benefits, not the lender, as the value of the dollar declines. Also, the long term for which money is committed makes mortgages nonliquid and you cannot sell them without offering to give a substantial discount.

What argues against mortgages in a deflationary period is the disappearance of the security as real estate prices decline. Borrowers have wised up to these disadvantages, with the result that the days of the fixed-rate, long-term mortgage are gone. In its place are various types of participation agreements whereby the lender attempts to participate in part of the borrower's profits on sale as a condition to making the loan in the first place.

Even with these protections and participations, mortgages have little justification for either the speculator or investor. They are the antithesis of the liquidity that these times demand if you are to prosper. If you have gathered that buying mortgages is not favored by a Swiss banker, you're right! The reason one should be aware of the problems of mortgages is not only to avoid them directly but to avoid the thrift institutions and S & Ls that hold them.

CHAPTER 8

Gold

Where The Money Is

A Senate investigating committee, looking into crime in the U.S., once asked Willie Sutton, the notorious bank robber, why he robbed banks. He replied, logically enough for his day, "Because that's where the money is!"

Before we understand the role of gold in our economy we must know a little history. Like Willie Sutton, we must determine *where the money is.*

Since money is historically something valuable and paper itself has very little intrinsic value, the question naturally presents itself: Why should anyone accept a piece of paper as valuable money?

If barbarians invaded any country tomorrow, they would carry off the gold, jewels, paintings, rugs, furs and everything else that felt and looked good. The one thing they *wouldn't* steal is paper money. They're not stupid. How come we treasure it and they don't? In a word, we've forgotten what's real. We have been victimized by the operation of a million laws and circuitious manipulations designed to hide and confuse what the government and the bankers have been up to until we no longer remember what real wealth is. Real wealth consists of goods produced by human effort, not paper money. But we need something that can be used symbolically to measure conveniently the *relative* value of such goods. What could be used?

A Fairy Tale

In the beginning, there was gold. This was money. People carried it when they went out to buy things, but it was heavy and bandits could steal it, so goldsmiths (old name for bankers) said, "I'll keep it for you," and for a while that's all they did. Every day the goldsmith would go in and look at the gold. All that money sitting there idle made him start to think. One day, the goldsmith remarked to his accountant, "In a year only 20% of the people ever come to redeem their gold, so why not loan out the rest?"

"How?" the accountant asked.

"Deposit receipts are just paper. I'll have some extra ones printed and the next time somebody brings in a dollar's worth of gold, I'll issue $5 of these newly printed deposit receipts against the gold, give the depositor one, then loan out the other four of them at interest. At 3%, that's twelve cents a year!" (This was all before inflation. Twelve cents was a lot of money and that is why he was so excited.)

"But isn't that dishonest?" the accountant protested feebly.

"Of course not," the goldsmith replied. "That's leverage."

And soon everyone admired the banker-goldsmiths and they hobnobbed with royalty. Then when the king found out about leverage, he fired his chief alchemist (old word for economist) and decided it was too good a deal for the goldsmiths and he would take over the job of warehousing the gold and issuing the receipts himself. He called the receipts paper money and even had "In God We Trust" printed on them, hoping that would make them more acceptable.

Just like the banker-goldsmith, the king shrewdly kept a little gold in case any of the citizens got nervous and wanted real money—gold. Knowing they could get it kept them from asking for it. In this way, the *illusion* of redeemability persisted. Remember, the paper was just a receipt for the bullion, and at this time people hadn't forgotten which was which. With just gold bullion sitting there doing nothing, kings had to content themselves with very small wars, but as soon as they got into the banking business by loaning unbacked paper money, they found they could take on (and soon defeat) almost everybody. *This is when people started to need protection from the whole world. Inflation, in other words, is a convenient way of financing war.*

Over the years, the king found out that if he reduced the percentage of gold backing, he could issue more paper money. This additional paper money caused prices received by businessmen to rise faster than wages paid to their workers, and this stimulated business at home even between wars. With all the new money, everyone felt happy and prosperous. The do-gooder king wanted that—desperately. It kept everybody—even the peasants—quiet. But the gold was always there as an anchor to reality. Soon the king noticed that prices kept going up and the paper money always seemed to be worth less. With rising prices limiting the worth of paper money, the king found he couldn't fight the right wars or make his subjects happy enough. That is when rulers first began referring to gold as that "barbarous relic."

Then, there was a recession and six men who were out of work couldn't pay their taxes. The king had to decide whether to curb his spending or print more money to cover his deficit. He chose logically enough to print more money.

The country had started out with full theoretical convertability for all the paper money, but like the goldsmith before him, the king found that so few people asked for gold, he could issue more—a lot more—paper than he had gold. The king became so powerful that everyone got to thinking that it was the king that made the money strong, not the money that made the king strong. In this they forgot history's fundamental golden rule, which is:

HE WHO HAS THE GOLD MAKES THE RULES.

By now, everyone had forgotten so much and had fallen so much in love with paper and other wood products that it was easy for each successive king to cut down the gold backing for the paper. This is how it went:

King Roosevelt (1934):	From 100% to 35%
King Truman (1945):	From 35% to 25%
King Johnson (1967):	From 25% to 0%

But there was one limit and restriction that was hard to shake. The paper money would always have some value in the kingdom (if for nothing else than paying taxes), but the question remained of how to handle the money owed other kings (like King De-Gaulle). These other kings had their own paper money rackets going and understood ours well enough not to want mere paper. They still wanted gold. Finally, a solution was found. We gave them so much of our paper money that they became afraid to offend us for fear we wouldn't give them any more. In 1971, when they finally decided the paper money wasn't worth collecting and tried to convert it to gold, King Nixon said "Nothing doing."

So they were stuck with tons of paper money which no one wanted or needed. They had no alternative but to put U.S. paper money in their treasuries and issue more of their own paper money against it. This meant that their paper money was backed by our paper money, which was now backed by nothing. When their subjects asked for gold for their share of our paper money, these other kings told their citizens "no way," so the people got the idea they were being set up and put their money in Swiss banks instead. Everyone knows that the Swiss are the greatest loan brokers in history. There it remains—in a giant computer—and these foreigners all make lots of money loaning these dollars to each other. This electronic money is called *Eurodollars.*

Gold As Money

Since this story has strayed pretty far from gold, we can sympathize with all those that have forgotten that historically *gold is money.* Because gold still retains some of the elements of money it has been necessary to understand the past so that we can better understand gold's future. With all this as background certain questions naturally present themselves.

Does gold have to be our money? What role does gold play in our monetary structure? What role should it play? What is gold worth today? Is it worth anything if we don't use it as money?

Much is made of gold's industrial uses as well as its beauty for jewelry, but if these uses actually determined its price, gold might well be selling below $100 an ounce.

IN SPITE OF ITS USEFULNESS AND BEAUTY NO ONE NEEDS A SINGLE OUNCE OF GOLD.

That is a fact. Yet, directly opposed to this fact is another: Government's attempt to back paper money with hot air is not working —and historically never has worked. Foreigners have no need for dollars to settle trade balances. This fact, added to our government's propensity to run deficits and finance those deficits with printing press money, leads one to believe that eventually the dollar must be devalued. By definition, there is no other way to devalue the dollar than by raising the price of gold. Thus, it is the *future need* of gold by governments to back their paper money that gives gold its present speculative value. Governments—who know what is going on better than their citizens—believe in gold's future. In 1980 alone, governments, acting through their central banks, purchased 6 million ounces of gold for over 3 billion dollars. Foreign central banks already own more gold than South Africa could probably produce in half a century. Given the present atmosphere of chaos and distrust in the world, it is difficult to conceive of these governments selling their gold *en masse.*

It is in the struggle between the lack of present need, and yet great future requirements to inspire confidence in new paper currency, that the price of gold shall be determined.

Gold As A Store Of Value

Gold is a proven way to preserve purchasing power over long spans of time, but since it is already up around 1,000% since 1971, there is some doubt about its efficacy as a way to make money in the future. Since volumes have already been written about precious metals, we will concern ourselves with only so much of the past as is necessary to construct a scenario for a dramatic price increase in the future.

The next upward move in gold will come after the hiatus of stable prices has given way to a more virulent type of inflation and the flaws in a paper money economy become more clear.

The more inadequate paper money proves to be, the more people will look to gold. Gold holders wait patiently in anticipation of the day when gold is summoned back like a Winston Churchill to lead the Western world out of chaos. But waiting can be painful. Figure 1 shows just how painful.

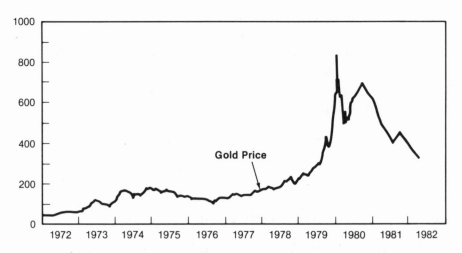

Figure 1. Even after its recent decline, there has still been a dramatic rise in gold (decline in paper money?) since the "barbarous metal" was set free to compete in the open market place. Perhaps some day redundant paper money will be known as "that barbarous relic."

What Real Money Consists Of

Historically, money has had two characteristics: It has been acceptable as a medium of exchange, *and* it has represented a store of value (which means it must *have* value).

Today, the dollar is the world's medium of exchange, yet is merely a piece of paper depending exclusively on confidence. Confidence in what? In the power of the United States. Otherwise, the only thing dollars represent is evidence of a pseudo-debt—a piece of paper totally without intrinsic value that may or may not be honored in exchange for goods at some date in the future. Analyzed on this basis, dollars are not money at all.

What about gold? Is it money? It certainly satisfies the "store-of-value" requirement. It is scarce, beautiful, and its extreme malleability makes it very useful in both the arts and science. As for its acceptability, as a medium of exchange, gold has been traditionally accepted as money until the last few decades when politicians' caustic comments have tried to dull its luster. However, as George Bernard Shaw once said, "If you have to choose between a politician's promises and gold—pick gold."

The issuance of the Krugerrand and other popular gold coins has created what amounts to an underground conservative money. These coins are tradeable within a few percent of their bullion value and hence are quite liquid. To the extent that gold has become more of a medium of exchange, its usefulness as money has been enhanced. But what gold really has going for it is the politicians' proclivity to run deficits and print new dollars to cover the deficits. With every new printing the "store of value" of all existing dollars is diminished.

For the time being, gold is in limbo after a drastic decline to under 40% of its former value. The decline can be explained by a combination of factors. First, when interest rates go up it costs more to hold gold and high-yielding alternative investments drain money out of the gold market. Second, gold reacts directly to the rate of inflation. As inflation declines there is less need for it as an inflation hedge. When interest rates decline or inflation heats up again, it will bring an end to the gold slide. But what gold is really good at is calming people's nerves. This is especially true in time of financial panics, wars, riots, rebellions, and general malaise—the kind of things that fill our daily newspapers. Some as yet unforeseen and blissfully unknowable future crisis will undoubtedly call gold back to resume its disciplined, objective, and statesmanlike role in the financial world of the future.

Gold As A Liquid Hard Asset

If you like puzzles and projections and want to calculate how high the price of gold could go in a runaway inflation, just total the amount of *real* things that are liquid (easily marketable, like gold) and divide that into the total amount of paper money. There aren't many liquid hard assets other than gold, are there? There is an awful lot of paper money to balance against gold, isn't there? This shortage of real, liquid alternatives will determine the price level that gold could reach in the future.

The U.S. As Banker To The World

During the last two decades, the other nations of the world favored gold and the U.S. Treasury fought it, enunciating the somewhat dubious doctrine that the dollar was as good as gold. It's true. The dollar was not only as good as gold; for the U.S., it was better.

The United States benefited enormously by having the dollar used as the medium of exchange in international commerce. As Jacques Rueff, the French economist, pointed out so ably for so long, the country whose currency is used for international commerce gets the banking business involved, and that means retaining dollars to use in local commerce even after ownership of the dollars is transferred to a foreigner. Every time Americans buy anything produced in another country with dollars, U.S. banks get the spent dollars back almost immediately. This happens because foreigners don't need any dollars to settle trade balances since they already have a surplus.

Here's how it works. Mr. American Consumer sends a bank draft to Frankfort to pay for his Volkswagen. The draft arrives at 10:00 A.M. in dollars. The money is deposited back in a German branch of the Bank of America by the Volkswagen company before 3:00 P.M., so essentially the money never leaves New York.

The dollar has had a string on it. We have spent it and then quickly jerked it back in our pocket, or at least the New York banker's pocket, so that it can be used as a reserve to make five times more loans and help finance a skyscraper. Bankers can't do that with gold. This is the fundamental reason why bankers have opposed gold: It ties them down to reality.

Nor is this all. In the past, through the mechanism of an overvalued dollar, we have obtained the products—cars, TV sets, oil, wines—of our trading partners at prices that were much lower than we would otherwise have had to pay. The U.S. has financed a huge, post–World War II construction boom and built an industrial capacity exceeding anything the world has ever seen. Part of this was accomplished by using as a credit base the vast amount of foreign dollar holdings deposited in U.S. banks.

All this overvaluation of the dollar has been positive. Recently, however, a combination of declining inflation and high interest rates have strengthened the demand for dollars. This has made U.S. goods cost more abroad and caused our foreign trade to suffer. Being crowded out of foreign markets has added to unemployment here at home. It is a fact that countries that can devalue their currencies gain a competitive advantage in trade. Since the dollar is the new reserve money, the only way to devalue the dollar is—by definition—to raise the price of gold.

How much more trade can we lose to other countries because of an overvalued dollar? How much more unemployment must we sustain because of our overvalued dollar? The U.S. will be forced to do something to raise exports and lower unemployment. The pressures are building fast. We can be sure that when our national interests dictate a rise in the price of gold, the U.S. will see that the gold price rises. This is because for the last thirty years the fundamental rule for predicting the future has been: **What is in the economic interests of the United States is what will happen.**[1]

Almost every gold bug you talked to in the last decade would tell you that gold was powerful and the U.S. was weak, and that was why gold was soaring and the dollar was declining. *Exactly the opposite was true.* Our amber waves of grain gleam more brightly than all the world's gold. Our productive capacity, technology and highly trained workers make us the most powerful nation. Just travel abroad to appreciate the incredible power of America. At the end of the World War II the U.S. possessed 47% of all the world's monetary wealth. Being shackled to the expedient and profligate spending programs of short-sighted leaders has caused us to give up a great deal of wealth and power, but an emaciated eagle still dwarfs the sparrows.

Let us explore what is clearly in America's economic interest so we can determine what goals the U.S. will most likely be using its power to achieve. It is in America's interest to increase trade, rebuild factories, and lower unemployment. All these things require lower interest rates.

Financing The National Debt

High interest rates are partially a result of having to defend the dollar. The U.S. has a huge paper mountain of debt, the interest payments on which are becoming more and more burdensome. So much goes to pay the interest on this debt that the government must compete with business for the funds that business

---

1. When this rule no longer works it means power has shifted from the U.S. elsewhere, and it will constitute a great danger signal for the dollar and for our very survival as a nation.

needs to remodel its industrial plant and equipment. The government could get its financing a whole lot cheaper if the dollar were backed with something more tangible than politician's promises. If that were the case, there might be some funds left over for business to borrow at low interest, too. Remember, business is the politicians' golden goose. If they let it die, how can they keep getting those great eggs?

Marking Up Gold Prices

What might the politicians do? First, they could increase the value of U.S. gold reserves to make paper dollars look like they had more backing. How could the U.S. accomplish this? By marking its own gold holdings to market (that is, from the $42 official rate to the current market price.[2])

What would increasing the price of gold to this new higher level accomplish? First and foremost, it might give the Fed an excuse to increase the money supply enough to alleviate the acute shortage of cash that is presently developing in our economy. This would help put an end to the twenty-year high in business bankruptcies caused by the illiquidity in our financial markets. A glance at figure 2 below will show what it could potentially mean in terms of increased reserves for the U.S. Treasury.

Second, it would acknowledge what is already a fact— namely, the devaluation of the dollar in terms of gold.

Third, it would create a whole new reserve base of something real that could act as a backing for all the dollars that have

---

2. But remember, in order for gold to prove an effective store of value, gold must be reasonably priced (that is, determined by the interplay of real supply and demand, not mere speculation).

What constitutes a fair price for gold? Since its $35 price was established in 1934, consumer prices have increased close to 500%, raw materials prices 600%. Using the higher figure would give a gold price of $210 an ounce. Assuming real inflation to be even higher, say 1000%, would still only make for a gold price revaluation to around $350.

This provides another clue for gold's recent weakness—that it has been seeking its own true relative value prior to a revaluation.

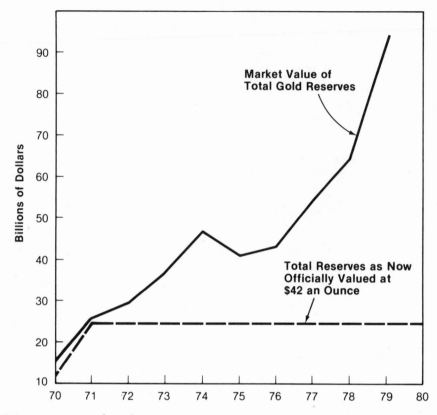

Figure 2. Even after the recent decline our gold reserve position could be greatly strengthened by the simple expedient of marking our gold reserve to market. This seems a next logical move on gold's historical comeback trail.

already been issued. This would both strengthen the dollar, and lower interest rates. Whether interest rates would stay down long enough to enable business to take care of its capital needs would depend on what happened next.

What Would Happen Next?

If a move to revalue our gold reserves were timed to facilitate new money creation to avert a financial panic it might prove a big help. If the new money was issued gradually and with restraint, interest rates might decline and remain low long enough to enable business to make profits with borrowed money again.This would help bring about a period of real prosperity. This, plus a rising bond and stock market, could provide the 1927–1929 period of "new era" euphoria usually necessary to put a capstone (or tombstone) on a huge credit cycle. If the increased reserves were used as an excuse to print too much money, and were part of a program to rescue a stagnating economy with printing press money, these extra billions would create a very great inflationary impact on everything and set the stage for a hyperinflation in which business would eventually be worse off than ever.

Which will it be? How about both? First, the party, then the hangover. We can only wait and see but it is difficult to believe in a politician's restraint over the long term. In the past, whenever the prodigals of Washington have come into an inheritance, they have taken awhile to get used to the idea (the euphoric stage) then *spent it as fast as they could.*

History points to the fact that any mark up of gold reserves would be used to eventually create a new supply of money equal roughly to the reserve as it existed before the revaluation. This means the government would theoretically have new power to balloon the money supply over eight times.

Politicians, regardless of party, seem to have a compulsion to do good with someone else's money. Once you start the handouts, it's hard to stop, and yet there is only so far the politicians can go in channeling money to welfare. The savers and businessmen don't have much more to give, but with all these new reserves the politicians would be home free. They could spend on welfare without robbing anybody, and thus be loved by everybody and maybe be elected for life.

The same banking-interest faction that fought to maintain dollar supremacy would be there, arguing that we should keep on inflating so that we could continue having our cake and eating it, too.

There is also the false hope that over the long term we can cheapen dollars *faster* than foreigners can raise prices so that we can continue getting bargain purchases.

These cheap dollar advocates will be arguing persuasively that we shouldn't worry about a deficit in our balance of trade—that it's all a wonderful con game. We've got the whole world working for us, they will say. How? In order to explain this, they'll ask us to stop resenting the Japanese and Germans underselling us in our own markets. They'll assure us that actually it's really just the opposite—that the American consumer is the Tom Sawyer of the modern world and the reality is that we have conned everybody into working for us by telling foreigners how much fun it is to paint a picket fence and collect dollars. The argument is seductive and worth examining.

The End Of The Fairy Tale

The Germans and Japaneseare possessed by a kind of corporate euphoria every time they sell us a car or a TV set. That's because all the foreigners who receive our dollars think (now don't laugh) that they are acquiring a *future store of value.* This game can go on for a long time with foreigners who want to believe that American citizens are going to sit still while America is purchased with paper dollars.

What will eventually end the wonderful game of sticking foreigners with all this potentially worthless paper money in exchange for their valuable cars and TV sets? It is like CONFIDENCE for the banks. This Tom Sawyer ploy of letting foreign trading partners paint our picket fence could be ended when the foreigners finally understand what's going on. If they ever get smart enough to realize that *there is no dollar redemption at the end of the rainbow,* the game will end fast. They will start demanding vast amounts of interest again just to hold dollars and it will be a rerun of the problems of the 1970s on a giant cinemascope screen.

The world is slowly becoming more sophisticated and that's one reason interest rates have tended to rise. People around the world are starting to think—to stir things up—to want to be compensated for inflation. The eternal dilemma from here to the end of the credit boom party will be how to dampen inflation for the benefit of foreign creditors and bondholders without causing unemployment and economic stagnation for American workers and business.

What would happen if, after a gold revaluation, we tried to hold down interest rates at the same time we were printing more money to stimulate our faltering domestic economy? Our foreign trading partners would be forced to retrench behind trade walls and refuse to take any more of our printing-press money. What would happen then to the trillion or so dollars they already have, plus the mountain of new money we could print after a gold revaluation? They wouldn't need dollars to settle trade balances or *anything* else, so they would try to spend them fast on every *real* thing they could buy. And what would happen then?

SPECULATIVE POINT:
   Gold will come unglued from its new revalued price around $300 to $400 and this time, could go to several thousand dollars an ounce because gold would be the first thing foreigners would try to buy with their dollars.

So don't be discouraged if gold consolidates or dips or even continues to retrace a good part of its rise now or even stabilizes later at a lower price. Just like Winston Churchill—its day will come.

Why should a gold price of several thousand dollars be hard to believe? If, during the 1970s, the gold price increased twenty times, why can't it go up ten times more in the 1980s? Certainly the situation today is potentially more explosive than it was in the 1970s.

No one is saying gold will repeat its 1970s performance, only that it *can*. Only time will tell. But we're counting on you not to whisper a word of the Swiss banker's analysis to those who are holding all those dollars abroad. If you do, you can be sure, *gold will soar.*

So don't tell anyone until the time is ripe to use gold[3] to help you in your battle to retire rich.

A Footnote To Gold

The present times dictate a speculative approach to wealth accumulation, and we have already seen that speculation requires thinking beyond the ordinary—looking ahead. Gold is nice and should perform very well indeed, but it is an old game. Speculators like new games. What is being touted today that represents what gold did in the early 1970s? In other words, what is glamorous, tangible, in short supply, and relatively liquid? The answer, according to the Swiss bankers, is:

Strategic Materials

What are they? They are mostly metals—titanium, cobalt, rhodium, germanium, magnesium, manganese, molybdenum, tungsten, vanadium, columbium, lithium, chromium, cadmium, beryllium, zirconium, and a host of others.

Our modern technology has evolved to the point that we cannot fly planes, build cars, computers, TVs and radios, launch missiles, drill oil wells, or practice chemistry or modern medicine without these metals. There is a quiet yet intense war being waged for these necessities. Almost without exception, they are minerals not easily obtainable in the United States. They are not only rare and not locally produced, but no readily available substitutes exist for them. Most importantly perhaps,

---

3. Much of what is said about gold applies to the other precious metals as they may be expected to move together over the short to medium term. Long term, however, a good case can be made for an increasing industrial use for both silver and platinum that could cause these metals to increase in price, on a percentage basis, even more than gold. Silver, for example, has an indicated demand of a billion ounces more than production over the next five years.

their source—principally Southern Africa—is threatened internally by racial problems and externally by Soviet aggression. Though rich in these treasures themselves, the Soviets look forward to a time when they will enjoy a monopoly of them like OPEC monopolizes oil today.

These materials have favorable supply-demand relationships that make them perhaps even stronger and more compelling investments than gold was in 1970. For those who can forego the income and are patient, these exotic metals represent a valuable commodity in short supply that is relatively liquid. These characteristics are hard to find in any investment and they spell potential profits for the future.

Traditionally these materials have been traded and stored in London. No matter how or where you buy them, the future appears bright for strategic materials and their owners. If you have a lot of long-term money to place and are looking for the "new gold," these materials merit your investigation. But remember this kind of investment is not without risk. The recent sharp decline in price proves this.

SPECULATIVE POINT:
Strategic metals may prove in such short supply that the government might be forced to confiscate them from you for any amount it chooses to pay.

So, if you are rich and decide to speculate with these, try not to be so successful in helping to corner a tight market that the government is obliged to use Draconian measures to protect the national welfare against hoarders. As in many types of investments, don't be greedy or you may be sorry.

CHAPTER 9

Collectibles

Collectibles include rare coins, stamps, paintings, sculpture, jewelry, prints, antique furniture, old masters, Chinese porcelains—things that give their owners large amounts of psychic income or pleasure while they wait for their cash rewards.

There was a questioning process that went on before listing collectibles as an investment category. A recent article in *Forbes* magazine decided the issue. The article described in some detail the financial acumen of a famous mutual fund manager in picking stocks. At the end of the article, the interviewer asked where the manager put his personal investment funds. "Antiques," was his reply, "for which I always pay cash. I have enough leverage and risk in my working life. I don't need any when I come home." This sounds like a man who will have a lot of fun, never go broke, and even make money along the way. This is the kind of conservatism a speculator can understand and empathize with.

Anyone who has had anything to do with rare stamps, coins or gems in the last decade knows that the income percentage profits are often astounding. Even run-of-the-mill collections have done well.

ANNUAL PERCENTAGE RETURNS ON COLLECTIBLES[1]

U.S. Stamps	22%
Chinese Ceramics	19%
Rare Books	17%
U.S. Coins	16%
Diamonds	15%
Silver	14%
Old Master Paintings	13%

These figures are averages and probably understate just how well first-quality collections have done. However, the costs of insurance and safeguarding plus the loss of interest return must be deducted from these figures to create a fairer picture.

If and when price controls are enacted, these uncontrollable assets could really soar in price. In addition, there is an obvious tax advantage in putting your money in non-income-producing assets that are appreciating. A Rembrandt etching is like a tax-free bond that you can hang on your wall. You are taxed only when you sell, and then only at capital gains rates.

The most important point in collecting these things, however, is still the fun. The joy of possessing and living with objects of great beauty and rarity is a wonderful experience—the psychic income mentioned earlier.

Like most hard assets, collectibles may not do well over the short term because of declining inflationary expectations, but when the period of disinflation inevitably ends, their prices should resume their long-term advance. Remember, rare items and land holdings constituted virtually all that was included in the concept of wealth for thousands of years—in many countries right up until World War I. (In some others right up until the present time.) The popularity of these treasures certainly will not disappear just because there is a financial crisis. Perhaps the age of paper assets—shares, checks and currency, bonds and mortgages, etc.—is just an aberration, a blip on the

1. These percentage returns are compounded in the decade from 1970-1980 and compare with an average inflation rate of 7% per year.

financial charts of history. Maybe some day all personal wealth will again be reckoned in what is real and/or provides pleasure.

To prepare for that day, here are a few hints to guide you in collecting:

1. *Love what you buy and buy what you love.* That way you will be assured of getting something for your money— namely, pleasure.

2. *Initially, invest more time than money.* Try to learn before you earn.

3. *Buy the best you can afford.* Strive to acquire that which is so rare, so beautiful, that everyone will always want it. Unfortunately, in such a sophisticated market, the best usually means the most expensive.

4. *Buy fewer pieces and put more money in each piece.* Continually upgrade your collection and eliminate your weakest pieces. Your collection is almost always judged by its weakest rather than strongest items.

5. *Eliminate all fakes as soon as they are discovered.* Anyone you can fool by displaying a fake isn't really worth fooling. In this regard, don't be afraid to pay for expert advice to guide you in building a collection.

6. *Enter the market for the long pull.* It is almost impossible to trade collectibles unless you are a dealer. Being a dealer means more than having knowledge; it means having the physical facilities to show and sell your wares, and this costs a great deal of money. The knowledgeable dealer, like other professionals, earns his or her money.

7. *If you buy through auctions, try to be unemotional.* You can usually accomplish this by consulting an expert in the field. Having an expert advise you, and even buy for you, is good insurance. Most dealers will do this for a small percentage of the purchase price.

8. *If you sell through auctions, be realistic about what your net proceeds will be.* Also, put your piece up for sale far enough in advance so that you don't miss the market at major turning points. Collectibles decline when inflation

abates. This is because interest rates are then high and paper assets are sought after for their high interest return.

9. *Buy and keep your collection in the best condition possible.* You owe it to posterity to protect these rarities. No one really ever owns them, but rather has the privilege of acting as guardian or caretaker while they live with them.

10. *If and when inflation heats up again, be sure that you have a better use for the money before you sell your collection because you just might have the ultimate investment already.*

SPECULATIVE POINT:
Many people will live well and retire in style on what looks to the uninitiated like a foolish hobby.

CHAPTER 10

Commodities

What are commodities? Essentially they are the wheat, corn, cotton, soybeans, cocoa, coffee, lumber, copper, cattle, and other staples and basic industrial products we need to survive. They are traded in specific amounts deliverable at some future date in packages known as contracts. These contracts are highly leveraged, which means only a small number of dollars control a vast amount of goods. In essence, each commodity contract represents what amounts to an option on a quantity of something real—which is very much like having purchased the actual commodity with borrowed money.

Leverage

Why consider future contracts? Why not just buy the underlying commodity—copper, for example? Because of a thing called *leverage*. An example will help explain.

If you own a load of copper, say 25,000 pounds at 80¢ a pound, the metal would have to sell at $1.60 a pound in order for you to double your money. If you have a futures contract for the same 25,000 pounds, you would have put up so little money that the price would only have to advance 3¢ or 4¢ in order for you to double your money. If copper actually doubled in price

112

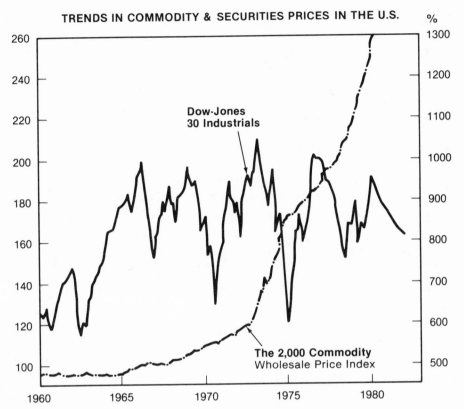

TRENDS IN COMMODITY & SECURITIES PRICES IN THE U.S.

Dow-Jones
30 Industrials

The 2,000 Commodity
Wholesale Price Index

Figure 1. This chart shows how, beginning in 1979, the price action of commodities began to greatly outperform stocks. This is understandable given the rate of inflation. The commodities market provides the perfect way to control great quantities of real assets with small down payments— a speculator's dream if and when inflation heats up again.

your investment would go up over fifty times. Those who bought silver contracts on the commodity exchange using this kind of leverage in August, 1979, saw the $5,500 in their margin deposits become a million dollars in 1980 (just five months later) as the price of silver moved from $8 to $50 an ounce. How is this possible? To understand how leverage works, think of yourself putting $1,000 on a $100,000 house with someone loaning you the balance. If the house goes up to $101,000, it has advanced in price only 1% yet your profit is 100%. If the house goes to

$110,000, it has gone up only 10% but your $1,000 "margin" has increased ten times or 1000%[1]

Considering the amazing leverage in our example of the silver contract, is it any wonder that in a period of inflation commodities tend to outperform stocks? See Figure 1 above.

Real Goods Versus Paper

Let us examine not only how, but why, the Swiss feel commodities could someday make you rich enough to retire in style.

The same two principles that applied in discussing gold also apply here. First, the value of paper dollars is based on the myth that governments are trustworthy. Paper money has no intrinsic value in the real world and depends exclusively on confidence and belief to maintain its fictional value. In the later stages of an inflation, there is less and less confidence and belief in paper and, as the myth evaporates, the illusion of paper wealth vanishes.

As the illusion vanishes, the quantity of paper money in circulation is inexorably forced to align itself with the quantity of real things in the world. Since paper money can be printed and real things cannot, there results a great deal more paper than real assets. The way these two types of assets align themselves determines the way goods are *priced.*

This may seem elementary, but it must be thoroughly grasped if you are going to be able to imagine the price levels that can be attained in an eventual hyperinflationary situation. To take an extreme example, if the only real things in the world were ten houses matched against a total of $10 billion in paper money not needed for other purposes, then the potential price would be $1 billion a house. Paper money is useful and significant only to the extent that it can be converted into or exchanged for real

1. Also, it should be noted that the margin required for commodity contracts does not have to cost you lost interest. A $10,000 Treasury bill may be used instead of cash so that the speculator can continue to earn interest on his money.

things. Once we start applying this principle of *obligatory ex-changeability,* a whole new way of thinking emerges.

Is there a limited quantity of valuable real assets? Very limited. Let us consider the commodity of gold, for example. If all the gold mined since the beginning of time were to be formed into a cube it would fit inside a baseball diamond. All the superb gem quality diamonds ever mined could be put into one dump truck and all the investment type rubies, emeralds, and sapphires in existence could probably fit comfortably inside a few large pickle barrels.

What about the quantity of paper money to be measured against these real things? To give you some idea, the Eurodollar market alone would make a stack of dollar bills that—laid end to end—would reach all the way to our sun 93,000,000 miles away. There is *no need* for a foreigner to hold a single one of these dollars as long as these countries run a trade surplus with the U.S. and settlement is never called for in dollars.

Why do foreigners continue to hold dollars in the face of perennial trade deficits by the U.S.? These dollars were originally held because the dollar was convertible into gold or silver, making it the strongest currency in the world. Now, they are held because the dollar is the almost-universal medium of exchange for all international trade. Still, maintaining the value of the dollar requires an interest rate high enough to reward foreigners for holding dollars. In addition, foreigners must always have confidence that they can buy something with these dollars at some future date. Otherwise, no interest rate, however high, will suffice.

But a foreigner holding our dollars abroad is not participating in an isolated event. We are affected, too, in the level of our own domestic interest rates in America. At an earlier stage of inflation, being able to use the dollar as a reserve currency lowered interest rates in the United States by making more money available. This is no longer true. Today, because of the world-shrinking effect of international banking, the high interest rates necessary to give foreigners the incentive to hold dollars abroad spill back into our domestic system and help keep interest costs high here. This makes it harder and harder for the Federal Reserve to prime our own economic recoveries without forcing interest rates so high that business can't borrow enough money to replace obsolete equipment.

American politicians find themselves in the position of the laboring man that Williams Jennings Bryan defended—a prisoner, not of gold, but of this new Eurodollar hoard, crucified on a cross of high interest rates. When the politician tries to get the Fed to artificially maneuver these rates down, what happens? The foreigners' confidence erodes and the dollar declines in foreign exchange markets.

Just as price is the function of relative quality of paper money and real goods, so confidence depends on the interest rate. Foreigners want us to be prudent with *their* money. When the Fed supports a tight money policy, the foreign holders of dollars forebear exchanging their dollars for the best available substitute.

What substitutes are available for our dollars? At first, foreign monies, until talk of "hard currencies" is heard no more. This happens when it is realized that they are just paper, too. At this point foreigners turn to real things. That usually has meant gold and silver, but as the metals get too high relative to the historic prices of other goods, substitutes are sought.

Commodity Prices And Inflation

Is all this related to commodities? Yes, very much so. It provides the theoretical and mechanical basis for how and why commodity prices can soar to undreamed-of heights after inflation resumes.

At present, high interest rates are keeping the dollar strong, but over the long term there is no way foreigners will hold dollars without the incentive of either continuing high interest rates or the future possibility of cashing them in for something of value. As budget deficits grow larger and new money is created to pay them, inflation will ultimately heat up again. This will make foreign dollar holders nervous and the Eurodollar hoard will play a significant role in the U.S. financial markets. How can you profit from this?

SPECULATIVE POINT:
The real speculative opportunities—the great fortunes to be made that will equate with shorting stocks in 1929— will be in buying commodities during the last stage of the recession that historically precedes a big inflation and then holding them through at least part of that inflation. How long you hold them will then be determined by how rich you want to become and how much risk you are willing to take to accomplish your goal. This will be the time when exchange controls are enacted around the world. Before that happens, a few thousand can theoretically become $100,000 or even $1 million or more in a matter of months by speculating in commodities.

To grasp fully what the foreigner is up against emotionally, picture yourself in a foreign airport. Your plane is scheduled to leave in a few minutes and you realize that the money in your pocket will be unspendable once you board the plane. In such circumstances you will buy items you'd never buy at home for prices you wouldn't even remotely consider—*as long as you can take the items with you.*

We let the Arabs put their money in Treasury bills and maybe a few houses in Beverly Hills because this is to our advantage. But, if they seriously began to acquire our banks, industries, airlines, or farmlands, how long would the American people stand for it? The answer is not very long. So, these dollars foreigners are holding are second-class dollars.

This brings us to the rule that

A DOLLAR HELD BY A FOREIGNER IS WORTH LESS THAN A DOLLAR HELD BY AN AMERICAN.

We may temporarily hide this by enacting exchange controls for Americans and using a double standard of interest that would make possible paying foreigners more on funds held abroad than Americans received in banks at home. This or other temporary expedients would delay, but not put to rest, foreigners' fears. To inflation-conscious Europeans, the ultimate question will be, "What real assets can be bought with my depreciating dollars?"

What can foreigners buy that they really need? The great wealth of the United States is in its food production. The large populations of Western Europe need these foodstuffs desperately, to survive. In food we have our equivalent of the Mideast's competitive advantage in oil (and food, being the source of human energy, is potentially more valuable than oil). All of this means that when foreigners begin cashing in dollars the natural mechanism is in place to push food prices to extremely high levels.

If food prices did skyrocket, what would happen? It would be a disaster for our citizens, but our banker friends would insist we deliver our agricultural production against foreign claims so that massive withdrawals wouldn't wreck our financial system. This would mean that although it would spell hard times for most, fortunes would be made by farmers and those lucky few who had positioned themselves in the commodities markets.

How long would these opportunities last? Not very long, because these conditions would eventually lead to rigid price controls, but long enough for you to profit greatly before such controls were imposed.

Making It Work For You

Trading commodities is not easy. Ninety-five percent of speculators in commodities lose for basically the same reason that horse players lose at the track. In a closed betting system, too great a percentage is constantly being removed from the wagerer's equity position by commissions for there to be sufficient and consistent winners. This problem can be greatly ameliorated when commodities are *invested in, not traded.* In the absence of special circumstances—a breakdown in paper money described above—the chances of making money are not good. The *time factor* makes the commodities market dangerous, speculative, and treacherous. But remember, if all real assets were on the threshold of a giant move up and you could identify such a move in advance you could profit handsomely. You could then look at the commodities market as a great way to buy something real with a small down payment and borrow the rest. Doesn't this make commodities trading sound a whole lot better and more conservative?

ONCE IN A LIFETIME THERE IS AN OPPORTUNITY TO LOOK AT COMMODITIES NOT AS CHANGING NUMBERS ON A TOTE BOARD, BUT AS REAL, VALUABLE, USEFUL THINGS THAT CAN BE PURCHASED WITH A VERY SMALL DOWN PAYMENT.

Viewed in this way, positions in commodities, properly structured as a part of your total portfolio, would then be appropriate for even the most conservative investor.

How do you play it? You must be able to ignore the daily fluctuations that are the bane of commodity speculators and think only in terms of a big move. To do this, you should consider a more distant contract (one farther out in time) and put up sufficient deposits of your cash in your margin account so that you will not be fluctuated out by minor price moves. This type of commodity speculation is called *position trading.*

Because of the very high volatility in commodities, putting a lot of margin in a distant contract (one that is far out in time) makes it easier to have patience. Trying to make too much too fast and thinking of commodities contracts as mere lottery tickets rather than calls on real assets are what usually cause commodity losses.

Because stocks should move earlier, whatever money you had at the outset should have already been increased substantially. You don't need much to tie up great quantities of corn, wheat, or soybeans in the commodities market, so the potential profits are enormous.

To summarize:

1. Over the short and medium term a stronger dollar, together with high interest rates and lower economic activity, will keep a lid on commodity prices, but the worldwide need for food should prevent them from falling too low.
2. Trading commodities for long term moves can be looked at as a way of buying a lot of something tangible with easily (and cheaply) borrowed money.
3. The leverage inherent in the commodities market will provide great profit potential when all commodities start their next big inflationary advance. This is because the reason for their increase in price will be based on the fact that they are real and can be taken out of the country. This is going to become critically important to foreigners abroad trying to spend their second-class dollars when inflation finally resumes.
4. One way to play this is with distant contracts—position trading—plus the use of sufficient margin to avoid the dangers of day-to-day fluctuations.

Assuming that the speculation works out and produces profits, there should be time to place these profits in other real assets because commodities historically top out ahead of business in general.

SEEN WITH YOUNG EYES (EVEN IF THEY'RE IN AN OLD HEAD), COMMODITIES ARE AN UNLIKELY, BUT APPROPRIATE, VEHICLE FOR A CHOSEN FEW OF YOU TO WIN THE BATTLE AND RETIRE RICH BY 1986.

CHAPTER 11

A Pause to Reflect on the Unfairness of Life—Followed by an Explanation of a Crap Shoot that Could Make You Enough Money to Correct the Injustice

No one knows better than a Swiss banker that it is one thing to show those who are rich how to keep their money, and quite another to show someone how to make it initially. One fact is certain: Both to make and preserve money, you must have a plan, a general approach based on sound facts and logical projections. With a plan, you are a hundred times more likely to succeed than you are without one. However, there is still the arbitrary nature of fate to contend with.

Timing

Since most mistakes involve doing the right thing at the wrong time or vice versa, let's say a few words about *timing*.

The big money is usually not made by the great prophets or seers—they see *too far* into the future. *To be right too soon is the equivalent of being wrong.* To counteract this, try to cultivate patience. Just after a definite trend begins is usually the perfect time to make your move. Most price rises have the pattern shown in Figure 1 on the next page.

The ideal is to buy when the price is just moving from A to B. This way you avoid the long wait involved in buying too

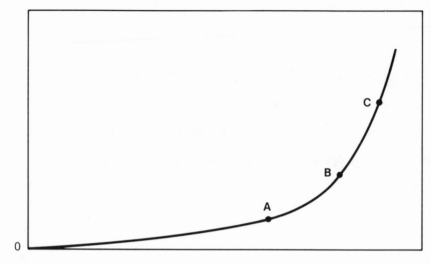

Figure 1.

early. You are paying a higher price when you buy at A rather than at O but it's worth it.

Another point to help you in your timing is to remember that financial events usually take longer to manifest themselves than is generally supposed. The reason for this is that once your mind forms an idea of how external reality should manifest itself in the future it has already happened in your mind and your brain projects it instantaneously into the world as if it had already occurred. But the real world is made up of millions of different minds, each viewing things differently, and until enough others see the future as you do, there is sufficient resistance to keep the event from happening. You may have an insight into what will eventually be reality, but others resist and their resistance can keep your reality from manifesting itself in the real world for a good long time, even though you eventually will be right and they are temporarily wrong. There's one consolation for all you quick thinkers: As inflation shifts into high gear, the *denoument* of financial events accelerates until, in the last stage, no one can think or act fast enough to keep up with actual events.

No Speculative Funds?

What if you accept the logic that there are great opportunities to get rich on the horizon but—having only a pittance to speculate with—you can't see how you can take advantage of them. Being short of money is no disgrace. In fact it makes you a regular guy (or gal) part of what can be called the Great Impecunious Majority. Consider these facts: In 1972, one fourth of all Americans had a net personal wealth of under $1,000 and one half had total assets of under $3,000. This bottom half of the population owned little more than 5% of the nation's wealth. About 70% of the population possessed less than $10,000 each and 90% had a net worth of less than $30,000. Only 6% had assets of $60,000.[1] If you're fretting because you lack capital and haven't been able to put much aside to speculate with, you can see you have a lot of company.

Seeing how few have real capital causes a flood of insights. First, you understand how precious and rare capital really is. Second, you begin to see how the poor are inflation's natural victims. Third, you realize that it takes capital to obtain real freedom.

Not having the means to speculate is one of life's many tragedies. It is not really a consolation that you have little to lose. Perhaps never in your lifetime will you get another chance to make the kind of money that is necessary to live decently, and make it so fast, as in the crazy period of crisis and inflation that lies ahead of us.

1. All these statistics are taken from Data On the Distribution of Wealth in the United States, published by The U.S. Government Printing Office, September 26, 1977. Even assuming the figures have changed since 1972, the figures still demonstrate dramatically how most of the population are without the means to protect themselves from, or profit by, inflation.

You have two choices: (1) You can be philosophical and take satisfaction from just understanding what is going on, or (2) you can play a wild speculation. For those of you who are inclined to gamble, here is a real crap shoot:

Imagine that you walk into a bank and want to borrow $5,000. When you are asked what you have as security and you say $3,000, you are turned down. That part I'm sure you can imagine. (The next part is a little more difficult.)

You go across the street to a commodities broker and a nice person says in a voice filled with awe "So you have $3,000 of your own money. That's fine. Let's see . . . on that kind of security, I can let you buy a futures contract on a million-dollar Treasury bill." When you realize he isn't joking, you hold your breath. You see that the futures contract is selling for 87 (which represents $870,000). That's roughly the equivalent of someone loaning you about $867,000.

What's the catch? You don't get the thousands of dollars of interest that a real million-dollar T-bill would pay every year. All you get is the change of value that the Treasury bill may experience over a period of time—in other words, its price movement.

We all know that anything worth hundreds of thousands of dollars can experience a great change in value even over a relatively short time, so this isn't so bad either. The real catch is that you have to pinpoint your timing and be right or you will lose your $3,000. Basically, that's the worst thing that can happen to you (but, of course, it can happen fast).

How It Works

The price changes in financial futures such as T-bills or Treasury bonds are determined by changes in the interest rate.

If interest rates decline, a U.S. Treasury bill will increase in price, and *since you own the price movement,* you make a lot of money. Conversely, if you correctly guess interest rates will rise and you sell the same treasury bill short, you will profit because then the Treasury bill will decline in price to reflect the higher interest rate. Remember, you are paying your money so that you can profit from the price change of the financial instrument up or down depending on how you are positioned. As interest rates rise, the price of financial instruments declines. As interest rates decline the price of the financial instrument rises.

To show that this kind of speculative opportunity is going on in the real world, providing big profits for some astute speculators, see Figure 2.

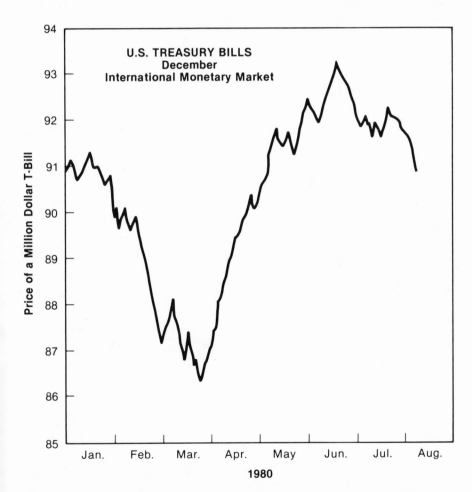

Figure 2. This chart shows the actual price changes in December Treasury Bills in the period from January to August of 1980.

You can see that if you had bought Treasury bills on March 25, 1980, for every $3,000 you put up in cash as a margin deposit you could have had $9,000 by April 23, 1980 (four weeks later) and $14,000 by June 14 (seven weeks later) through the magic of the amazing leverage available in financial futures.

By using your profits to pyramid,[2] you could have made even more all in seven weeks and all never risking more than $3,000.[3] If you had really been a financial genius, you could have next observed that the advance had stalled and was forming what technicians call a head and shoulders, a very bearish reversal pattern signaling a down move. It looks like three mountains with the highest peaks in the center. (Look at Figure 2 and see if you can find it.) With this as a clue you could have then taken your profits and gone short the same T-bill to repeat the whole process in the other direction. As interest rates rose, the price structure of T-bills collapsed, thus providing even greater profits on the subsequent downside move that continued into the third quarter of 1981. The point is this: the leverage in commodities provides once-in-a-lifetime opportunities to increase your capital dramatically in a very short time. What other type of speculation gives you an opportunity to make so much so fast?

Most of what has been said about commodity futures contracts also applies to trading in currency futures. These markets are so big that there is no worry of manipulation, but they are still the ultimate crap shoot because you are buying and selling paper money itself—speculating on the constantly changing relative value of the dollar *vis à vis* the Swiss franc, the German mark, or the Japanese yen, for example.

Though this is certainly a ripe field for interesting speculations, never forget that you should approach all commodity

---

2. 'Pyramid' means using profits to buy additional contracts.

3. It must be understood that the figures used are approximations to show the general principles involved and don't take into consideration commissions or special requirements of financial responsibility that may be imposed by individual brokers as a prerequisite to the opening of a commodities account. Never risking more than $3,000 will entail using close stops or utilizing options in carrying out trading strategies.

trading somewhat like a one-armed baseball pitcher approaches a buzzsaw—with a great deal of respect.

Can these types of fantastically profitable moves reoccur in the future? Yes, with greater frequency and intensity. As inflation progresses, spike markets (rapid price changes up and down) become more frequent. This is when the speculators really get the movement they need for profitable trades and even use that movement to make a fortune all by risking very little in each trade.

In summary, no speculation is a sure thing, but a combination of hard work, knowledge and luck can lower the odds against you and provide at least a fair chance to win big.

What we have been exploring in this book is how to: Preserve what you have if you have a lot to preserve, make more if you have a fair amount to invest, and, if you have a very small stake, participate in a crap shoot in the same way you would gamble in Las Vegas or at the races, only with the chance to get a lot bigger payoff (with far better odds) than those offered at any casino or track.

Knowing how a roulette wheel works will not change the odds against you, but knowing how interest rates work can give you a competitive advantage. For those of you who are inclined toward this type of speculation (which isn't for someone who needs the money to pay for the groceries or the rent), more information on how to project and predict interest rates is set out in the Appendix. The fact that it is in the Appendix doesn't mean it is not important, it only means this type of speculation or gambling is not for everyone.

You will have to consult a commodities broker for details such as margin requirements before you attempt to try your luck but the principles outlined here are substantially correct.

Why Gamble?

A word in defense of risk taking. America was built by people willing to take risks—literally gamble everything for the wealth and freedom that Americans now take for granted. The whole history of America is replete with examples of successful long odd speculation by real gamblers. Imagine taking on the British, the world's most powerful nation in the 18th century, being optimistic enough to even consider the merging of 13 diverse and economically competitive states into one nation, fighting the War of 1812 against insuperable odds, the luck of Napoleon's needing funds and the resultant Louisiana Purchase, the hardiness of settling the frontier, the bonanza of California's annexation, the odds against preserving the Union in the Civil War when faced with the militarily superior forces of the South, the gamble of successful assimilating millions of immigrants—the most diverse elements of humanity, the incredible victories in two world wars. Even Columbus himself was one of history's greatest gamblers—an Italian explorer betting on finding the East by sailing west in three tiny ships; financing the whole shaky enterprise by a loan secured by a Spanish queen's jewels.

The lesson seems clear—America is not only a nation of gamblers, it is a nation of winners.

To defend speculation on an individual basis, how many of you have returned beaten or dejected from a hard day at work, only to be faced with bills and money problems at home?

Is taking a shot at the big money justified? Is it worth risking the little you may have for the chance to end your financial problems in one fell swoop? These are questions you have to answer for yourself. Some may conclude it is better to gamble and lose rather than die slowly by being squeezed between the rock and the hard place—continuing to see a few dollars become worth even less tomorrow. Only you can answer the question, but remember if you decide to go for broke it won't be your first risk. You are already taking a thousand chances every day.

You cannot win without acting and you cannot act without risk. Even when we lose we have the satisfaction of at least having tried. Losses may make us suffer, but they also make us grow. The person who doesn't know risk doesn't know life and is chained to his riskless, rickety, rocking chair. Only a person who knows how to take risks is really alive. Such a person may be temporarily down, but never out.

If it is true that the only ones that have a chance of coming out ahead in periods of crisis and inflation are the speculators, and if you think you're a potential winner, then you have made a beginning in finding out how to do it. The rest is up to your intelligence, timing, hard work and luck.

A STOP TO LOOK AT A ROADMAP—
WHERE WE'VE BEEN AND WHERE WE'RE GOING

If something is true, its truth has a universal application. The gambling techniques of the world of high finance, based as they are on empirical truth, must embrace the same correct principles that filter down to explain why the average person can't win at the $2 betting window.[4] Knowing what is an intelligent speculation and what is *not* is half the battle.

So far we have stated the problem in individual terms and offered a solution for you—intelligent speculation. The solution has been developed by discussing the different types of speculation available to see which ones had the largest future potential to make you a winner and to transform the theoretical solution of speculation into the reality of riches.

The last part of this book will demand your greatest concentration. Some of it may appear theoretical but it will all help you to think for yourself. It is the part that will, with proper application, make for the economic sophistication necessary to accomplish miracles on your own behalf, miracles necessary in today's world if you are to live really well and retire really rich.

But, in order to accomplish miracles you must first become a believer in the probability of renewed and intensifying inflation *after* the current recession terminates in some kind of money crisis that threatens depression. You must further believe that a group of knowledgeable speculators will become rich from the opportunities that will present themselves at that time. Above all, you must believe that you can be one of them and be ready to put forth the effort necessary to make it happen.

---

4. Horse players lose over time because of the extraction of such a large commission by the state that there is a constantly shrinking pool of money for potential winners to draw from. This guarantees statistically that if you play long enough, you will end up a loser.

On what evidence is the idea of accelerating future inflation based? The *extent of present debt* is offered as proof that we will have even bigger inflation in the future. The mechanism of how such debt came about and its inflationary implications is detailed in Chapter 12.

Chapter 13 provides a historical review of our inflation so that you, as a speculator, can situate yourself in time—gain a perspective where we stand in history so that you can profit from the *denoument* of historically predictable events.

A series of twenty-one questions to help you deepen your understanding of critical issues is set forth in Chapter 14.

Chapter 15 treats the subject of present trends which may logically be projected in the future and attempts to stimulate your thinking in this regard so that you may begin to make your own projections and decisions.

A more advanced study of how to predict interest rates, keep a dynamic balance sheet and a glossary of terms is to be found in the Appendix.

CHAPTER 12

The Drama of Debt

Prologue

Earlier in the book we saw how the government justifies its punitive taxes on the rationale that it is protecting us. If excessive taxes were the whole story it would be bad enough but there's more, much more. In its ever-increasing role as protector, the government so debases the money that savers become cynical and stop saving. This makes it impossible for our businessmen to get the long-term credit they need to replace the factories and equipment that produce America's wealth. Production *is* wealth, and anything that interferes with the production process makes us all poorer. This is why America is becoming poor today and is likely to be still poorer tomorrow.

As debt increases, it has a secondary effect. Large debt causes a decline in the worth of previously issued low-interest bonds and mortgages. The banks holding them suffer losses in their reserves and become insolvent. Unpayable debt becomes like the proverbial albatross around our economy's neck, pulling it down into the depths of poverty.

Debt has become the central economic issue of our times, and to be a successful speculator you are going to have to understand it well. Making a fortune in the next few years will depend on your understanding the subject of debt better than others do.

If the average person's lifestyle deteriorates to a poverty level and remains there for the next twenty years, it might well be because he or she didn't quite understand the subject of debt and how it could affect lives. Whether you eat dog food or caviar, drink tap water or champagne, will depend not only on your own debts but on the debts of government, business, and the American consumer. What will separate the winners from the losers depends on how well they understand what's going on and how well they take action, first to protect themselves, then later to profit from inflation's absurdities.

The General Problem

Citizens have never been able to control their politicians' search for easy answers. The easiest way of all for politicians to solve social problems is the creation of money. Money creation takes two forms: printing it and borrowing it. The latter is by far the biggest source of money creation. A very sincere but woefully expedient economist named John Maynard Keynes convinced us that because of our nation's natural riches and hardworking ancestors we had been bequeathed a very productive industrial machine that would continually spew out riches to all if only the people had the money to buy these goods. He was thus stressing the *demand* side or the ability to buy. How do you increase demand? By creating new money and credit. Keynes felt the supply side would take care of itself. He was saying, "There is too much saving, let's get some money in the hands of consumers—especially the poor—to spend." This philosophy has a great appeal for demagogues but it results in making us all poorer. How? Production is wealth and production takes new machines and new machines can only be purchased out of savings. Who wants to save when Keyne's inflationary policies reward borrowing and punish savers? We have seen our savings eroded for decades. Over that time we have lost our tools—our factories and machines—through obsolescence. It takes big, modern, efficient tools and factories to produce cars, TVs, farm equipment, and all the rest. These tools must be paid for by long-term borrowing, and in an economy dedicated to cheating savers, the savers eventually refuse to loan money for long periods of time. Thus producers are deprived of long-term credit and we learn to depend on others (like the Japanese) to produce our cars and TV sets.

Let's explore how the problem of debt has come about in more detail so that we may understand it well enough to at least save ourselves from its destructive consequences. To keep things as simple as possible let's make it in the form of a play. So that we don't miss any part of the plot let's divide it in three acts.

Act I

The play opens where we left off in Chapter 3 with an army of bureaucrats occupying center stage. Having provided us protection from external enemies and finding themselves temporarily unemployed, this army of bureaucrats joyfully discovers that we need someone to protect us from each other. Do-gooders appear to point out all the problems that need correcting. This eventually leads to a greatly expanded concept of government. The need for welfare replaces warfare. Ostensibly this is an improvement but financially it can be equally devastating to a nation's wealth and solvency. All this welfare costs money— more money than the government receives in taxes. Where does it get the extra money? Government borrows it by tapping the savers of the country for it. Not only does government need money for welfare, business needs to borrow to keep up its plant and equipment, to create the production that constitutes the wealth of our nation. Both are competing with each other for the citizens' savings. Business encourages government to cheapen the money to make its own ballooning loans easier to pay off. Government has its own financing problems by this time and tacitly agrees. Soon the ability and desire to lend has been destroyed because of the "free money" formula worked out between businessmen and politicians. This ultimate gentlemen's agreement is: We will inflate the money supply, thus assuring an inflation rate greater than the interest rate, which will guarantee *free money for borrowers.*

For those of you old enough to remember pre-Keynesian, old-fashioned pragmatic economics, savings meant rewards. Without a reward there is no reason to save. Without savings there is no wealth, and that becomes the problem—how to cut a constantly shrinking economic pie into more parts and convince people that there is progress. Before Keynes, when the creators of wealth saved, they were consciously forebearing from the satisfactions of consumption at an earlier point in time in the expectation of even greater satisfaction in the future. Throughout the 19th century savers got that satisfaction because the borrowed money created even more wealth thus lowering prices. The money the savers got back constituted a real reward.

The way things work out now, it becomes a game of how to increase inflation faster than interest rates. The end result is that savers get very little satisfaction because they are loaning their money for free.

When you understand this simple plot, you will quickly realize that our fifty-year credit boom has been fueled by low interest rates which have resulted in very cheap, even free, money. These "free money" loans negotiated by business made the boom possible. The boom could not have existed without it. But what's good for borrowers is bad for lenders. Because the inflation rate has been close to or even exceeded the interest rate, savers have become discouraged. Thrift has all but been extinguished among America's once frugal and hardworking people.

Act II

The Carrot And The Stick

The savers have been patient and complacent but they are not completely stupid. In Act II they begin to anticipate the cheapening of the dollars they lend and start demanding that something be added to the interest rate to compensate them for the loss of purchasing power. This begins the long upward climb

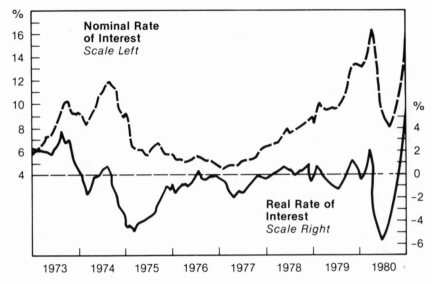

Figure 1. A graphic description of why there aren't more savings. It will be seen that until recently, when corrected for inflation, interest rates have not been yielding anything.

in interest rates. As prices increase, the interest rate becomes a reflection of inflation and less and less a charge for renting money, (which historically is only 3%). Finally, when borrowers complain of high interest rates they are only really complaining of high inflation (see Figure 1). To keep the free money scam working, the government is forced to become more subtle. It gets all it can by taxing and more by borrowing, but when it still comes up short it gets the rest by running a deficit and printing IOUs that it calls dollars to cover the shortfall. Dollars aren't printed directly; that would be too crude. Money creation takes on ingenious subtleties as freshly printed greenbacks are made to look like loans to the government backed by treasury bonds, bills, and notes.[1] Upon close examination, however, the Federal Reserve's greenbacks turn out to be just paper that has

1. Technically, the way money increase takes place is that the Federal Reserve buys government securities from a securities dealer crediting that dealer's bank account with funds that never existed before.

printed on it that this piece of paper is "legal tender" (whatever that is) for all debts public and private. Translated, this means that this piece of paper known as a dollar, having been issued to buy debt, can also be used to pay it off.

If you are thoroughly confused by now, the politicians are happy, because that is exactly what they intended. To keep it simple, just remember that the result of all this finagling is that the goodhearted politicians (who are always ready to share your last dollar) can get money whenever they need it without asking you for it and with hardly anyone understanding what's happening. And they get it for *free*.

The savers, as the lenders of the country, have historically been easy marks. But the danger is that they are wising up.

In the late 1960s, savers balked a few times and threatened to forget all that forebearance nonsense. Maybe they took a vacation to the West Coast or bought that sports car instead of saving their money. In order to lure them back to the bank, it was necessary to offer higher interest rates.

In 1970, the interest rate went to 8%, then 12% in 1974, and finally hit 20% in 1980—a figure that convinced many savers to begin depositing again.

Act III

All this borrowing and dependence on the nation's savers and all this activity in the printing business would not necessarily be a disaster in itself except that there are now three powerful interests whose very existence depends on creating new money—business, banks, and bureaucrats. Matched against this great demand there's only one sucker—the nation's savers—to supply them.

The Assault On Savings

The businessmen threaten to go bankrupt and fire their employees if they aren't guaranteed their free money by the politicians. U.S. bankers depend on the ability to create loans for their lifeblood—profits. But the entity that really needs all the money it can possibly borrow is the American government. Once the money was needed for the protection it was providing, but lately it needs the money to give away to the less fortunate (sometimes known as freeloaders)—the ones with clout at the ballot box.

What the freeloaders have learned is that it's easier to vote for wealth than work for it. Poor freeloaders. In spite of all the handouts, they've never had it so bad. They'll soon be voting themselves welfare in money that's worth so little they'll have to put catsup on it and learn to eat all that paper directly without trying to run it through a grocery store.

But the ones to feel really sorry for are the ones dumb enough and persistent enough to keep on saving. A world of would-be borrowers and tax collectors seems determined to live off them.

How long can these inequities persist? To see, let us ask another question. Just who are these savers? The savers of the country are usually well-trained and well-educated. They have always had to practice self-discipline and they work hard to send their children to college, to buy a house, to expand their small businesses, or to work for promotions. They are literally the backbone of the nation, the keepers of its morality and guardian of its destiny. They think inflation is everyone's problem. If they looked harder they'd see that the rich aren't worried about inflation. They live in big houses behind what are known as tax hedges. The poor know they will be cared for. They live in public housing, which is the most neatly clipped hedge in town. But specifically who are these savers—the ones that own the assets that everyone has been tampering with and lending out to others? The answer is *you*.

If you have had a checking account, bank or savings and loan passbook, are a contributor to Social Security or a purchaser of any kind of insurance, annuities, or government bonds, paid union dues or contributed to a pension fund or professional organization, credit union or farm cooperative, you have played the dumb, ungrateful, middle-class role of saver in unwittingly making loans (through your representatives in financial institutions) over the years.

Now that you know that the politicians have been making you work half the year without pay and that the borrowers (government and business) have been stealing your savings by taking it without any real interest, isn't it surprising that you've done as well as you have?

Consumer Debt

Just as they'd forgotten that they were supposed to be able to get gold for their paper money, savers have forgotten that they were supposed to be able to get real interest on their money. Savers have become so used to being cheated that they have come to believe that it is their *patriotic duty* to support the politicians and bureaucrats, that supporting business is part of *free enterprise,* and that supporting welfare recipients is *charity.* They haven't even realized they were supporting the bankers; they have always been grateful just to get their checks cashed. But it's changing fast.

Lately, the savers have stopped saving and started to spend. Why? They have learned that borrowers have the best of it; so they have decided to live it up, even take on the role of borrowers themselves. This is called *consumer debt. The problem is that they have borrowed so much so fast (consumer debt is up 80% since 1976) that most of their after-tax income has to be used to pay off past debt. In other words,*

DEBT BECOMES A WAY OF LIFE FOR THE ONE WHO IS THE TRADITIONAL SAVER—THE ONE WHO IS THE SOURCE OF BUSINESS FINANCING, BANK DEPOSITS, AND GOVERNMENT BORROWING AND TAXATION NEEDS.

A quick look at Figure 2 will make it clear.

Postwar consumer debt increased from under $5 billion in 1946 to over $200 billion by 1975. It has almost doubled again since then.

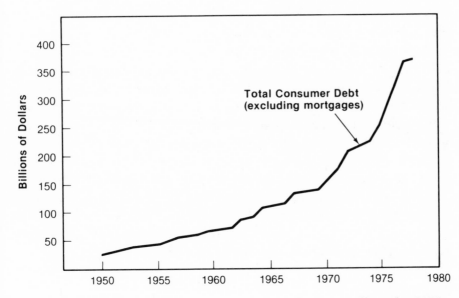

Figure 2. The amazing growth in consumer debt, especially since 1975.

In 1948 consumer debt amounted to 12% of after-tax income. Now it takes 30% of each paycheck to pay past bills, bills that total over $300 billion. So here are the savers, the purveyors of the money, the source of savings and investment (for everyone else) on a spending-speculating binge of their own. This spells bad news for the banks, business, and government; the gang who, having systematically picked the saver's pockets, were desperately counting on stealing their shirts. Apart from austerity (a really dirty word), the politicians offer no solution to cure the borrowing sickness.

Less-Developed Nations

There are just two more characters in the play depicting our fifty-year anniversary credit boom party and the cast will be complete. The first is the guy from the less developed countries. He literally has nothing and needs everything. Having no assets makes him a poor credit risk but, as a human being, he feels he's entitled to help and hopes the others won't discriminate against him because of his poverty.[2]

To be able to understand what is about to happen, you must keep in mind that the bankers aren't loaning their money at all. They are loaning *six times* the saver's little nestegg and they make profits on the total amount, which helps explain why there always has been and always will be a great number of eager would-be humanitarians in the banking business.

The bankers have been worried about American business's (and even consumers') ability to pay, which has made their bank's own balance sheet look pretty rotten. They decide if they can just make a lot of money fast, they can cover up for all the deadbeat debtors and save themselves so they devise a scheme to loan money to less-developed countries! These countries include:

Afghanistan	Guinea	Mexico	Panama	Thailand
Angola	Haiti	Morocco	Philippines	Turkey
Bangladesh	India	Nepal	Poland	Uganda
Botswana	Iran	Nicaragua	Romania	Yemen
Brazil	Jamaica	Niger	Somalia	Yugoslavia
Egypt	Kenya	Nigeria	Sudan	Zaire
Ethiopia	Korea	Pakistan	Syria	Zambia

A more likely list of bad credit risks may you never see. The combined debt of the Communist nations alone due to Western banks is over $80 billion (Poland owes $26 billion of that). "How can that be?" you ask. "Aren't they the enemies that the government is supposed to be protecting us from?"

The answer isn't easy. You see, ever since John Maynard Keynes taught us the language of Double-Speak, people have gotten used to new ways of thinking and seeing. Up and down,

2. Just so you won't be too hard on the poor underdeveloped nations, consider the fact that in 1800 the per-capita income in developed countries was only three times that of the underdeveloped countries; in 1914 rich countries' income was seven times greater. Today the average person living in a developed nation has *twelve* times the income of a person in an underdeveloped nation.

right and wrong, rich and poor have all been seen to be only relative. In this new world of relativism it becomes perfectly logical for America to help its enemies bury it because most of its politicians think capitalism isn't very workable anyway and they only pronounce the word "capitalism" on rare occasions and even then in a soft whisper.

When you see things as politicians have seen them—through the beady, dreamy eyes of rich Socialists—it is easy to understand their profound logic in trying to convince Americans that they needed more military protection from the Communists at the same time the Federal Reserve was worrying about whether the bankers had enough money to loan these same Communist governments. But there's more than the Communist loans. Here's how the total LDC's borrowings have increased.

THE EXTERNAL DEBT OF THE LESS DEVELOPED COUNTRIES

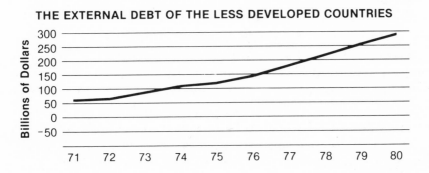

OPEC

But why dwell on one absurdity when we have so many to work with? No party would be any fun without someone really rich to look down on all the others, and that is why the businessmen invite a representative from the OPEC countries. These businessmen have decided that if savers can't lend them any more, the least they can do is to pay more for their oil. OPEC agrees to charge more, and the politicians say they'll sit still for this if OPEC promises to loan it back by buying Treasury bills *and* if the businessmen agree to split the take with the government by paying extra taxes. "Sure," the others say. When

U.S. politicians are promised they can even create a Department of Energy to hire thousands more bureaucrats, they agree. When they are told the new agency can have a budget larger than the combined earnings of our eight largest oil companies they are ecstatic. So the businessmen say, "I guess I do," and OPEC says, "Of course I do," and our politicians say, "I now pronounce us all partners." On cue the businessmen say, with a straight face, "There's a lot of greedy Arabs creating an energy shortage in the Mideast. Ain't it awful? I'll have to raise prices at the pump to cover my increased costs."

And the bankers say, "Ain't it awful? All this new demand for energy has increased loan demands. We'll have to raise interest rates so we can loan the big oil companies enough money to aid in the search for oil even if they use the money just to buy each other out."

The politicians say "We're forced to create a Department of Energy to protect everyone from everyone else."

And even OPEC says, "Ain't it awful? We'll have to work day and night to find ways to spend it all."

But in spite of all the protests, everyone thinks it's pretty good except the savers, who nobody cares much about by this time anyway because they aren't much use to anybody any more.

The savers turned out to be misers when they started spending money themselves and ran out of money to lend. Not only are they no good to anyone as savers, as borrowers they have become deadbeats and can hardly pay off what they already owe.

The representative from OPEC comes by about this time counting his new bankroll and when he hears the bankers are loaning OPEC money to the less-developed nations, he decides to raise the price of oil again just to be on the safe side.

In 1980, when asked how they are going to get us out of this energy mess, the politicians chuckle and say, "Don't worry. We're going to fool OPEC. We're printing so much money that we'll take their good oil and just give them worthless paper in exchange!"

The savers look suspiciously at the government, the freeloaders, and the bankers, and finally decide to elect a whole new conservative bunch of politicians in hopes of averting disaster.

The drama of debt is almost over except for the last few scenes that are going to make most of you poor and a few of you rich. At present the U.S. is going through the painful process of recession as politicians try to convince skeptical savers that money is worth saving again because of high interest rates.

This is where we are now. Hard times are upon us. But don't worry. In the near future, the politicians will come up with the same old solution to everyone's problems—more money. You see a long time ago a very lazy magician (read economist) thought up the sorcerer's all-time one and only biggest hoax in history when he whispered in the King's ear:

WHAT WE CAN'T BEG, BORROW OR STEAL ANY OTHER WAY . . . WE'LL PRINT.

(And understanding this unfair game is how one can make enough money to retire rich by 1986.) But in order to make the magic of inflation work again, the U.S. economy will need a lot of gullible savers, not to loan the money next time but really to make a gift of it. There's just one problem. If politicians are to convince the savers that the money is worth saving again, inflation will first have to be squeezed like a sponge. The money will have to look good again. Cash will have to be king. Government will have to put some new material in their act. It will have to convince savers to forget all that inflation protection in houses, collectibles, and gold and make them concentrate on building up paper nest eggs in things like tax-free All Savers Certificates and IRA and Keogh Plans.

You are already saving up so you can loan (give?) money to the government and take advantage of those high interest rates. Since free money for government and business requires an even higher inflation rate, think of what inflation rates are going to be needed to get free money for them the next time! Even the S & Ls are getting in on the act pretending if you make periodic deposits of a few thousand a year at current high interest rates you and your spouse will be millionaires at age 65. They forget to tell you that sometime before that it just might take a few hundred dollars to buy lunch.

144 | THE OMEGA STRATEGY

By the way, the less-developed nations have been able to borrow over $300 billion to date. The interest over a three-year period received by America's banker-humanitarians on these loans now amount to more than all the money the U.S. has given away since World War II. Ah, those humanitarians!

We have to stop now. Not because we have run out of absurdities to expose but because now you are sophisticated and know what we have set out to accomplish. You have seen how "free money" leads to debt and how debt leads to trouble. You now understand what others call "money" more thoroughly and technically than the people who print it, because they are not conspirators or even stupid but, when it comes to power, just plain greedy.

The following chapter will show you how all of this has translated into history. Study the past if you would know the future. You will see the repetitive nature of cyclical forces. You can learn where we are in the current inflationary cycle, then use your new found economic sophistication to help you retire with something more than the sore back and empty pockets that the politicians intend.

CHAPTER 13

The Lessons of History

Now that you have accepted the abusive power of taxation as a fact of life, examined the ins and outs and ups and downs of specific investments, and have become somewhat sophisticated in how paper money, debt, and inflation interact, you are now ready to turn to constructing an historical framework to use in projecting the future.

The German Inflation

Just how scary can a ride on the inflationary roller coaster be? Let us start with the end of an inflationary cycle and work back. To see what hyperinflation looks like, let us consider the one in Germany in the early 1920s. As for all those who say it couldn't happen here, we can only say, suspend your judgment a moment and think of the extent of the debt to be liquidated in present-day America compared with the relatively small debt and reparation payments confronting Germany after World War I.

- The quantity of paper marks circulating in Germany increased from 2 billion in 1914 to about 500 quintillion at the end of 1923.

145

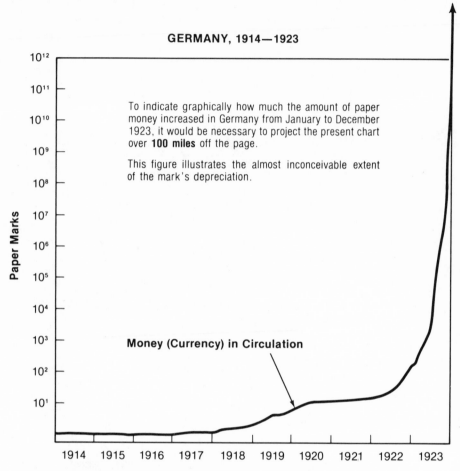

GERMANY, 1914—1923

To indicate graphically how much the amount of paper money increased in Germany from January to December 1923, it would be necessary to project the present chart over **100 miles** off the page.

This figure illustrates the almost inconceivable extent of the mark's depreciation.

Money (Currency) in Circulation

Figure 1. A descriptive measure of hyperinflation.

- At the peak of the inflation in 1923, the value of money declined 10% *an hour* until it took one trillion paper marks to equal the purchasing power of one prewar German mark—about 24 cents in U.S. money.
- The cost of a postage stamp for a local letter climbed to 100 billion marks—fifty times the *total* currency in circulation just ten years before!

- To conserve paper and printing-press time, notes were printed only on one side. Then they appeared in billion- and finally trillion-mark denominations.
- Prices rose so rapidly in 1923 that wages and salaries were paid daily (or even twice a day). Shopping breaks were demanded from employers to facilitate quick spending of earnings.

Is there any relevance in these horror stories? Do things have to get this bad for us? Do we have to experience hyperinflation? Couldn't inflation moderate? Some may think it already has but this is short-term window dressing designed to lure back savers. In order for inflation to moderate significantly, long term problems would have to be solved. Business would have to be willing and able to pay a *real* reward for savings and banks would have to stop making dubious loans with money they don't have. Also, the politicians would have to curb spending, live within a balanced budget, and stop printing IOUs that they deceptively call money.

Perhaps this will happen. But remember, this book is about acquiring and preserving capital to retire on, not what to do in case of a miracle. Making money requires a pragmatic approach, which means running all these lovely dreams through a practical meat grinder to measure their probability.

Inflation is able to get started and continue because there are always those who feel inflation will moderate and that prices (or at least the rate of price increase) will decline. Over the short run, this remarkable phenomenon actually happens enough times to give substance to such hopes. It is happening now. When there is recession and a lot of people are out of work, prices do temporarily stabilize a little. But we must never forget the bad guys (the politicians, the Federal Reserve, and the banks) and their proclivity to print money and create credit. Whenever these compulsive do-gooders, these happy humanitarians, look like they have stopped, be wary. Consider the probability that they are just resting.

Having tasted the easy buck, no one—not even as lovable and well-meaning a fellow as a President—can get all the special interest groups to eat beans again. That is why inflation can moderate, but most probably will eventually accelerate. This is a rule gleaned from studying past inflations, just a few of which may be cited as examples of the devastating German variety.

Roman Empire —	3rd-4th centuries
France —	1790s
Russia —	1921
Germany —	1922-1923
China —	1940s
Greece —	1944
Hungary —	1946

As to historical examples of inflations providing examples of when the issuance of fiat money has moderated and disappeared, *there are none.*

Is this new inflationary binge going to begin tomorrow? No. The pendulum has swung toward conservatism and the liberals will make sure to give the President enough time to fail. It will also take time to build up a new mass of lendable funds and make savers forget about past losses to inflation. After the current hiatus, however, inflation is practically certain to resume because of all that has gone before. We say *practically* certain because if there is an accident in the form of a financial panic inflation could be shot down fast and it would take an awful lot of fuel (read printing-press money) to get the rocket launched again.

If we have learned the lessons of history, we know that inflations are rockets. They can slow down while they're shifting stages, like now, but, barring an accident, only accelerate until they fall to earth.

What are the potential advantages to you in this chamber of economic horrors that accompany hyperinflation?

KNOWLEDGE OF WHAT HAS HAPPENED IN THE PAST IS POWER, AND THIS KIND OF POWER WILL ENABLE YOU TO KNOW HOW, WHEN, AND WHERE TO SPECULATE IN THE FUTURE.

This is because history (with certain minor modifications) repeats itself. History can teach us many lessons—like which groups have survived recessions, depressions, and even inflations. Knowing history will enable you to turn each new public disadvantage to your own private advantage.

The winners of the 1980s will not be economists but historians, because to be a winner, one must make right and timely moves. One doesn't live long enough to learn what the right moves are because the type of economic developments we are discussing only occur once in a lifetime. Consequently, one must be willing to *learn through experience—the experience of others.* These experiences of others will show you what a select few can do, not only to protect what they have, but to make more by greatly profiting from inflation and deflation.

Is it immoral to win when others are losing? To profit when others are suffering? No. You are not taking this wealth from others, merely preserving it from destruction at the hands of madmen. By being humble in the face of history, by understanding what is going on in the world, hard-working pragmatic optimists who have learned the fine art of speculation will come through these difficult times with their money multiplied, their sanity intact, and, especially, their optimism justified, for they are the chosen few who will retire rich!

America's Heritage of Depression

The 1970s saw new lows in the American dream: decreased productivity, rising prices, and an OPEC-induced shortage of the basic stuff of civilization, energy. Financially, as the U.S. played banker to the world, there developed a vulnerability to foreign claims on the dollar as money gave up its last remaining gold backing and U.S. products, factories, and real estate become the last line of defense for the promise of dollar convertibility.

But these are only symptoms of more basic problems. History teaches us that it takes a long time for the politician's continual application of expedient short-sighted acts to enmesh a nation in long-range problems. When we pick up the long-term threads, we can trace them back all the way to the 1930s and see how the mechanism of the Drama of Debt described in the previous chapter translates into history.

In order to understand fully America's heritage of depression, we must contrast the German experience of the 1920s with the American experience of the 1930s. The kind of inflation that Germany went through was a nightmare. Because of their disastrous losses with printing press money, the German people came to fear inflation more than anything else, even war. But the American losses seem to have been caused by just the opposite. Its *bête noire* became deflation.

Throughout the troubled 1930s America was still on a gold exchange standard so no inflation could take hold. That meant its economic problems caused money to be worth more. Deflation and depression became associated in America's cumulative psyche as synonymous. Since deflation conjured up visions of closed factories and unemployment, this allowed for a little of deflation's opposite, inflation, to be tolerated as a lesser evil in post–World War II America. Believe it or not, it is this fear of deflation that has been at the psychological root of America's inflation for the past four decades.[1] The lingering fear of depression and widespread unemployment is so great that nobody cares about the future problems which might be caused by pursuing a cheap money policy now.

Every four years our elected masters of expediency have been forced to fight the latest crisis with more short-term solutions, putting bandages on the nation's latest wounds while hoping the recalcitrant beast of an economy wouldn't die on their door-

---

1. What makes it even stranger is that the link of deflation and bad times cannot even be proven. A good case can be made that *falling prices* are as easy to live with as inflation is difficult. It is *not* true that depression and deflation have to go together. One of our nation's greatest eras of progress, from 1870 to 1913, was— generally speaking—a period of deflation. In the 68 years prior to the creation of the Federal Reserve Board in 1913, the consumer price index rose a mere 10%. In the sixty-eight years since its creation, the consumer price index has increased 625%. In 1833, the wholesale commodity index stood at 75.3. In 1933, just before going off the gold standard, the index was 76.2. Today, the index is 612.3.

step while they were in office. Washington's armies of neo-Keynesian economists have steadfastly advocated pouring money into the system to make sure we're never short of dollars again. The fact that each dollar has so far been cheapened by about 94% doesn't seem to faze these paper-lovers. The deficit spending that the New Deal started in the 1930s is still with us and even under a Republican administration seems to be getting worse every day.

That's the surface. Beneath the surface are the motives for why people act. The real lesson of the 1930s was not lost on the politicians. They learned that regardless of their efficacy for the nation, massive government programs made them–the *politicians* more powerful. The first taste of power was provided by the New Deal, then the war. After the war, the bureaucrats had to come up with something new or face the worst kind of economic crisis and layoffs—loss of their own jobs and power. Given the challenge, they came up with the Economic Recovery Act of 1946, committing Congress to full employment. The spending that it entailed was like sentencing a fox to eat chickens.

Seeing that more problems to solve meant more work, and more work meant still more problems to solve convinced the politicians that the people needed them. They began giving money to almost everyone until the voices of protest finally were stilled. What they really had learned was how to make themselves more needed through buying everybody off with paper money.

This lesson, once learned, assured that income redistribution would continue through the postwar period at a constantly accelerating pace. It is important to understand that the basic reason for the increase in welfare payments has not been charity or humanistic concerns, but simply that it provided a lot of bureaucrats with a lot of powerful jobs to dispense all that money. Because of the scope of the task, the figures are startling. Out of 100 million workers in America today, fully 40% are employed by the government, its agencies, or government contract-holders. In certain areas it requires a ratio of three administrators to dispense the welfare payments for each recipient.

In brief, the fundamental characteristic of a welfare state (and the reason America will have a job getting rid of it) is that it guarantees full employment for bureaucrats. How could they pull off this giant power grab? Simple. They used other people's greed. The Keynesian approach to economics at first didn't look absurd at all. Money and credit creation made the economy grow bigger and created, initially at least, a vague general feeling of prosperity. There was a promise of something for every-one—*something for nothing*. There always is. A naive concept of "progress" makes a nation fall in love with the idea of *growth*, which becomes confused with prosperity. Politicians love growth so much (especially growth in the number of bureaucrats) that they make people forget the absurdities. No one has ever seriously contended that the growth of anything else in the world can or should be purchased at any price. Only the American economy has been singled out for this dubious distinction.

Politicians discovered long ago that the way to perpetuate their power was by pretending to be great humanitarians, fostering growth. After that there remained only to have their statiticians prove how much better off everyone is by manipulating inflated and meaningless raw (uncorrected for inflation) data.

If the only effect of this apparent redistribution of wealth was to make a few rich kids feel bad or cut down on their mothers' wearing of mink coats or make their daddies pay more taxes, we'd be the first to applaud it. But exactly the opposite is true. The rich love inflation and high taxes. It is easy for people with lots of money to protect themselves against both. The citizens it hurts and eventually destroys are—the ones just barely getting by now, hoping to retire in dignity later—in other words, *the middle class.*

The problem is inflation's effect on a society—facilitating war, causing unemployment, reducing real wages, diverting investment from production to hoarding and wasteful consumption, encouraging tax evasion, spawning an underground economy, ensuring trade deficits, fostering crime, drugs, and immorality. Apparently, these minor evils have not been considered relevant when measured against the solid benefits accruing to all those well-entrenched bureaucrats in Washington.

This is how the evils developed: As money was diverted from commerce, first to fight World War II, then to finance social welfare, companies were deprived of their earnings through taxation and forced to borrow more for plant replacement and expansion.[2]

But the tax drain on earnings eventually drove business to drink in the trough of the debt market like thirsty cattle, and when they got there an elephant of a government was already there drinking all the money up unmercifully. The need to borrow created chronic financing problems and periodic crises in the capital markets. The government's response has always been the same—to keep the cattle alive, increase the money supply, and let them drink, too. The Federal Reserve Board did this in 1949, 1954, 1957, 1960, 1966, 1974, and most recently in 1980.[3]

After decades of this nonsense, everything was in place for a few crazy Congressmen who call themselves "liberals" or "humanitarians" to have the power to bankrupt the U.S. with huge welfare programs financed by piling up debts that they perversely call money.[4] This periodic restimulation—this liquification by fiat money—has created an antiquated industrial machine, a moribund middle class, and an economy whose credit structure has been weakened internally to the point of collapse.

2. Business wouldn't have allowed this confiscatory taxation in the nineteenth century, but as the giant corporations evolved, management became separated from ownership and the shareholders were not able to organize to protect their interests. Government lessened the blow by letting business pass on the taxes in the form of higher prices. Also, giving government contracts to "worthy" (read docile) management of large corporations helped keep them in line.

3. It is not just the Federal Reserve Board alone. The bankers have played their part. Bankers have been given the job of filling the gap left by the government's drain on corporate profits. Today the government takes the loot and gives the banks power to create enough money so that business can borrow it back.

This is exactly what the Nazis did in the 1930s. They left the farmer his cow and only took the milk.

4. From 1975 to the present, the Federal Reserve has monetized an average of 11.6% of the budget deficits. This adding to the currency makes everything cost more, which causes budget deficits to rise, which causes more money to be printed, in a never-ending circle. This is the engine of inflation.

To summarize,

1. America, having associated deflation with depression, unwittingly accepted its opposite, inflation, after World War II.
2. This coincided with the politicians' desire to increase their power by espousing the concept of growth. More inflation meant a bigger economy and a greater need for bureaucrats to handle all the new money.
3. In posing as champions of working people with "full employment legislation," politicians pretended to be serving the people, but in reality have served only the very rich and the very poor. They have almost destroyed the middle class and set up a potential disaster of financial chaos that threatens massive unemployment for the whole country.

The Panic Stage

Historically, the absurdities of unpayable debt, soaring demand for funds, and astronomic interest rates follow a natural progression. This progression does not stop short of a credit shortage so severe that it results in a panic stage in which money is unobtainable at any price. This finally causes enough bankruptcies to stop the bankers' mad quest for profits and end borrowers' unquenchable thirst for borrowing (at least temporarily).

The real business bankruptcies are caused not by the government's deficits themselves, but by soaring interest rates that result from such deficits. This is the way it works: Government purchases and payments (about $700 billion a year) are paid for in two ways: (1) taxes, and (2) the sale of government securities. When government bonds and notes are sold, it soaks up savings. The more government borrows, the less money there is left for other borrowers. These other borrowers must bid for what is left of the available savings by offering higher interest rates. Rising interest rates increase the cost of doing business and decrease business profits. Lower profits slows business and that causes unemployment, making business conditions deteriorate further. As inflation progresses toward a panic stage, corporate liquidity deteriorates to the point that government ends up competing with business for loans that business needs just to *survive.*

High interest rates are always the other side of the inflationary coin. Why? Because you can't cheat savers forever. Lenders always end up demanding some after-inflation reward for the use of their money. High inflation eventually guarantees even higher interest rates until that rate exceeds what business can earn with borrowed money. At this point business collapses.[5]

The vicious circle is that all this falls back on government and produces a shortfall in revenues. If the government gets less tax revenue, it is in turn forced to borrow more in a never ending circle of unfortunate causes and effects.

Nor are the burdens of high interest rates distributed evenly and fairly. The most creditworthy borrowers learn to live with high interest, but marginal borrowers (small businessmen) are forced into bankruptcy and whole groups of residual borrowers like those seeking mortgage money are deprived of loans. As this continues, the effects escalate and unemployment becomes chronic.

The progression is relentless and implacable. Inflationary expectations grow organically, dictating that the highs in the rate of inflation and interest costs of one cycle become the lows in the subsequent cycle.[6] In this process the point is finally reached

---

5. This is related to what economists call a collapse of the Marginal Efficiency of Capital.

6. The approximate figures of the most recent "steps" toward printing press liquidation of debt are as follows:

	1970	1974	1980	198?
Interest Rate Highs	8½%	12%	21%	(?)
Inflation Rate	8%	11%	15%	(?)

Notice the recent high rates have not been caused by a booming economy as in the past, but by the soaring budget deficits of free-spending *politicians.*

where only government is able to borrow money because only government has the means (the printing press) to repay.

Crowding business out of the capital market goes hand in hand with another phenomenon—the increasing impotency of the Federal Reserve Board either to stimulate a recession or cool off a boom. The reason an increase in the money supply progressively loses its power to stimulate business is the same reason a patient becomes immune to penicillin. The form this immunity takes in the economic world is an increasing ineffectiveness of paper money to convince people to work or save. The more people there are who know about inflation, the more people there will be who will build it into their calculations and work as little as possible and borrow all they can. The less they work, the less they produce and the less there is to buy with money. The more they borrow, the more inflation there is. The more inflation there is, the more they want to borrow. As far as slowing down a boom, things are even worse. Inflation becomes so efficient in its later stages that when the Federal Reserve Board finally does act, it finds "cooling off a boom" takes such astronomical interest rates that it freezes us into a recession and brings on deflation. Since the Fed started to "fine tune" the economy with a scalpel when the prime rate was ½% (1946), it has been forced to use an axe—the axe of short-term interest rates over forty times higher, 21½% in 1980, to try to get the job done. Finally, a point is reached where everyone knows about inflation and there isn't anyone left to fool anymore. It is at this point that *deflation* starts to fool them.

In a later stage of inflation, more and more of the absurdities catch up with the perpetrators of the hoax and the Federal Reserve Board is forced by the basic nature of the braking mechanism to put up short-term interest rates so high that they even exceed the inflation rate. Borrowed money is no longer free, and by this time business is so inefficient it can't stand any additional costs. The result: Corporations draw on their liquid assets until their needs become so desperate that there is a financial panic followed by an economic collapse.

To understand the panic stage, remember that skyrocketing

short-term rates are merely the thermometer measuring the heating up of our economy. The real panic occurs in our financial markets. Short-term rates affect long-term rates and these, in turn, affect the prices of *preissued* debt—that is bonds that have been issued at earlier periods when interest rates were lower. What is a long-term bond issued to yield 5% worth when current long-term bonds are being issued to yield 10%? Roughly half. This is the real Achilles heel in the system, for these bond prices are not just little numbers printed in our financial pages. These "old" bonds are the assets that serve as backing for our financial institutions, the things which make them solvent. The declining value of these foundation assets undermines our whole financial credit structure. When the prices of these bonds and mortgages decline far enough it finally bankrupts our banks, savings and loans, and thrift institutions. These financial losses finally spread to everyone as governments destroy the value of money by trying to make good on impossible promises and guarantees to the depositors of the very institutions they have ruined.

A little recent history will illustrate how these problems interrelate and manifest themselves in the real world. In order to understand what is happening, keep in mind that high interest rates are not an isolated event. They cause bond prices to decline for *preexisting* bonds and other evidences of debt. They have this effect because in order to continue inflating, you need bond (and mortgage) *holders* as well as new buyers. Every day, savers (really their representatives in pension plans, banks, savings and loans, or insurance companies) have to continue to make the decision whether to hold bonds (or mortgages) or liquidate them.

At first, the institutional money managers tolerated a decline in the value of savers' bond (and mortgage) portfolios because it was less upsetting to lose someone else's money than their own. But as prices declined throughout the decade of the 1970s, they became disturbed. As the decade ended they finally decided to abandon the bond market (and stop making fixed-interest mortgage loans). In the fall of 1979, they decided to dump bonds *en masse.* They got their first surprise when they said "sell," and the bond brokers casually asked: "To whom?" It seemed all of Wall Street's financial gurus had seen the light at once—they all discovered that there was a thing called inflation and that it was bad for bonds. As a result, bond losses from January to March of 1980 totalled over $525 billion. If the prior three months are included, *losses amounted to $1 trillion—more than the then total value of all the stocks listed on the New York Stock Exchange!*

To compound the problem, worried bankers holding these rapidly declining assets asked their congressmen for help. Certain crisis legislation was passed during the troubled spring of 1980, seemingly based on the theory that what problems new money can't solve, new laws will cure. To handle the problems that seemed imminent, the banking interests managed to railroad through Congress the Monetary Control Act, the most potentially inflationary piece of legislation since the creation of the Federal Reserve Board itself in 1913. This legislation guarantees that the banks will be able to meet their obligations even if it means destroying the value of our currency to do it. As R.T. McNamara, Deputy Secretary of the Treasury, said in an interview in February 1982: "As long as the United States can print money, the insurance fund (for Savings and Loans) will be there." With the enactment of this new law, the last piece necessary to complete the hyperinflationary jigsaw puzzle is now in place. It will enable the Federal Reserve to buy and monetize almost any asset without prior Congressional approval. In the future a hundred of America's banks can be saved simultaneously until all the Keogh plans, social security, IRA plans, and other forms of individual savings are rendered worthless in the process.

All this has had to do with periods of panics in general. How does it concern you personally and specifically? The secret of surviving a financial panic is *liquidity.* Nothing is more liquid than short-term government Treasury bills. As the panic strikes interest rates will reach such levels that good grade long-term bonds (or financial futures) will become super bargains. You can profit handsomely as the damage is repaired and interest rates decline. Afterwards, anticipating the effects of reinflation and easy money policies to "get the economy moving again," you will again seek out the traditional inflation hedges—land, gold, and collectibles—sell your bonds (and financial futures) and go short before others see what is happening. This is where you will make enough to retire rich—perhaps richer than you ever dreamed—by 1986.

To summarize, the current problems are severe because

1. Business employs labor and cannot continue to employ it if it doesn't make a profit.
2. Most business is done on credit which means business must borrow money to make money. This indirectly makes labor dependent on the credit market and each 1% rise the interest rate causes a determinable amount of increased unemployment.
3. The rate of interest payable on loans must be less than what business can earn with the money, or it won't (or can't) borrow.
4. Government competes with business borrowing to finance its deficits, thus pushing up the interest rate and lowering business profits.
5. Government tries to remedy the situation by "stimulating the economy." The Federal Reserve does this by printing more money and making more credit available through the banks.
6. As the Federal Reserve creates the additional money, it simultaneously increases the demand by borrowers who borrow because they fear more inflation. This new borrowing puts upward pressure on interest rates and lowers the worth of preexisting debt instruments.
7. This forces banks to sell bonds to maintain their reserve requirements in their shrinking bond portfolios.
8. The shrinking of reserves causes banks to call in loans. The liquidation of debt feeds on itself until enough bankruptcies ensue to cause loan demand to decline sharply.
9. The secret of surviving a financial panic is *liquidity*.

Today, we are fast approaching a panic stage. Every day that goes by puts a further strain on our financial institutions. If banks and savings and loans had to use the same methods of accounting required of their depositors, most would show a *negative—less than zero—net worth*. Take heart. If you think you are being impoverished by inflation, it is nothing compared to the impoverishment of that giant bank or savings and loan on the corner. Yesterday your net worth might have passed hundreds of large American businesses—Itel and W.T. Grant, perhaps soon even larger and more powerful corporate dinosaurs. Who will it be tomorrow? Close analysis of the situation will prove how preposterous things have become. On second thought, you'd better not look. It might scare you to death and you'd miss your big opportunity to profit from it.

Where Are We Now?

You can learn to profit from inflation, *but it isn't easy,* because there are periods of *disinflation*. We are in one of them, so it behooves us to examine such periods in some detail.

In the first quarter of 1980, inflation at the consumer level reached a 19% annualized rate. Then, with a recession upon us, it dropped to under a third of that as we walked the inflationary tightrope, trying not to topple into the deflationary abyss.

What should concern speculators in such a period is maintaining valid long-term inflationary hedges without being shaken out of them by temporary bursts of sanity that a conservative President has stirred up to muddy the inflationary waters.

Let us dissect the effect of inflation on prices to see what the present deflationary problems are. In every current price, whether it be for a city lot, an ounce of gold, or a Picasso print, there is built-in the anticipation of future price increases (or decreases) projected from past inflationary (or deflationary) experiences. For example, the present price of a piece of land might be $50,000 in a perfectly stable economy (one without expectation of inflation), but the actual price is $100,000. Why? The extra $50,000 has been tacitly structured into this price based on the assumption that inflation will *continue* at a certain rate. If inflation looks like it is abating or even slowing down, this $50,000 inflation premium can quickly be reduced to zero or even turn into a negative figure.

These recessionary pauses cause problems for speculators as well as small businessmen and unemployed workers. To guard themselves against a change in the anticipatory element in prices, speculators must understand beforehand (*a priori*) that inflation is not a constant or continuum whose shape is a gradually ascending curve, but rather an ascending curve punctuated with sharply spiked declines that look like the configuration shown in Figure 2 on the next page.

If investing were easy, all you would have to do would be to acquire assets, contract debt, and sit idly by as inflation made you richer and richer. The majority of people who consider themselves speculators are doing just that today. But it is the perverse nature of economic truth that *the majority cannot be right because there is not the total wealth available to accommodate them and fluctuations will result to make things tough.*

This is why in past inflations there have been increasingly severe jolts that shake out the weak holders, usually the small players who end up transferring their assets into stronger hands. This kind of shakeout is one reason so few can live well and retire rich.

SPECULATIVE POINT:
Speculators must have sufficient reserves so that they are not forced to sell during a temporary pause or minor reversal in a major inflationary trend. Whenever possible, they should use these temporary recessions to buy, not sell, long-term inflation hedges.

But the real world is run by emotion, not logic. After the unlucky ones have lost their heavily leveraged assets, the gov-

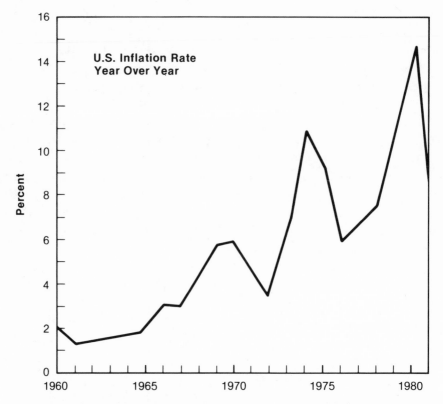

Figure 2. A graphic depiction of a nation's disintegration through monetary sin. Notice especially the periods of repentance, the *declines* that chastise the speculators in inflation hedges.

ernment creates enough fiat money to work its nefarious magic again and a new boom starts, but at this point the recovery achieved is very selective and spotty. As for those forced to sell, there is no recovery at all, for they are out of the inflationary game. As they say in "21", they busted before the dealer did.

The concept of inflationary pauses is important to understand. As inflations mature, economic upswings tire, just as people do in old age. Inertia overcomes them. It takes more to get them going again. There is a war of strength between two opposing forces, inflation and *deflation*. Everyone has found

out about inflation, but few have found out about the deflationary forces at work beneath the surface that are tiring
inflation and dragging it down. What appears initially as inflationary is the extent of government's need to finance its deficits.
A chart showing the growth of government deficits is worth a
thousand words. See Figure 3 on the following page.

The early significance of huge dollar amounts of government
deficits is that as these deficits become monetized (turned into
money), this new money increases prices (inflation). But inflation in turn drags up the interest rate, causing government to
borrow still more money to finance its new deficits. Finally, at
a given point the mountain of debt built up through decades of
inflation becomes deflationary. It happens because the amount
needed (currently $93 billion) for just *interest* on the govern-
ment's past debt approaches the amount of *new* savings available from *all* lenders (currently $117 billion). Finally, upon the
occurrence of a financial panic enough business bankruptcies
ensue to instill a fear in the hearts of borrowers that they won't
be able to repay and business gives up and stops borrowing. In
this way government's engine of inflation sputters to a stop and
becomes deflationary.

Is there any hope these deficits will be reversed? No. History
tells us that no matter what accounting tricks are used,[7] what
is off-budget or on, or which administration is spending what
on its pet projects, the irreversible spending trend in an inflationary period is *up.* Interest alone on the national debt is now
greater than the entire Federal budget of 1960!

In summary, what we are witnessing presently is a hiatus in
the rise of the Consumer Price Index—a typical slowing down
of inflation accompanying a recession. This recession could be
more severe and last longer than generally supposed because

7. The government reports on a cash basis. A 1974 study by the accounting firm
of Arthur Anderson and Co. showed that on a more accurate and appropriate accrual
basis accounting the government's *real* deficits were several times those stated by
the cash basis.

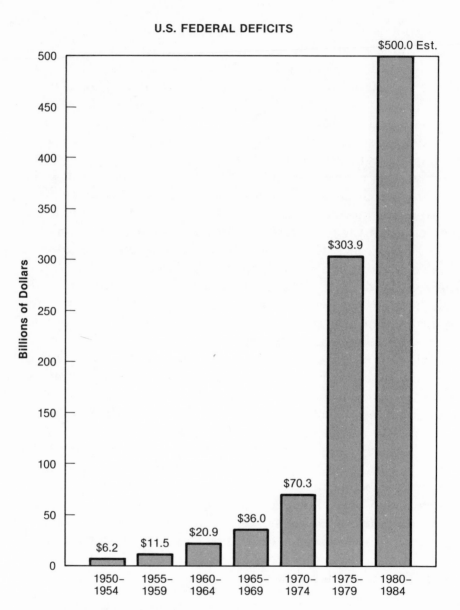

U.S. FEDERAL DEFICITS

Figure 3. The budget deficit for Reagan's four years may exceed the *total* deficits incurred in the entire 206 years before him.

the need for reliquification and reaccumulation of new savings necessary to fund the next upmove is bigger. If it culminates in a panic stage, a crisis of confidence could paralyze business. This, in turn, would lead to a clamoring for more money to end the recession. When this happens it will produce an inflationary explosion as liberal economists see the problem as *too little* liquidity and use their "Johnny-one-note" mentality to print more money.

All this adds up to a growing dynamic struggle between the forces of inflation and *deflation.* If deflation gets the upper hand, it could hold down the economy and keep unemployment high until *only* a virulent inflation can overcome it.

To put it in a workable multifaceted perspective, dangers in three different time frames work against the nonspeculator:

- *Short-term*—an era in which inflation declines, causing losses in inflationary hedges for the investor. For the small businessman, possible bankruptcy. For the working stiff, unemployment and deprivation.

- *Medium-term*—a spotty economic recovery brought about by a tremendous amount of new money creation. It will stimulate the financial markets more than the economy and get only a small part of the unemployed back to work again. Such stimulation, based as it is on fiat money, can only be short lived. The ensuing downturn from the monetary binge will signal the start of a catastrophic economic hangover; a paralysis that will not respond to stimulation.

- *Long-term*—A period of great economic difficulties and personal deprivations. Replacing a period of affluence with a period of want will bring about a restructuring of our institutions, our economic and even our democratic political system. If non-speculators weren't optimists in the old world of plenty, they'd better become optimists to survive the world of hardship and dictatorship that a collapse of America's paper money economy could bring about. Even as an informed and sophisticated speculator, it's going to take all of your ingenuity to accumulate wealth before the collapse of paper money and hold on through the tough times to follow.

Since timing is everything and the majority is usually wrong, here is a suggested formula for profit to help feather your retirement nest:

SPECULATIVE POINT:
  The majority have for years and still expect more inflation now. Hence, put your bets on deflation. Later, as the forces of deflation gain the upper hand the majority will have switched and will be expecting deflation to continue. Then, and only then, will hyperinflation be possible. This will be the time to move into inflation hedges (real things).[8]

You can use both these minority opinions to make you rich. For those of you who missed all the prior trains and are just sitting around on the sidings waiting for the last train, don't worry.

THE LAST TRAIN ON THE INFLATION HEDGE RAILROAD IS THE SUPERCHIEF.

All prior trains were strictly locals.

The real winners—the people who will retire rich—will be on this train. But be careful: It runs on time. There won't be any whistle blowing or anyone shouting, "All aboard." When others think the train yard is closed, they're going to be watching for the first wisp of steam coming out of the giant boilers. By knowing the inflation that it signals, they just might run fast enough to catch it—the Rocket Express to riches.

---

8. The government will be forced to inflate the money supply to combat deflation. You will know when this is happening by using the timing tool of money creation figures obtained from the Federal Board (Chapter 4). This will enable you to anticipate the inflationary effects of money creation before others are aware of the impending change although by then the two year period of time lag in our formula may be shortened to months or even weeks.

CHAPTER 14

Some Questions—and Answers—to Help Deepen Your Understanding of Important Issues

Speculators don't succeed by simply following the advice of others—even Swiss bankers. They succeed by thinking for themselves. In order to do that they need to thoroughly understand *basic* issues. When they do, they are able to take a subject and turn it over in their minds, seeing it from many angles. From this results the insight—the little bit extra—that gives them the edge to win. If something seems theoretical to you, or you feel that you are reviewing material you already understand, be patient. Try to master the theory so well that you can explain it to others. When you do, strange and wonderful things will begin to happen as you put your economic ideas into practice. The answers to the following questions constitute important background material—essential information you need in successful speculation.

1. Who was John Maynard Keynes and what did he stand for?

John Keynes (1883–1946) was the English economist and writer largely responsible for demand-side economics. In essence, he believed that over-saving was the most serious economic problem. His theory assumed that production would take care of itself; that if you put enough money in the hands of consumers, goods would be produced to fulfill the demand. He never satisfactorily explained where the money came from (except borrowing and printing it) or how you stopped the inflation that inevitably would result from all this new money. His ideas, coming as they did during a depression, appealed to a lot of politicians anxious to do good to lots of people all at once. Predictably these simple souls became the power structure of the modern economic world. Today, Keynesians have lost face. They are in retreat but not beaten. They are still there, waiting for Supply Side economics to fail. No matter what the verdict of history, no one can deny that Keynes' influence on our lives was enormous. He was one of the men that shaped the modern world.

Directly opposed to Keynes' ideas were the ideas of the eighteenth century author of *The Wealth of Nations,* Adam Smith. Adam Smith said that there are no leaders capable of making economic decisions for us and that the interests of *all* the people would best be served by each individual following his own interests. He felt that the marketplace should determine what is wanted, what will be paid, and who will provide it (and also who will fail and have to try something else).

Central to Adam Smith's ideas were the puritan ethics of hard work, savings, and investment so that our work aids—our capital equipment and machines—could make us ever more efficient. This was the origin of the concept that a worker is no better than his or her tools. We are seeing how true this is today as we try to compete with the Japanese.

But tools cost money and money must be saved. Keynes mistakenly thought *too much* saving was the problem. His ideas have now left us with antiquated tools that are threatening our supremacy in one field after another.

Keynes said, "We have been trained too long to strive and not to enjoy. I look forward to the day when the social customs and economic practices . . . useful in promoting the accumulation of capital, can at last be discarded." The following figures show what Keynes' fly-now-pay-later advice really meant. It meant financing by borrowing instead of saving. These are the results:

In 1960 the total debt in the U.S. was $750 billion
In 1970 the total debt in the U.S. was $1.5 trillion
In 1982 the total debt in the U.S. is over $5 trillion

This debt consists of:
—owed to holders of U.S. bonds, notes, and bills, $1 trillion;
—owed to commercial banks, $1 trillion;
—owed to insurance companies, $340 billion;
—owed to mutual savings banks, $160 billion;
—owed to holders of municipal and state bonds, $400 billion;
—owed to S and L's and individuals on mortgages, $850 billion;
—owed to holders of corporate bonds, $1.6 trillion;
—owed to holders of commercial paper, $160 billion.

A recent article in Forbes magazine estimated gross interest payments—the amount of interest being paid by all borrowers—to exceed $920 billion (larger than the total debt in 1960). This figure is higher than generally expected because of the structure of our financial institutions. Interest is often being paid by them—as well as received by them—on the same money.

> More significant than the size of current debt is the fact that by 1985 the total debt is estimated to be *many times greater.*

For Keynes, the problem was how to stimulate an economy by injections of paper money, never how to control the inflation that such infusions of money cause. He explained how you use credit and money creation (he called it increased demand) to get things rolling (he called it going from a depressed state to equilibrium). Once things were rolling and the economy passed equilibrium (which happened about 1969), his theories didn't provide an answer as to how you got back to a point of equilibrium. "Equilibrium," by the way, is another word for Shangri-La where production, consumption, savings, investment are all in balance.

Neo-Keynesian economists following in his footsteps have taught subsequent generations to look to politicians for their beneficence—that all good things flow from Washington. The Keynesian professors have taught a whole generation that wealth comes from an inexhaustible harvest of money trees grown in government-subsidized forests.

Who listened to these Neo-Keynesians ideas? The politicians. Their object, as always: More power over the people. Keynes made politicians feel they were needed to dispense all the newly created money. Can you think of a better reason his ideas were so quickly accepted and implemented?

The power to dispense this money has led to a politician's paradise—a government of, by, and for special interests—a system of fully legalized bribery and corruption ruled over by a well-entrenched bureaucracy in Washington. At the core of the "big spender" political philosophy is the erroneous idea that the politicians are somehow protecting the weak from the strong who would otherwise exploit them. Nothing could be further from the truth. Historically, government itself has always represented the *real* oppressor.

The free market guarantees only liberty and *equal opportunity*. The demagogue seeks to legislate absolute equality which is the antithesis of liberty and always ends up depriving the people of not only liberty and equality but prosperity as well.

All this is important to you as a speculator in the future because the neo-Keynesians are still around and will come out fighting for printing-press money to end the paralysis they have caused. The greatest thing you will be able to do is to understand the Keynesian ideas well enough to capitalize on their failure.

2. It has often been said that inflation misdirects resources. What does this mean? Is it important?

To take the last question first, it is not only important, it is *essential*. One of the greatest cruelties of inflation is that it impoverishes some and enriches others in an arbitrary manner. On a personal level, it punishes those who work hard, save much, and borrow little. For a whole society it is the misdirection of resources that finally causes the smash. The seeds of inflation's own destruction are carried within it. Let us see how. Imagine that as a sales promotion, General Motors extends ten-year credit to all buyers who purchase a new automobile. The plan is so successful that 3 million Americans end up buying new General Motors cars. This stimulates sales to such an extent that General Motors is able to raise prices, which enables Ford and Chrysler to raise theirs. The auto business booms. There results a shortage of auto-related products (replacement parts, radios, etc.). Existing GM dealers can't handle all the business, so hundreds of new franchises are set up. They crowd out existing cleaning plants and florists and food markets, among others. Rubber companies can't handle the demands to supply the tires, so they build new factories.

But when the payments start, as a consequence of all the money spent on autos, the new buyers have less money to purchase groceries, pay their rent, and even buy gas for their new cars. The ten-year credit promotion was a one-shot deal. Auto sales drop drastically over the next two years. New franchises are now competing with the old for half the business. There is a recession in the auto business. Rubber factories close and workers are laid off in that industry. Desperate, General Motors executives go to their congressional friends in Washington and get special legislation enacted to give a tax credit for purchases of new autos. This saves the industry until next year.

What can save it after that? The government has already used the tax approach. The only solution left is to print so much money that people will buy more of everything, including cars. This is the inflationary solution facing us today.

The following year even this will work only if a greater amount of new money is printed.

Here is the rule:

THE STIMULATIVE EFFECTS OF ARTIFICIAL DEMAND BASED ON CREDIT INFUSIONS, TAX CUTS, OR MONEY CREATION CAN CONTINUE ONLY SO LONG AS THEY ARE INCREASING AT A CONSTANTLY ACCELERATING RATE.[1]

---

1. This is akin to the economic Principle of Acceleration, which deals with the relationship between remote and near goods used in the production process. It is based on the idea that a small increase in demand at the consumer level gives rise to a much greater (and unsustainable) demand at the capital goods level. Those readers interested in pursuing a study of economic cycles would be well advised to study this principle first.

For those of you who would delve still deeper, the case against inflation continuing indefinitely lies in the workings of the Principle of Acceleration, plus the impossibility of compound interest as outlined in Question 3 below.

When the artificial energizers stop, the merry-go-round plays a sad recessionary tune as the economy grinds to a halt.

Technically, when money is introduced into the economy through an artificial means (not based on solid consumer demand), various price relationships and investment flows are disturbed, leading to a misdirection of resources that can only be cured by subsequent retrenchment or bankruptcy.

3. Why is making money so difficult? Or, statistically, why don't more people die rich?

There is an eighth wonder of the world called compound interest that theoretically should work to concentrate wealth in a mechanical way in the hands of a very few. We are told by the thrift institutions and banks that if we save $2,000 a year, magic and wonderful things will happen to us. They offer the following chart to prove it.

Here's what an annual $2,000 investment will grow to become assuming various annual rates of return.

Years	Total contribution	(Interest rates)			
		12%	13%	14%	15%
5	$10,000	$ 14,230	$ 14,645	$ 15,071	$ 15,507
10	20,000	39,309	41,628	44,089	46,698
15	30,000	83,506	91,343	91,960	109,434
20	40,000	161,397	182,939	207,536	235,620
25	50,000	298,667	351,700	414,665	489,423
30	60,000	540,585	662,630	813,474	999,913
35	70,000	966,926	1,235,498	1,581,345	2,026,691

This principle of compound interest doesn't work for a number of reasons. You've all heard about how the $26 paid to the Indians for Manhattan Island in 1626, compounded at a 10% interest rate over the intervening years, would total over $30 quadrillion. This is not only more money than New York is now worth, but many times more than the worth of all of the world's goods plus all of the world's production since the beginning of recorded history. As for the thrift institutions chart, they don't tell you it might cost $1,000 for a phone call and $100,000 for lunch.

Compound interest doesn't work as outlined in the story and wealth is *not* concentrated because what one group loses the other doesn't necessarily win. A roulette board isn't divided into just red and black, for example. There is a third color—green— the house color (or number 0) where *both* groups lose. The statistical reason why more investors aren't successful is because they refuse (or are unable) to take their bets off seductive but risky paper assets (or worse, commit to a series of illiquid investments) just at the time a series of house numbers are going to hit. These string of house numbers occur most frequently at times of great inflation or deflation.

Even the smartest investors fall victim to illiquidity at these crucial turning points. *They are either in real assets and can't get into paper when deflation strikes, or they are in paper and can't get into real assets when inflation strikes.*

You would think that if investors held paper, they already had liquidity (by definition). The only thing wrong with being in paper is that paper assets are subject to being destroyed by bankruptcy or by inflation itself.

What about being in real assets? In order to survive inflation, the real asset must also be *liquid* so that it can in turn be sold at the proper time to take advantage of the subsequent low prices of the depression phase. The reason investors can't find a real asset that is liquid (salable at just the right time) is that by definition the investment items that fit this category are extremely limited. We have seen that gold, for example, is so scarce that all the gold ever mined would only make a cube eighteen yards to the side, and there are price limitations for anything. Gold is only an efficient preserver of capital for those lucky enough to have purchased *early* at a low price.

Also, there are other pitfalls. Even for the limited number of winners, there is a punitive form of government expropriation. Consider how it works: First, currency has depreciated around 90% in 50 years. Then there is the confiscation of taxation. In the past, every time an individual's income has increased 1%, the government's share increased 1.6%, or over 50% more. Add this oppressive income tax to a large estate tax, and only a few cents have remained out of even a winner's dollar. When one understands how hard it is to win, is it any wonder that few people die rich?

There is another aspect to compound interest that explains why inflation can't continue forever. Over a long period of time, inflation can't continue reducing the *value* of the dollar for the same reasons compound interest can't continue increasing the *number* of dollars. You have probably heard the story of the wise man who did a favor for the ruler of an ancient kingdom. To reward the man, the ruler promised him anything he wanted. The man humbly replied that he would be compensated enough if the ruler would merely place one grain of rice on the first square of a chessboard, two on the second, four on the third square and continue doubling the measure until the sixty-four squares had been accounted for. The ruler granted the man's apparently modest request and watched first with a smile, then with a fierce frown. As the doubling continued, the ruler saw he was going to be completely impoverished. Now imagine, if you will, *the reverse of this.* From the point of view of the saver, price rises that exceed interest received really result in an inverted form of compound interest. That is, inflation is compounding each saver's capital down toward a zero level (below which it obviously cannot go since at some point *all capital disappears*). In 1980, we saw a manifestation of this phenomenon when the value of existing government bonds declined more than the value of the newly printed money.

The key to understanding either the impossibility of compound interest or the similar impossibility of an unending inflation lies in the difference between real and nominal rates. The nominal or widely publicized rate of interest can go to astronomical levels during periods of high interest rates such as those we are experiencing now. The real rate (the one corrected for inflation) always remains much, much lower, or even goes to a minus figure. This means the nominal rates are fictional. This is just another way of saying that real interest rates can't be compounded over any period of time.[2]

The only long-term measure we have of a real cyclical rate of possible sustainable price increase (or yield) compoundable over a long period of time is the factor by which something real, scarce, and valuable goes up to reflect the increased wealth or production of a society. The nearest we can come to measuring this is the amount by which art treasures—paintings, silver and other objects of great beauty and rarity—increase in value. It is a positive rate, but very low (only 1 or 2%) over a long period of time. The impossibility of compounding fictional paper values that exceed real production gains explains why the mass of apparent wealth is periodically destroyed and why more people don't die rich. In a word, *the wealth was never there* to be realized *en masse.* Paper values can be realized by a lucky few but are never capable of being realized beyond the real wealth involved. The rest is simply an illusion based on paper or numbers that cannot be fulfilled by the limited amount of real wealth available to satisfy the paper claims.[3]

Inflation eventually gives way to deflation because of the limitations inherent to its own inhuman absurdities. On the practical level, inflation is just another way of describing people being priced out of one thing after another, forced to give up one thing after another because they can no longer afford it. Only the government gains in this grotesque game. For example, private business people do not have the luxury—like the government—of monetizing debt. They must pay it back, with interest, at rates that eventually become higher than their profit margin.

2. See Figure 1 in Chapter 12 on page 135.

3. This is analogous to the economic model discussed previously regarding the stock market. The model there was constructed to show that the numbers listed in any newspaper's financial section are mere statements of opinion, not wealth that can be utilized *en masse.*

From the worker's point of view, the situation is even worse. Inflation results in profoundly human limitations: There are a lot of people who can't take the cut in real wages that inflation entails. The worker gets priced out of *necessities*. Looking at the real average weekly wage (adjusted for taxes and inflation), we see proof of this fundamental point. In real wages, workers averaged $92 a week a decade ago but currently earn only $82 a week. Their standard of living can't drop to zero. They are pushed to the wall now trying to make ends meet. Their families have to be clothed and fed. If they aren't, our society is close to the breaking point. Inflation will come to a halt, because at that point the people will take political action or even confer dictatorial power to someone who promises to put an end to inflation's inequities.

4. The best way to protect yourself from long term inflation seems to be to purchase real things (land, gold, collectibles). Periodically, however, real things decline sharply in value during temporary recessions. What's the best way to handle this?

If you had the right formula, you would make a great deal more money (and avoid selling at temporary bottoms). How can you get such a working formula? By discovering the secret of what determines the price of real assets such as gold, diamonds, rugs, antiques, art, and real estate. Can this be done? Let's try.

In a sentence, *the price of hard assets is determined by the **real rate of return available on alternatives*** (paper assets, and especially bonds). The real rate of return on such alternatives is simply the nominal rate of return less the inflation rate. Assume a bond, for example, has a coupon or nominal rate of 14%. With an inflation of 10%, the real rate of return on this paper asset is 4%.

As long as the rate of inflation exceeds the real rate obtainable on paper assets (for example, bonds or money market instruments), money will flow into real things for protection. However, when the real rate of return on such paper assets exceeds inflation and a *real* reward can be obtained from holding paper assets, there is no need to hold real things for inflation protection and their values decline.[4]

SPECULATIVE POINT:
By charting the real rate of return on paper assets, you know when to buy and sell real assets. You should sell inflation hedges when the rate on paper turns positive (yields a positive return after inflation). You should buy inflation hedges again when the rate on paper assets turns negative. This rule can take you a long way toward your goal of retiring rich by 1986.

---

5. What about Reaganomics?

Ronald Reagan is a man of good will and forceful personality. His persuasive powers as president have rivaled even those of F.D.R. Unfortunately, he is surrounded by rich men. These are men that understand the truth about excessive taxation and have responded by offering a supply-side economic solution designed to increase production by decreasing taxes. This is supposed to eventually create more jobs for all by increasing the incentives to save and invest for the few.

On the surface it all seems simple enough—By cutting taxes people will respond by working harder, earning more, and paying more taxes so that the government's tax receipts eventually will be higher even though the rates are lower. Theoretically, the new money not paid in taxes will be saved and invested in the creation of new jobs for all. Surprisingly enough, there's nothing new about the idea. It's just good old fashioned capitalism as set forth by Adam Smith. Instituted earlier it might

---

4. The rule should be modified by recognizing that *anticipatory feelings* rather than actual rates are what determine the beginning and end of flows in and out of such items and that you must be convinced the move represents a change of trend. With this slight qualification, and by using this rule, the investor has automatic buy and sell points for real assets (gold, diamonds, land, etc.).

have proved a great success and polished up the somewhat tarnished image of free markets. Now, the hour is late. The problems, like cancerous growths, have been allowed to grow and for their removal a dose of laetrile is proposed.

If the men around the President understood the *real* problem of debt as you now understand it, they would have had a chance of succeeding. If it is true that the major economic problem today is one of debt, then it can easily be understood that Reaganomics, like Keynesian economics, is only half a theory. Any theory that refuses to recognize the plight of our bond and capital markets is doomed to failure. *No long-term capital can be obtained to modernize America's productive capacity until confidence is restored and savers feel justified in extending longterm credit.*

How does Reaganomics fail in this regard? Restoring savers confidence means cutting spending, as well as taxes. Unfortunately, an increase in defense spending calls for higher, not lower, taxes. You cannot finance a military buildup with a tax cut. The tax cut plus the military buildup spells deficits and deficits mean more money creation. More money creation means higher interest rates and higher interest rates mean lower bond prices, and this in turn guarantees the continued difficulty of obtaining long-term credit. The unavailability of long-term credit means the basic investment sought by Reagan's economic plan will *not* be achieved.

As for a lowering of inflation, remember that each action creates a reaction. The lowering of inflation that has been achieved has been purchased at the price of *slower economic recovery.* When it is seen that the economy is still plagued with high unemployment, low profits, and uncontrollable federal deficits, there will be the usual call for government to "do something about it." The American people have not—like the Germans—been used to making sacrifices to control inflation, and we can be certain there will be no lack of politicians clamoring to get the economy moving again by making money easier.

Pressures to reinflate could thus reach a maximum just as the restraints of Reaganomics begin to produce a new, soundly based boom. If this happens, as it well might sometime in 1983, a new inflationary binge could build fast. As deficits soar out of control, we will pick up the same old book, with Reagan's attempts at conservatism and fiscal reform just a short chapter in the inflationary story.

History will judge us harshly for having missed this golden opportunity for real reform. Inflation won't be stopped after this because there will no longer be the possibility of disinflation without collapse. Inflation on the next upswing will be ineradicably built into the structure and fabric of our society. Once a given point is reached, inflation can only accelerate toward a hyper or irreversible stage. This is because at that point too many decisions will have been based on inflation continuing—a perfect formula for a self-fulfilling prophecy.

6. Where is the greatest weakness in the financial system of the western world?

The Swiss bankers believe the greatest weakness is in money itself, especially Eurodollars, for the following reasons.

There has been a phenomenal growth in the number of Eurodollars during the last decade. We have already touched on the Soviet Bloc nations' vulnerability to crisis and the great number of less developed nations that are teetering on the edge of bankruptcy. If any one of these countries officially defaults on its obligations, a crisis of confidence could domino through the whole Eurodollar banking system in a matter of days.

There is, however, an even more fundamental weakness emanating from the implied promises contained in the use of the dollar itself as a reserve currency to support the world's monetary system. The world's foreign reserves of dollars are held short-term based on our money's continuing integrity and value. This value cannot be maintained without discipline and restraint on America's part. This in turn limits our politicians' power to reinflate. Is this a potentially serious problem? A glance at Figure 1 showing the extent of dollar reserves in foreign treasuries supplies the answer.

In the decade of the 1970s, total international monetary re-

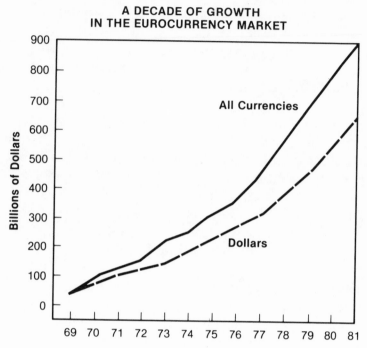

**A DECADE OF GROWTH
IN THE EUROCURRENCY MARKET**

Figure 1.

serves have been pushed up an average of 50% a year (to total an amazing 500% increase). Originally, these reserves were gold or dollars convertible to gold. Now they are in dollars convertible into nothing but promises. The dollar isn't even an IOU. Viewed internationally, the longer foreign nations continue to finance the U.S. trade deficit by taking in dollars as reserve units and continuing to issue their own currencies against this kind of specious paper backing, the more they are flirting with financial bankruptcy themselves. Foreign nations have long been trading real goods for a depreciating fiat currency but the real danger comes as our economy recovers later on and more and more of their money has to be printed to buy our depreciating dollars. This can only result in greatly increased inflation for them without solving the dollar problem for us.

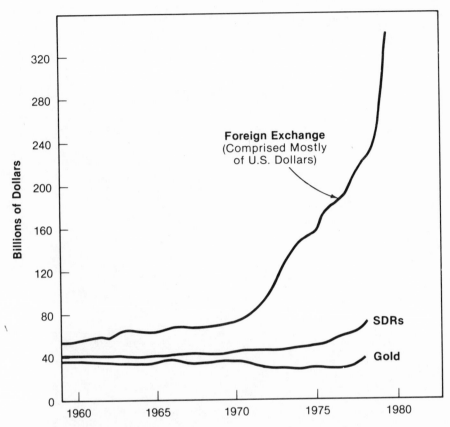

Figure 2. This chart shows the dramatic increase in dollars held by foreign central banks.

Using the dollar as a reserve currency confers certain duties and obligations as well as benefits on the U.S. The major obligation incumbent on the U.S. is to provide a money whose value will be maintained. The dollar must offer, ostensibly at least, some kind of store of value. A decade ago, U.S. banks held almost all the U.S. bonds. Over the last few years, foreign governments and individuals have purchased them from the banks. At the heart of these purchases has been an implied warranty that the dollar's value will be maintained and that these investments will be safe. If this promise is broken, these short-

OWNERSHIP OF U.S. GOVERNMENT SECURITIES

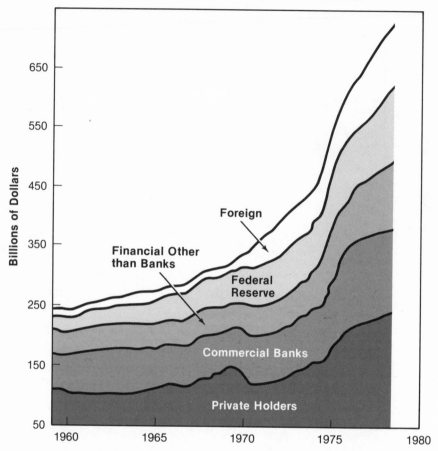

Figure 3. The ownership of U.S. government securities has recently shifted from the commercial banks to foreign governments and individuals.

term deposits can be withdrawn and foreign exchange purchases stopped. This would wreck our financial community fast. In the years to come, America could thus be impaled on the horns of the following dilemma:

If we don't inflate, we stagnate. If we do, we will have a massive withdrawal of foreign dollar-denominated holdings that will produce financial chaos.

The U.S., as banker to the world, has thus brought itself within the grasp of all the classical financial traps that bedevil bankers. Our whole country will pay the price for the dollar "privilege," which is nothing less than a banker's subsidy.

What could still be done to mitigate this problem? The U.S. could stop insisting on the world using paper money reserves that have no intrinsic value when it has no intention or interest in defending those paper values. Foreign nations, for their part, could either stop printing money to buy dollars, or buy gold on the open market with their dollar surpluses as soon as they receive them. Also, each nation's banking system could require the same reserves for Eurodollar balances that the Federal Reserve requires domestically.

As it is now, everyone is blundering along with policies destined not to defend the dollar but to bring about a financial crisis so severe as to threaten the very survival of the Western economic world.

7. What are the ABCs behind the huge borrowing needs of American business and government?

The tax policies have been revised for business to encourage capital investment. Capital investment takes money. Since corporate liquidity is at an historic low, the money must be borrowed. The more inflation makes America's huge industrial machine larger, the more fuel (money) it takes to make it go, and the money is not available from earnings. This happens because the depreciation schedules of our tax structure are based on historical cost, not replacement value, so current earnings are drastically overstated and, hence, overtaxed. For example, in 1980 GM paid 55% of its *total* revenues in taxes, National Steel and Norfolk & Western paid over 70% each, and Exxon paid over 75%.

The significance of this is that dividends plus taxes often total more than real earnings. For example, in 1981 AT&T had real earnings (figured at real current replacement cost of depreciating assets) of only $2.3 billion, while it simultaneously paid out dividends of $3.4 billion. The company ate into its capital by over a billion dollars and at this rate would liquidate itself at some ascertainable future date.

Replacement of plant and equipment gets progressively more difficult as inflation continues. The only way American business can beat this horrendous consequence of inflation is by borrowing. Corporate treasurers take it as a truism that debt payments get progressively easier as inflation increases, so they attempt to offset the ravages of inflation by borrowing their way out of it. Then something goes wrong. An attempt at fiscal restraint and a declining inflation rate suddenly plunges a few marginal businesses into bankruptcy. This dominos to other businesses and before you know it there is a financial crisis, a real recession, and mountains of unpayable debt. In other words, a conservative administration's temporarily trying to do the right thing by slowing inflation proves catastrophic because so many are committed to it. This is the tightrope now being walked by the Reagan financial planners—to do enough to slow inflation without precipitating a financial crisis.

8. Can the basic economic problem confronting us today be intelligently summarized? How did it originate? What will it lead to? What is the best investment approach to survive it?

In a word, the basic problem is DEBT. How did the problem originate? Borrowers at first found borrowing profitable. Nothing succeeds like success. If borrowers have found debt utilization profitable, so have banks when they create credit. The banks' desire for profit maximization has led them to continue lending far beyond the bounds of prudence.

Doing away with the natural restraint of the gold standard has left a giant void and put the burden on borrower restraint and lender prudence. But what happens to the concepts of restraint and prudence when both feel the government will bail them out if they get into any real trouble? They disappear. The last remaining self-restraint has been undermined by the government's misguided interference. Its latest gigantic economic blunder has been to extend loan insurance guarantees and even intervene as an underwriter of bad loans. It's more than the

Chrysler syndrome. The Monetary Control Act of 1980 sets the stage for new and even more irresponsible bailouts in the future. If business and banks know the government will come to their rescue, there is no apparent punishment for failure and hence no natural self-interest to stop putting money into irrational ventures.

All this cannot continue forever. The ease of obtaining credit for dubious projects plus Uncle Sam's paternalism have caused debts to grow more rapidly *than the incomes and earnings out of which they are to be repaid.* This is an untenable situation that must lead to a financial crisis.

SPECULATIVE POINT:
The coming financial crisis will be precipitated by a default of one or more undeveloped countries on their bank loans. One should stay liquid until that crisis develops, then—realizing the inflationary implications of the ensuing bailout—shift to gold, silver, and other hard assets. This should also provide an opportunity to buy commodities and later sell short T bond and T bill futures in order to profit from the ensuing run-up in interest rates.

---

9. If deflation always follows inflation, why can't you just sit on your cash, Treasury bills or money funds, until inflation blows over and beat it that way?

We have seen that the main impediment to retiring rich is being caught in an illiquid position at crucial turning points. For those who have a lot to protect and preserve and who are not psychologically inclined to speculate, a few words are in order about the idea of beating inflation by waiting it out with liquid assets.

The wait-it-out approach is based on the idea that over the long term, *investors who lose the least may be big winners.* That is, an absolute loss in dollar amounts does not preclude a relative gain in purchasing power (the reverse of the phenomena experienced in the inflationary expansion phase). But investors should be careful about one thing—the *danger of the change in currency used as dollars.*

Investors may reason that they have money now and are only comfortable in a continually liquid position. Eventually deflation always follows inflation, so all they have to do is take a long-term approach and wait for money to become worth something again.

Their reasoning is right but their facts are deficient. The problem is central to the thinking of Dr. Franz Pick, the currency expert. Just when the patient cash-holders are about to be right, the government changes the currency on them and issues new money—usually one for every five or ten of the old. This is how, historically, we have created so much worthless paper. The old money disappears into drawers and furnaces and becomes just a name in a history book—Continentals, Confederate money, Old Francs, marks, shekels, pesos, or lira. Nor is it without precedent here. This is how our country got its start—issuing $1 of government bonds for every $100 of Continental Currency.

Incidentally, this is what will destroy retirement funds that have been trapped into tax free Keogh and IRA plans and make mockeries of retirement annuities. The money will be there all right, but what value will it have after a massive devaluation that changes the value of the dollar? When you fully understand this, even the most timid and conservative investors will be more willing to join the *only* group that has a chance of winning—the speculators.

10. Is a third-stage runaway inflation inevitable?
Historically, the way inflation unfolds is as follows: If a nation's economy goes to Stage A, Stage B will usually follow. If it goes to Stage B, Stage C will almost certainly follow, but if it goes to Stage C, Stage D is *guaranteed* to follow. The American economy has already left B and is moving toward C.

The situation is bad, but for the moment, at least, not totally hopeless. The concepts promoted by Keynes and used by a succession of liberal Congresses to justify huge government interventions in the free market are coming to their predictably sad and weary end. A wave of new conservatism offers some hope for a belated recognition that we cannot print wealth, we must work for it. But if reason doesn't triumph (and why should it start now?) and the sacrifices inherent in controlling inflation prove too much for the American people to bear, we are heading for a runaway stage of inflation—a horror so severe, or opportunity so tremendous, that few can imagine it.

After the temporary hiatus of the present recessionary rest period, we will again have even larger inflation in the future. This will happen for a number of reasons:

- When there is a mountain of debt (consumer debt, business debt, and above all, government debt), it must be paid, and the only way such debt has ever been liquidated historically is by inflation or bankruptcy. That is, cheapening of the monetary unit in which the debt is denominated. The bigger the debt, the bigger the inflation necessary to pay it. So if history is any guide you can count on hyperdebt leading to hyperinflation.

- It is apparent that there will be an increasing pressure for arms buildup occasioned by cold war confrontations and Russian-induced terrorism around the globe. The present administration is reacting to the threat by attempting to rebuild a war machine at the same time it is cutting taxes. If this plan is carried out in its entirety, there will be resultant deficits of over $100 billion a year through 1984. This means creation of enormous amounts of new money to fill the gap between government's expenditures and its income.

- Because of the built-in higher floor on interest rates, the next inflationary binge will start from a higher level than any previous inflation and thus force prices into orbit sooner.

- Western Europe's soaring unemployment will cause European nations to pressure us to reinflate so that they can do the same.

- President Reagan's economic reforms, while they are steps in the right direction, were too little and too late. Paradoxically, Reagan was accused of too much restraint when exactly the opposite was true—his program would have required much more drastic restraints in order to succeed. Reaganomics—under the pressure of Congress—has already been abandoned.

- Growing unemployment in the United States will lead to trade restrictions of imports, thus allowing inefficient American producers to raise prices on goods produced and consumed domestically.

- The poor nations continually use their inability to repay their existing loans as an excuse to extract more. This cannot continue without bankrupting our banks. Unless we let these nations charge higher prices for the commodities they produce, they will default. It is all a not-so-subtle form of blackmail, but the banks will lobby for these price increases to avoid their own bankruptcies. These forced commodity price increases will fuel inflation at the primary level. There also will be increasing pressure from the third world nations to solve their desperate problems of food and fuel.

These problems are not solvable short of a rebirth of humanitarian impulses in the nations of the world to switch expenditures from war to peace. This is a worthy idea, but not a likely occurrence.

11. How will you recognize third-stage inflation?

Your pocketbook will tell you. Although the dollar now buys only 10¢ (or less) of what it would in 1933, and although world inflation in the 1970s was four times what it was in the 1960s, we are not even close to what hyperinflation looks like.

We all have some favorite bargains—a place to eat, someone who repairs things cheaply, a place to shop. The bargains all will be gone. Bargains will disappear because the holdouts—the nice guys—will have to pay too much themselves.

As an investor, you'll feel it, too. At first, there were several investment alternatives: gold at $35.00; silver at $1.30; cheap commodities; real estate that gave a good net spendable income; stocks at historically low prices; and bargain-priced art, antiques, etc. Now there are just stocks (if you assume that the period of earnings overstatement through inadequate depreciation is coming to an end). As inflation abates temporarily and stocks move up, there'll be little that can be called "cheap."

12. How will the money created by the hyperinflation finally be destroyed?
In sequential declines as the forces of deflation overcome the forces of inflation. This happens historically as follows:

- Business bankruptcy
- Falling bond prices ($400 billion went to money heaven in 1980 alone)
- Falling value of the dollar, especially abroad
- Falling stock prices (in real terms—even if prices advance)
- The declining marketability of inflation hedges (even if advancing in nominal price)
- Bank failures
- Government calling in the currency and reissuing megabucks (devalued dollars)

You can see how difficult it becomes to have assets that don't fit under these categories. Traditionally, precious metals, being real, useful, and liquid, maintain their value better than anything else.

13. How can you use history to understand the mechanics of inflation?
History is merely prior experience gained vicariously by study. By realizing the characteristics that all inflationary periods have in common, you may learn to recognize what stage you are in. By observing what is going on around you and then

consulting history, you may ascertain what usually happens next. In this regard, it is instructive to read *Fiat Money Inflation in France* by Andrew Dickson White, just one quote from which might whet your appetite for more:

> "New issues (of money) only increased the evil; capitalists were all the more reluctant to embark their money on such a sea of doubt. Workmen of all sorts were more and more thrown out of employment. Issue after issue of currency came; but no relief resulted save a momentary stimulus which aggravated the disease. The most ingenious evasions of natural laws in finance which the most subtle theorists could contrive were tried—all in vain; the most brilliant substitutes for those laws were tried. . . .
>
> Out of the inflation of prices grew a speculating class; and in the complete uncertainty as to the future, all business became a game of chance, and all businessmen gamblers. In city centers came a quick growth of stockbrokers and spectators. . . . Instead of satisfaction with legitimate profits, came a passion for inordinate gains. . . .
>
> So came upon the nation the obliteration of thrift. . . . There came cheatery in the nation at large and corruption among officials and persons holding trusts. . . . Faith in moral considerations, or even in good impulses, yielded to general distrust . . . patriotism was eaten out by cynicism. . . .
>
> Stagnation became worse and worse. At last came the collapse and then a return by a fearful shock, to a state of things which presented something like certainty of remuneration to capital and labor. Then, and not till then, came the beginning of a new era of prosperity."

It is helpful to use history to learn the sequence of events. If the usual sequence of stages in an economic cycle is A B C D E F and each of these stages has common ascertainable characteristics, you can use this information to know the future. If, for example, you decide we are at point D, then by taking the common characteristics inherent to stage E, you have a very valuable tool to help predict what the future will look like.

As an example of how this works, you may observe that you are in a severe economic contraction and see that such contractions are typical of Stage D. What will follow? A study of past inflations teaches us that stage E may be a period of hyperinflation because all big inflations come out of preceding inflationary lulls (economic contractions). This sequence of events is logical enough since it is only at the point of economic contraction when problems are severe, that politicians dare to run the printing presses to solve them.[5] Just think what a beautiful timing tool this is. You don't need to look for a third-stage inflation (stage E in our example) until things look really bad all around you first (stage D in our example). When you see stage D, you know the politicians, the Fed, and the bankers are likely to print money to solve problems.

Have we ever had a runaway-type inflation in this country? Not in peacetime or within living memory. On one occasion— during the Revolutionary War—the currency issued to pay for war was rendered almost worthless, but it was a relatively painless procedure affecting rich creditors. We have never had a runaway inflation affecting the majority of the people who are creditors through their IRA plans, bank accounts, credit and labor unions, life insurance and retirement plans. These kind of losses weren't experienced during the Civil War or in 1929 because of the natural restraints of the gold standard.

14. What about Social Security? How might the ability of the Federal government to continue retirement payments be affected by all that we have seen? Conversely, how do these payments themselves affect the financial stability of the government?

At age 65, 92% of Americans are broke except for their meager social security payments. Only one in fifty are financially independent so social security payments have become crucial to the lives of millions.

When Social Security began, there were 135 workers for each recipient. Today, payments are made to 25 million or a ratio of one recipient for every four workers (25%) This ratio is projected

---

5. This gives us a chance to use history to form a minority (hence potentially profitable) opinion to go against the prevailing trend by seeing ahead. For a speculator, this is the type of thinking necessary to formulate trading strategies and plan speculative campaigns, just as a general makes a battle plan.

to increase to one in three (33%) by 1990 and to one in two (50%) thirty years later. All this is because the average age of Americans is increasing. As the demographics shift to an older population,[6] not only Social Security but the private pension plans that have been instituted to care for the nation's aging will come under financial pressure. Even today, without these stresses, Social Security is paying out $12,000 more every *minute* than it takes in.

In addition to Social Security, there are presently 50,000 pension plans covering 40 million workers. A large portion of the population is depending on these plans for their subsistance during retirement. How are these plans funded and what are their obligations? Most of the private pension plans are unfunded and dependent on the employing company's *future* earnings. The total liabilities of private plans exceed $600 billion. Since 1974, there have been certain forms of government insurance to guarantee payments, but again, such payments can only be made *en masse* by a cheapening of the currency, so payment in real terms remains an illusion.

Unfunded welfare, medical, and Social Security payments have produced a present actuarial deficit of over four *trillion* dollars! These programs will soon be obliged by fixed commitments to pay out more than the total wealth of the country.

Seeing these figures, do you still think these obligations will be paid? Yes, they will be paid. No government could survive repudiating the promises made to the millions of recipients involved. The real question is what will the money be worth? Like the government debt or private pension funds, the only way to pay is in greatly depreciated dollars. Danger signs to watch for include withdrawing the indexing of Social Security payments that has protected such payments against inflation and raising the minimum ages for Social Security recipients to be eligible for benefits. A great many private companies may

6. In 1900 persons over 65 comprised only 4% of the population; now they are 13%. By the year 2000 they will comprise more than 20% of the population.

declare bankruptcy or renege on their promises to pay retirement benefits by not hiring or arbitrarily discharging old employees (even if this is illegal). Do-it-yourself retirement plans (IRA and Keogh are examples) may be substituted for the Social Security program until Social Security is severely curtailed or phased out altogether. Most importantly, a general cheapening of the dollar value of these benefits may occur through more inflation.

Inherent in all this are the seeds for great social discontent; riot points in future years. If there is an attempt made to actually pay these kinds of benefits, it will bring on a monetary collapse, followed by a period of paralysis, but if the obligations are not paid, a revolution could ensue. This isn't much of a choice is it?

Your only solution is to get smart fast and try to apply the lessons of history to save yourself and your family while you still can. This means providing for your own retirement *outside* the system (including IRA and Keogh plans) by learning now to be a speculator.[7] The real gamblers will be the savers. They are being offered tax incentives to save moribund financial institutions who have already proved their lack of judgment by investing money in bonds and making bad loans.

15. What would it take to stop inflation at this point?

Plenty. The FRB would have to stop the game of adding to the money supply while talking restraint. See Figure 4.

● In addition, the government would have to stop profiting by inflation. Historically the government has used inflation to reduce its debt burden; it gains every time it cheapens the value of the dollars in which its debts are to be repaid. Look at Figure 5 to see how painless inflation really is for the government.

● Congressmen would have to go on extended vacations. No

7. If you are not psychologically or financially equipped to be a speculator, you can hoard certain assets as your "savings." See the Appendix for a discussion of how to spend your money.

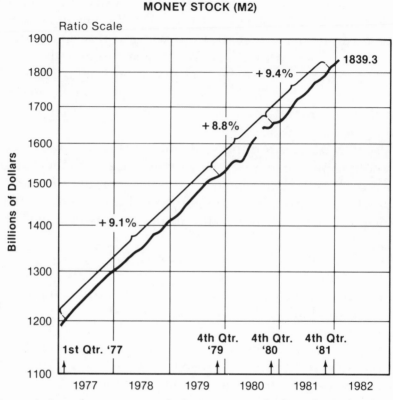

Figure 4. Actual money growth during a period when the Federal Reserve was almost continually giving lip service to fighting inflation. Notice especially the recent figures when the FED was supposedly pursuing a restrictive policy. The fact that the monetary base has been rising at a double-digit rate in the first quarter of 1982 tells the real story.

matter where they went, it would save billions of dollars. Since no greater assemblage of irresponsible spendthrifts, economic charlatans and pseudo-humanitarians has ever gathered under one roof, the only alternatives are move the spenders or move the roof!

• But stopping inflation requires more than getting rid of the big spenders; it also entails increased production and profits. Business needs desperately to raise capital to revitalize its an-

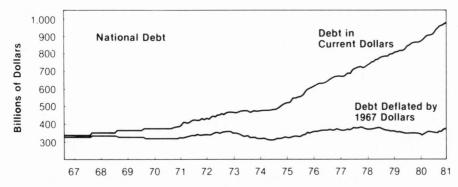

Figure 5. The real burden of increased borrowing remains constant while the dollar amount skyrockets. The difference is inflation, which makes borrowing painless to government and excruciatingly painful for everyone else.

tiquated plant and equipment so it can compete.[8] The average General Motors plant is 40 years old; America's steel industry is completely noncompetitive. We must have efficient machines to produce the goods necessary to lower prices domestically and compete effectively abroad; but it takes *capital* to buy efficient machines. Give U.S. workers the proper tools and watch how quickly and effectively they compete with the Japanese and Germans.

• To stop inflation now, it would also be necessary to provide the capital needed to modernize our industry by continuing to reduce capital gains taxes. This would help make stock investments profitable again and get money flowing toward produc-

8. The way the Reagan administration has tried to encourage modernization of industry's plant and equipment is based on the idea that the money saved would end up being invested in production. Increased production would create more jobs. This trickle-down theory is not workable because it doesn't protect the capital markets while all this is being accomplished.

What would work (though it might put a lot of high-priced accountants and tax lawyers out of business)—including myself—is a flat tax rate of 10% across the board with *no exemptions or exclusions*.

This would end up producing mountains of revenue. With a fair and equitable taxing system, the government would get enough of a windfall to operate in the black and end once and for all the deficits that are killing our financial markets.

tion and away from consumption. If this can be done and the income taxes are reformed to cut out all the gimmicks, enough money might magically reappear from the underground economy to make the obvious concepts of supply-side economics appear to be working.

• The income redistribution policies that have diverted money needed for industry's capital equipment to welfare and warfare must be abandoned or severely curtailed. You cannot pay people more to not work than to work and expect anything but chaos. This means stopping the flow of capital to increased government services and social welfare and letting business keep it instead so that we end up with jobs, not the redistribution of a constantly shrinking economic pie.

Paradoxically, this is also the soundest approach to a real welfare program. Today, welfare is a sham because it costs too much—not in dollar amounts but in its effects on business's ability to provide jobs and on people's ability to work. Properly handled, the government could pay more *real* welfare benefits because there would be more wealth (production) available to pay welfare from.

• The nation's gold reserves have to be pegged to the market with some kind of guarantee that the windfall in reserves will not be dissipated by an accompanying increase in the amount of currency outstanding. These additional reserves will go a long way toward restoring confidence in paper money, which will in turn, lower the interest rate, thereby increasing business profits and creating new jobs.

• Savings should be encouraged by paying a real rate of interest to savers in after-inflation, after-tax dollars. This could be accomplished by indexing bonds to take inflation into account or even issuing gold-backed government bonds that could probably be financed at 2% or 3%—the historical *real* rate of interest.

• Workers must be convinced that we are facing an economic crisis and that unless they take pride in their work and exercise restraint in their bargaining practices, they will be without jobs—permanently. Also, monolithic managements are as bad as bureaucrats in stifling the inventiveness and change that have made America great. We should let them know that they

are through being bailed out with tax dollars. If they can't produce what people want, at prices people can afford to pay, they
shouldn't be in business.

• The U.S. defense budget is out of control. How can we solve
the problem? With more than 50% of that budget going for
salaries for military personnel it isn't going to be easy. A Russian
soldier receives $7.50 a month and a Chinese soldier only $3.50.
We are fighting for our lives in a desperate struggle with those
who have a completely different approach to military pay. Paying personnel, not buying hardware, is what is stretching the
U.S. defense budget. Something has to give. Either America
begins now to cultivate some feeling of patriotism and duty
among its youth or resigns itself to eventual bankruptcy, military defeat, and enslavement by a foreign power. Harsh words?
Harsh world.

• We must stop letting a small group of OPEC nations shove
around the greatest powers on earth. We must use our power
to further our own ends or see that power disappear. Finally,
we must stop letting our trading partners take advantage of us
by exploiting our markets for their products at the same time
they discriminate against our goods in their countries. Letting
the Japanese close us out of their markets is a disgrace to our
Yankee Trader heritage.

If you think all or even some of these things will happen, you
can reasonably hope that we may avoid a hyperinflation.

16. What is likely to delay a runaway inflation?

The inflationary cycle will be interrupted when government
freezes prices and wages. Price controls are tried periodically
because (1) people forget how badly they worked the last time,
and (2) it's almost impossible for the public to grasp how the
government creates inflation but very easy to show how the
government is the champion of the people by restraining greedy
businessmen and labor leaders who want to raise prices. Controls thus serve to confuse the public in terms of who is causing
inflation. By enacting controls, the government can make it look
like business and labor are the villains.

Why don't controls work? The mere possibility of enacting

controls serves to defeat the purpose of stabilizing prices. Business uses the possibility of controls to put prices up sharply *in advance* so as not to be caught with low prices if there is a freeze. This accelerates inflation.

The usefulness of controls after enactment is no better. When prices are artificially held below the price determined by supply and demand for any length of time, tension builds and economic chaos is the end result. The tremendous internal distortions caused to an already highly misdirected economy leads to rationing. Since money continues to be printed, everyone has plenty of that. The shortages appear in items to buy with it, which soon include everything.[9]

Some speculative points to be aware of in a period of price controls:

a. In this type of environment, the prices of uncontrollable items like art, jewelry, and antiques are free to rise. Good profits are to be made in this phase by owning anything that is not, by its very nature, controllable.

b. Just before controls are removed, commodities should be bought and bonds sold short for the large, pent-up price rises that always follow removal of controls.

c. During a period of controls, the Federal Reserve uses the shield of stable prices to reinflate (greatly increasing the money supply). The catch-up move in the rate of inflation following the lifting of controls can provide tremendous opportunities for the speculator.

The terms used in describing this whole period of controls are *interrupted* and *frozen*. That we will have wage and price

---

9. In Germany in the 1930s, there even developed a "shortage" of zinc bathtubs and their price skyrocketed—not because anybody wanted or needed them but because they were not rationed.

control with eventual extensive rationing is not only a possibility, but a *probability,* based on our by now familiar rule that whatever puts more power in the hands of the bureaucrats is what will occur. When people get tired enough of these weird bureaucratically controlled distortions, a new prince will be elected to kiss the inflationary princess and wake her up so we can get on with finishing up our inflationary cycle.

One thing seems certain. When the situation becomes bad enough, there will be riot points. For every new regulation instituted on us to solve problems, people will become poorer and poorer, until too many will have nothing to lose by rebelling and rioting. The great productive forces of a free marketplace that produced a land of plenty will be replaced by a world of closed libraries, power brownouts, decaying neighborhoods, pot-holed roads, snarled freeways, unreliable mail service, garbage-filled alleys, housing shortages, strikes, crime, riots, and eventually food and water rationing. Finally, you might have to ask the government for a crust of bread and a piece of moldy cheese. Then you will need more than an investment plan; you will need a *survival plan.* The ones that have caused your economic problems might eventually decide that only the most worthy citizens should be allowed to continue living.

If you believe the Swiss are right and realize the impossibility of a nation permanently living beyond its means or borrowing its way to prosperity, get mad *now* and throw the rest of the big spenders out before it is too late. In the meantime, reread the section on collectibles again. A collection of anything real that cannot have its price fixed could comfort you with a pleasure beyond the mere aesthetic. That Rembrandt etching or diamond ring won't look quite so foolish in a world where there might be tons of money but nothing to buy with it.

17. How does OPEC threaten the very survival of the western world?

At the moment there is some respite on the oil price front but long-term the same old problems remain. Western civilization is built on energy, and energy is oil. Other resources—coal, solar, and gas—are out there somewhere in the distant future. Oil is *now.* And the Arabs have the oil. By the most conservative figures, Arabs will continue taking billions every year out of the already battered economies of the West.[10] This is not only inflationary, it is *impoverishing.*

In the last decade, the world's greatest industrial powers have become hostage to the whims of a few recently enriched tribal chieftains. We are now in a period of reverse colonialism, where rich Arabs are contenting themselves with buying our assets. Some say we should be grateful—proportionately, they are taking even more from the less-developed countries.

Nor is the problem limited to economics alone. It has to do not only with energy but with our special relationship with Israel. There is a strong, critical group woven into the fabric of Arab society that rejects Western civilization and would like to see it destroyed. These radical elements dream of past glories under Mohammad and Allah and future holy wars under Arafat, Ayatola Khomeini, and Colonel Khadafy. Since some Arab countries have more Palestinian residents than native citizens, acting on their dreams becomes possible. Money buys sophisticated weapons, including atomic bombs. We don't know it yet, but we are potentially at war with these people and the weapons they're likely to fight us with will be purchased with our own oil dollars. It behooves us to consider then what alternatives we have in limiting the power of their oil dollars. One way to handle the problem is to devalue the dollar, default on our dollar obligations. This is a very radical solution, one that will only be used as a last resort. Since the dollar is the reserve currency of the free world it would mean bankruptcy not only for us but most of the nations of Europe. What could we do short of this?

Some say we should encourage the Arabs to keep the oil in

10. Saudi Arabia's earnings *alone* have been estimated by some experts in the hundreds of billions through 1990. This drain of funds from our economy has a parallel in the reparation payments imposed on Germany after World War I. The burden of unpayable debt was one of the major contributing factors to Germany's inflation, just as oil payments may prove to be to ours.

the ground. This wouldn't help us. Limiting the supply makes the price of oil that is sold almost as high, and hence produces almost the same $100 billion surplus at the same time it deprives us of our cheapest source of energy.

Perhaps we should get them to spend it. We're doing this now. The richest Arab countries are spending so much in industrialization and water projects, hospitals, schools and housing that they won't be able to continue feeding our banks with massive deposits and buying Treasury bills as they have in the past. This could cause liquidity problems throughout our whole financial system. Massive withdrawals of their funds in case of another mid-east war could in itself precipitate a financial crisis.

If there are problems in U.S. banks, war in the Mideast or the dollar itself comes under attack, OPEC oil sheiks will be hard pressed to get rid of their dollars fast. Even if there is no short-term crisis, the long-term problem of a handful of Arabs controlling large liquid deposits in America remains. What will they do with their tremendous cash flow? They could buy cars and food, armaments, chemical plants, oil refineries, gas stations, and gold, or as we have seen, they could use our commodities markets to get rid of their paper dollars. But long-term, how much food can a handful of Arabs eat? How many Cadillacs can they drive? Why should they buy the downstream facilities of the oil companies, when by letting the oil companies continue to own these facilities, they can have them as allies and silent partners in one of the most profitable cartels of all times? What about selling them armaments? How many planes and missiles can we afford to sell Arabs without seeing the destruction of Israel and the start of a Moslem Holy War against not only Judaism, but possibly all Christendom? As for gold, how many billion paper dollars would it take to put the price of such a scarce metal in the stratosphere? Does recent history provide a clue to the answer for these questions?

Yes. The question of what the Arabs can do with their money has already been answered by what they have done with it. They can industrialize their own country but after that they seem to have a decided preference for putting it in the largest western banks in the form of short-term deposits. Does the money just sit there? No, the banks in turn seem to have a compulsion to loan it to less-developed countries. What do they do with it? They use it to keep from starving and paying for energy. Most of it somehow finds its way back to the oil sheiks to pay for higher oil prices.

How do all of these conditions weave together in a tapestry of absurdities to threaten the survival of the western world? If the Arabs just loaned (they'd never think of giving) the money to the less-developed countries, everything would work out. The less-developed countries, as debtors, could rip the Arabs off instead of Western banks everyone would benefit. However, ever since America became a nation of bankers, we have let them weaken our whole financial structure by co-mingling U.S. citizens' savings with Arab money. Worse yet, we have sat still while these bankers have loaned the money for the long term and convinced our government to guarantee the whole thing so that our whole banking system is now assured of going broke if the less-developed countries default. What really makes the situation acute is that these nations have already said they intend to default if we refuse to extend more credit.

No intelligent person ever seriously contended that these loans to the less developed countries would be repaid and U.S. bankers undoubtedly are counting on the government bailing them out. As serious as this is it would still be an internal problem. What makes the situation really critical is that a foreign creditor can be said to hold the first mortgage on U.S. banks. The Arabs have the means to coerce governments and especially banks into doing whatever they demand to protect their dollar deposits. If we don't obey, they can pull down the whole paper house of cards around our necks whenever they choose.

What specifically will happen when these less-developed nations begin to default? Our Federal Reserve will find itself the lender of last resort to the *whole world*. The Fed will print money day and night to allow our banks to pay foreigners while simultaneously destroying the value of about 200 years of accumulated savings of our nation's citizens. The only alternative to this would be defaults that would stop the flow of oil to the West and bring down the dollar. We can be sure the banks will be trying to avoid this even if it means pressuring the defaulting nation(s) to raise the price of their coffee or copper or cocoa and getting governments to buy so the debtors can pay off their loans.[11] Who will ultimately pay for this madness? *You* will, unless you devise a means to profit from the insanity.

SPECULATIVE POINT:
Here is where you can retire fast, not on Social Security or the "insured" pension plan from your by then bankrupt company, or your locked-in and depreciating IRA and Keogh Plans, but simply by holding ten coffee or cocoa or copper contracts on the commodity exchanges for about six weeks while foreigners are scrambling to get out of dollars.

You should be sophisticated enough by now to realize that paper money rewards the minority that learns to speculate with changing numbers on a tote board, and makes fools of the generations that have worked and saved. It's not that speculation *should* be the answer to hyperinflation's absurdities, it simply *is!* This is the essence of the pragmatic approach: If it works it's good. If it doesn't, it's bad.

By the time we wake up and the party is finally ended by a giant devaluation, the OPEC nations will go out and form their own economic world by first gaining control of the International Monetary Fund and raiding every last dollar of its deposits to give to less-developed countries to pay for OPEC oil. Then they will try to use a perverted instinct of survival of our allies to split off the more chauvinistic elements of the West—France, Japan, and others.

---

11. Then President Nixon started the whole process in 1973 when he got the Shah of Iran to raise oil prices to pay us for arms needed to police the Mideast after the British pulled out.

Where does all this leave the Western industrialized nations? In the Mideast—forced to defend their energy lifeline, with America right smack in the middle of a hotbed of trouble—a potential area of conflict with Russia (or even China) where our ties with Israel might very well force us to fight to survive.

All these problems stem from the devisive character of the modern world—the me-first, everyone else-be-damned disease of people and nations. There is a shortage, not of oil but of a sense of community and cooperation in the western world and especially in America. Today, no person can be well off alone. The world is totally and completely interdependent. The nations of the West had better change fast, or learn to their regret that in a dog-eat-dog world, everyone ends up eating dog food.

18. Can the problem of bank loans to underdeveloped nations be solved?

It cannot over the long term, but in this age of short-term expediency, many investment opportunities may be missed if an individual sits around waiting for the inevitable collapse of the banking structure. What early warning signals may be used to ascertain that the problem is becoming acute, so that you should close bank accounts and take cover in very short-term Treasury bills or even gold?

Domestically, the use of the Monetary Act of 1980 creates many alternatives to the bankruptcy of the banking system. Briefly, it provides ways to ensure that *everyone* is bankrupted in order to protect the banks. The quiet use of this new law to bail out distressed banks will be one early indication that the financial masterminds in Washington are running out of alternatives and a financial crisis is imminent.

On the international scene, there are more specific ways to detect problems caused by Third World defaults. The International Monetary Fund's equity capital consists of 104 million ounces of gold contributed at $35 an ounce. The difference between cost and market now amounts to almost $30 billion. This gold could be pressed into service to enable some underdeveloped nations to pay their bills. Such action would require 85%

agreement of the IMF members, but considering that the potential beneficiaries are the have-nots themselves, the votes are there to do it. When and if this happens, it will be one of a series of steps toward monetizing (revaluing) gold.[12] When this happens, can the official monetization of the U.S. gold holdings be far behind?

Revaluing gold will be a highly inflationary step because it will mean increasing the amount of cash credit available to gold-holding central banks without a concomitant increase in the amount of goods.

SPECULATIVE POINT:
Investigate potential profits in currency futures for big moves. It would seem that currencies of countries with the largest percentage of reserves in gold should outperform those with smaller reserves. Since a revaluation is potentially very inflationary, you might also consider selling short financial futures (Treasury bonds and T-bills) at this time. The main thing is to be out of bank accounts and Certificates of Deposit and into very short-term Treasury bills.

---

19. What causes major economic cycles to reoccur with such predictable and frightening regularity every 50 years or so?

Much has been written of the theories of the Russian economist Nikolai Kondratieff. He is known especially for his work on economic cycles that encompass long time spans. His studies (done in the 1920s) indicate we are approaching the end of a supercycle. If true this means a time of great depression and human suffering ahead in the 1990s.

---

12. Remember this does not necessarily mean an increase in the market price of gold, because the upward thrust of revaluation will apply to the official (and artificial) price of $42 an ounce that has prevailed for a decade, not the market price. The movement of gold will thus resemble the leap of a high jumper taking off out of a hole.

A look at the chart will give a visual impression of the structure of such cycles and the amazing repetitive characteristics of wholesale prices on which they are based.

Why do these cycles reoccur with such regularity? Perhaps, as Hegel, Spengler, and Toynbee suggested, a whole society has a life that parallels the individual's life and the society is being born, maturing, and dying constantly. The real question is how

THE KONDRATIEFF WAVE AND WHOLESALE PRICES IN THE U.S.

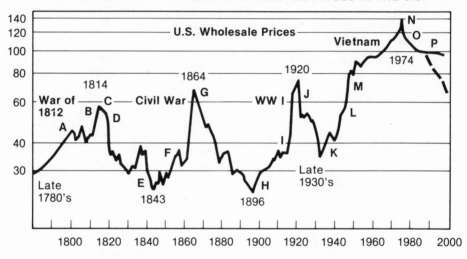

A Period of sharply rising prices in anticipation of War of 1812
B Primary recession after that war
C "Era of Good Feelings" plateau after War of 1812
D Start of Secondary major depression
E Mexican War
F Sharply rising prices in anticipation of Civil War
G Economic plateau during Reconstruction
H Spanish-American War
I Sharply rising prices preparatory to World War I
J "Roaring 20s" plateau
K World War II
L Korean War
M Sharply rising prices preparatory to Vietnam War
N Inventory Recession—1974
O Carter-Reagan plateau
P Possible start of Secondary major depression—early or middle 1980s.

Figure 6.

much credence we should give to the economic wave theories that say we are now entering a major decline that will cover the next 25 years? It is easy to believe in cycles. There are proven rain cycles, cycles of drought, as well as fertility cycles in animals and plants. The real question is not whether there are cycles but whether they provide any help to the speculator.

If we try to apply Kondratieff's work literally and superimpose his cycles on our calendar, we would come out with only general and vague time guides for speculative action. It isn't as if he had pinpointed D (for Disaster) Day as scheduled to occur tomorrow at about 3:00 P.M. Some think the theory not only doesn't help time speculative moves but isn't valid at all. They feel that it is too mechanistic; too pat. There are plenty of reasons for questioning the help such cycles provide in determining what will happen in the future. Some of these reasons for skepticism are based on common sense: Government, for example, may not be able to prevent major cycles from recurring but it has enormous power to alter their timing. Second, many people—especially optimists—have trouble believing theories that fail to take into consideration either the human brain's ability to change things or the power of the human spirit. Even if the pessimists prove correct, we doubt if they will profit much. Following mechanistic precepts, these macro chartists can underestimate what government might be willing to do to delay disaster. Those of you who waited through the decade of the 1960s for a gold price increase should have learned the power and ingenuity of desperate politicians fighting to hold back the inevitable. Kondratieff's seductive theories also ignore innovation as a possible cause of new economic booms. How can his graphs, based on different conditions and institutions than exist now, be used to predict what will happen in the absence of a gold standard, for example?

One cannot help but be impressed with Kondratieff's work but *timing* is what separates the winners from the losers. Mechanically applying Kondratieff waves to the current cycle will not make winners of pessimists because even if there are such cycles, his work provides a collapse date that is too broad to be meaningful. Someone telling a farmer that the year is divided into seasons doesn't help him to plant his seeds, harvest his crops or even tell him when they are occurring. Speculators today need stopwatches not long-term calendars.

The factors of worldwide economic interdependence in an age of great government power assure that no solutions will remain untried to stave off a worldwide financial holocaust. Desperation measures would almost certainly be taken to give us a final gasp of prosperity (albeit ill-conceived and falsely based). For an optimist looking to make a buck such a blowoff stage would be a shame to miss.

Kondratieff's theories, for example, would have had you use the middle 1920s as the top of the last cycle and you would have missed some fantastic opportunities to get rich in the period from 1927 to 1929. As unlikely as it may seem now, it is possible that there will be a similar era of prosperity—a crazy speculative blowoff stage resembling the late 1920s—before this credit cycle is finished. No matter how seductive graphs and charts can be, they don't pay the rent or put butter on your stringbeans.

As an ancillary question, should you be frightened by depressingly dire predictions of great economic suffering ahead of us? The optimist says no. There's one thing Kondratieff left out in compiling his statistics; the power of the human mind and spirit. Even if the worst happens and economies collapse, the optimists will survive because they keep in mind that all things pass (including that which is unpleasant). The cycles themselves prove that such declines do not last forever. Beyond the projected trough, new highs surely will follow. As proof of this look at Figure 7 for a smoothed version of Kondratieff long cycles smoothed out to project beyond the indicated trough to a new peak beyond.

20. To say that governments cause inflation is only a truism. What is really behind our leaders' acts of financial irresponsibility? Is it mere ignorance, incompetence, or faulty decisions

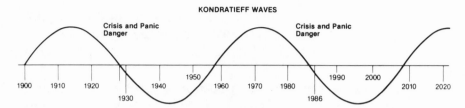

Figure 7.

by those in high places? Is it the politicians alone that are at fault?

No, what's at the heart of the problem of inflation is the greed of those wealthy members of our society who have already obtained great economic power and are trying to obtain more. They do this by using that power to activate the natural principle that money comes to money. Money does come to money because in an inflationary society, the credit-worthiness of the rich enables them to borrow more than others, thus greatly accelerating the accumulation of assets.

How can the beneficiaries of inflation (the very rich) perpetuate its concepts? Historically, they do it by influencing certain key members of a government to pursue easy money policies that make it easier for borrowers to contract and repay debt. The real world isn't really a question of black and white, good guys and bad like in our simplified version at the beginning of the book. These powerful people don't set out to deliberately ruin the country and cause others to suffer. At first, they see inflation not only as an easy way to build their own plant and equipment, to make profits quickly, but also to answer some worthy social problem such as restoring the damage done by a previous war or helping in the preparation for a future one. The impelling force of their idealized reasons and rationales just happen, however, to coincide with their desire to *maximize profits*. To do this, they borrow inordinate amounts of money that can only be repaid by a constantly depreciating monetary unit. As inflation progresses, they become more and more committed to its continuance, first for their prosperity and later for the very survival of their bloated industrial and commercial empires.

All their efforts are concentrated not on causing inflation in the first instance but in resisting monetary reform to correct it when it is called for. In this, they have the unexpected help of the misguided poor who imagine that because of large government transfer payments made possible by inflation, they are somehow benefiting from all the money creation even though more and more of their jobs disappear every year. The middle class finally wakes up and uses its power to fight back against these rich men, and their do-nothing friends in Congress or the civilization is destroyed beyond repair.

21. Can the speculative lessons contained in this book be briefly summarized?

Speculators win by having a strategy. The omega or final solution is grasping the big picture at the end of a credit cycle so that you can act, not react. The big picture is composed of the following components: Keynesian economics has led to excess consumption. The excess spending by government has necessitated excess taxation. This excess taxation has, in turn, destroyed the ability of America's industry to renew itself out of retained earnings and driven business to borrow.

This is the problem that supply-side economics addresses. If it were possible to give years of patient application to supply-side economics, its principles would undoubtedly work. But because of political opposition, the pressure of time limitations, and a weakness in the interlocking structure of the credit market mechanism, supply-side economics will not be given the chance to work as planned.

Excess taxation has caused a shortfall for business and individuals and resulted in excess debt. The great amount of this existing debt has weakened the interlocking structure of our credit markets. When the Federal Reserve now attempts to pump more money into the system to pay for the deficits occasioned by tax cuts, the new money raises interest rates and causes losses in preexisting debt (as reflected in declining bond prices). The decline in bond prices in turn causes losses in the reserves of our financial institutions (banks, savings and loans, and insurance companies). Since our banks have guaranteed huge dollar deposits and loaned vast amounts of money to less-developed nations, they are very vulnerable. Using the dollar as *the* reserve currency forces America to assume the role of banker to the world and guarantor of the world's financial stability. If the Federal Reserve had controlled the bankers instead of the bankers controlling the Federal Reserve then the system might have worked. As it is the government finds itself prisoner to the bad judgment of a handful of greedy rich men eager for profits. This means our government cannot act, only react to a series of financial predicaments. Even our most well-meaning leaders are no longer free to do what is best for our country; we must do what is best for foreign depositors first or face massive withdrawals.

In order to have another up-phase in our economy and overcome the forces of deflation, we must create more money. But every time the Federal Reserve tries to create more money, it adversely affects existing debt by a factor greater than the new money that has been created.

This is the dilemma we now face and will continue to grapple with in the next few years. Domestically, the Fed cannot create the needed money, and second, as the economic paralysis continues it will cause bankruptcies that in turn will activate guarantees that will necessitate even more money creation by the Federal Reserve. This will weaken bond prices even further and cause still more defaults and activate more guarantees in a never-ending circle. Internationally, American business cannot support a massive defense effort and still attract the savings necessary to modernize its plant and equipment so that it can compete effectively in world markets.

The only thing that will end the economic paralysis is a renunciation of debts and a return to a sound dollar based on one new bill for every 10 (or even 100) of the old ones.

How can you make enough money out of this potential chaos to retire rich by 1986? Getting rich requires speculation. In every era of chaotic change, a small group of speculators prospers. Past examples include

- The advance of commodities in general in 1974
- Silver in late 1979 ($5,500 became $1 million five months later)
- Treasury bills in 1981 ($3,000 became $14,000 in six weeks).

You can be certain even greater opportunities will come again soon. The forces of unpayable debt are not being reversed and time is running out. It might not take till 1986. It might happen much sooner. How the absurdities can perpetuate themselves beyond then is hard to imagine.

The Omega Strategy is not meant to endorse speculation or attempt to glorify gambling as a way of life. Speculation is not necessarily a *good* thing; but it just might prove the *only* thing that will preserve and create capital during these times. If this is true then in order to be successful, you must develop the characteristics of a good speculator as outlined in this book. You must learn the stages of an economic cycle and work out your plans with this "big picture," this Omega Strategy in mind.

THE OMEGA STRATEGY
Hold on to prime paper assets like Treasury bills during the recessionary declining-inflation phase. Speculate in stocks, bonds, gold, and commodities during the changing numbers phase of the new inflation. As we approach the time when debt must finally be destroyed by hyperinflation and default, try to profit by leveraged positions in real goods. Finally, try to end up with real items that are useful and/or provide pleasure and will not be destroyed by any changes in our money. If America is to have a chance of surviving, someone must be around to rescue those real goods from destruction and it may as well be you. This is the Omega Solution.

CHAPTER 15

Projecting Present Trends into the Future

Speculators win by trying to look ahead as far into the future as they can. The only way they can do this—without abandoning the empirical way to truth—is by projecting present, well-established trends into the future. This, plus consulting history for insights into the pattern of sequential occurences, is the way speculators succeed in not only their trading campaigns but in leading successful lives.

Looking Into The Future

We have examined the cause of the next financial crisis and found it to be fifty years of credit expansion and fiscal irresponsibility, which has as a subcause the earnest efforts of three powerful groups (government, business, and banks) that have profited by such expansion.

The most likely factor to precipitate us into a financial crisis will be a default by one of the less-developed countries that will cause several bank failures. This will finally replace fear of inflation with fear of bankruptcy, and usher in a period of economic paralysis and high unemployment. Before long, people will be clamoring for the government to stimulate our economy.

Translated, this means printing more money. This political pressure to spend us out of that paralysis will virtually guarantee hyperinflation.

By studying history, we have seen that the last depression in the U.S. was accompanied by deflation (lowering of prices). Because of our having abandoned the gold standard, this decline in prices will not repeat. However, all economic recovery from depression requires a readjustment of prices and wages to get the economy moving again. How will this be accomplished the next time? In past depressions, wages and profits have declined in both real and nominal terms. Next time, because of price and wage rigidity caused by business monopoly and labor unions, wages and prices will not be allowed to fall in nominal or apparent terms. The only way to effectuate the necessary drop in *real* prices and wages in the future will be by *decreasing the value of the monetary unit* in which such prices and wages are measured. This will also be the only way to pay the mountain of debt.

We may conclude that the shape of the next depression—its *form*—will initially be one of price inflation and money will lose all meaningful value in order to pay the huge debts and lower *real* wages to make a business recovery possible.

"What?" you ask. "A concurrence of depression and inflation?" Yes. The next depression will be characterized by a decline not in the quantity but the *quality* of money. The government will literally be forced to pay its past debts and discharge its bloated functions as guarantor to the nation's (and world's) financial institutions with new issues of fiat money. Thus, after the temporary decline in the rate of inflation caused by the current economic slowdown, we can look for the real value of money to resume its precipitous decline as we scale new inflationary peaks.

The future is, by the perversity—or blessing—of nature, locked in place beyond our grasp. Still, by projecting certain trends, we can go a long way in constructing an economic model of the 1980s. You must use your own knowledge and insights to add to, modify, and arrange this rudimentary effort as new events occur to give you new information and insights. For the present, however, the following trends and concepts seem a logical starting place in constructing a basic model of the future.

- Revolutionary terrorists, the cold war, and crime will make the world a more violent, dangerous place for anyone who has anything to protect (all Americans are in this category).
- This will require increased military spending to police our nation and the world, resulting in larger government expenditures with accompanying deficits.
- Grave social problems, aggravated by failed businesses, lost jobs, and reduced welfare, will call for countermeasures that will continue to add to deficits already assured by our military spending.
- These deficits will be monetized, thus adding to the money supply and the continuing pressure on the financial markets. This pressure will continue building until a financial panic results.
- To end the paralysis, pressures to reinflate will cause most governments in the western world to again embark on money creation to solve social problems. Inflationary pressures will again reassert themselves just at the time the tax reforms of "Reaganomics" finally succeed in stimulating production. Our economy will heat up again. When the tight money policies of the Federal Reserve again prove unsustainable in stopping inflation, investors everywhere will lose faith in paper money and buy gold, commodities, and everything real in an attempt to spend their dollars before it's too late. This will cause an inflationary boom. It will be short-lived and periods of recovery from then on will be spotty, characterized by huge speculative profits for a few and general malaise and distress for the great majority. As this speculative boom ends, it will mark the end of the long-term 50-year super-cycle. The decline will be steep and will eventually lead to an inflationary depression. Other nations will

attempt to insulate themselves against deflationary stagnation by first devaluing their currencies, then imposing tariffs. This will lead to still higher prices for us as cheap foreign goods are replaced with high-priced American products. After that, money will be printed in great quantities and inflationary chaos will eventually restrict the movement of people, money, and goods on a global basis. Having lost the benefits of free trade, America as a nation (and the world as a whole) will become poorer. Over the long term, the spending patterns of people worldwide will shift away from luxury goods to bare necessities.

• In essence, hyperinflation, will be caused by an unsuccessful attempt to end an economic prostration with printing press money.

Because of the interdependence of the modern production process this depression will be worse, the problems more complex, and the paralysis more complete, than anything America or the world has ever experienced before. You, as a speculator, will have plenty of warning. Before it happens, you will see some telltale signs of inadequacies (visible cracks in the monetary dam). For example:

1. The Federal Reserve Board will become more and more ineffectual in influencing the economy. Every time it attempts to *tighten* the money supply it will choke off money necessary to fund the government's deficit and finance business.

2. Every time the Fed *increases* the money supply, it will knock the bond market down by a factor greater than the new money introduced into the system, thereby actually intensifying the nation's liquidity problem by increasing interest rates and causing business bankruptcies. Stringent price controls and rationing will be tried but they will only aggrevate the problems by driving more and more people out of the tax system and into the underground economy.

3. Local and state governments will cut back on services until they are finally forced to rely on federal printing press money to avoid defaulting on employee pension plans and cure the colossal neglect of essential services.

The new great depression will be preceded (and accompanied) by a hyperinflation unlike anything this nation has ever seen. Gold and strategic metals will enjoy huge price rises but will eventually be appropriated by the government. The economic paralysis of the resulting inflationary depression will cause a swing to the left in Western Europe. The Atlantic alliance will continue to weaken as several countries drift toward socialism and communism.

In spite of the problems, life will go on but not as before. Decreasing water tables in the western plains of the United States will hamper food production. Deprived of its means of irrigation, and denuded of its trees by years of overplanting of grains, the seasonal winds that sweep down from the north will cause new dust bowls. The sequence of shortages will be first energy, then food, and finally water.

We have already seen the paradox of paying so much for military protection in Vietnam that we can no longer afford police protection in our neighborhoods. We will face other paradoxes, equally as absurd.

Americans will learn the hard lesson that social spending costs money and too much government spending can bankrupt a society so completely that government will not even be able to provide essential services let alone welfare. In this type of environment, riot points will be reached, bringing violence and mass hysteria as depression bites deep.

So that you can structure your plans to profit (or just survive), the sequence of events will probably occur in the following order:

Stage 1. A deepening of the current recession accompanied by recovery in the financial markets.

Stage 2. A period of disequilibrium and paralysis caused by the default of a major bank.

Stage 3. Highly inflationary stimulation leading to an era of much ballyhooed (but highly selective) economic recovery and a mini-boom characterized by large speculative gains. This in turn will lead to

Stage 4. A hyperinflationary depression as the new recovery proves to be unsustainable.

The essence of the problem is to be found in the government's hammerlock on the capital market. The government seems committed to welfare and warfare. The cost of both is enormous. The only way for the government to pay its bills is by borrowing or printing money. Crowding business out of the capital market will cause the financial panic stage that will lead inexorably to the depression that won't respond to stimulation. Stimulation will not succeed because once the economy breaks down, business will be too frightened to borrow, no matter how attractive the interest rates. Trying to end the stagnation by introducing more paper money into the system will finally cause the long-awaited and much-talked-about runaway inflation—in other words, superficially controlled chaos on a global basis.

At the depth of the ensuing depression, we might expect to see a series of dictators take control of countries around the world. Historically, the first dictatorships are of the political right, with a later counterrevolution leading to a dictatorship of the political left. Some may think this means the people ultimately win, but in this political charade—this ultimate battle of bureaucrats—the reality is that everyone loses. It is possible in such a situation to conceive of one leader emerging as a world dictator, perhaps even elected by the new oligarchy of the economic aristocrats of the world—the multinational corporations from various nations that will need social order to function efficiently.

The Omega Solution

All this gloomy picture is about the world. What about you? Can you survive and even prosper? The answer is up to you. Your ancestors did. There is still room for the individual to survive and even prosper in the most untidy of worlds.

The key to your success requires that you get enough to re-move yourself from the game before the game stops. You aren't going to be able to do much in the paralysis of a depression (stage 4). You will only survive by being brave enough to spec-ulate in stages 1 through 3.

Your survival requires you to make the right speculative de-cisions at critical times. To do this will depend on two things: First, recognizing that the recession preceding the crisis (stage 1) will be more severe than generally supposed and that cash can temporarily be king in such an environment, then switching at the bottom (stage 2) before others see the long-term infla-tionary potential in government intervention (stage 3) to cure the paralysis.

You will take inflationary hedge positions when you recognize that everything is in place for a resumption of inflation. You will know this is happening when you see a stagnating ineffi-cient and illiquid economy cause so much unemployment that you know that our politicians will at last be psychologically prepared to perpetuate the crime of hyperinflation. They will be forced to do this in order to avoid massive defaults by con-sumers, business, and banks.

When this new inflationary balloon bursts, it will finally bring on a depression that does not respond to stimulation. There will be no more lenders because there will be no more savings. It is at this point that you must be out of the game, your assets in secretable tangibles, your physical safety protected in order to survive. The depression will continue until people have had enough and replace the last dollar with a megabuck and the last of the Washington bunglers with one efficient authoritarian ruler. How hungry people with their hands out can think of liberty is a question that must be left for future generations to ponder. It is thus that democratic electorates eschew reason and countries turn to tyrants who give them bread but use stringent controls to seriously restrict their freedom. When this happens, governments around the world will supplant their citizens as the owner of the means of production. While thus appearing to be trying to solve problems, the bureaucrats will, as usual, be the cause and beneficiary of the problem.

If all of this happens, it is because, though the country is prostrated, *someone gains.* No solutions will be found, not because there aren't any, but because *failure rewards bureaucrats.* Even if millions are obliterated, governments and politicians will survive, emerging from the chaos and quagmire of depression with new undreamed-of power at their disposal—power to control people's lives and property at every point; power to live like the gods they fancy themselves to be.

The Possibility Of War

Wars are often fought to keep repressed people quiet at home. A third World War is not a realistic danger today. Russia doesn't need it to win. We're doing very well all by ourselves, as Lenin predicted, bleeding ourselves white economically. It will only become a real danger as economic chaos spreads around the world. So we may assume there will be no World War III in the 1980s. After we are economically prostrate and before we have caught up to the Russians in the 1990s will be our country's period of greatest military danger. The danger will become acute as our enemies find themselves troubled internally by dissention and Russia learns how expensive maintaining an empire can be. Such danger will manifest itself in a new "space race" rearmament program occasioned by a breakthrough in space weaponry that will make obsolete a great deal of the world's current armaments. World War III, if it occurs, will be fought in space with the earth as the prize.

Ending On A Note Of Optimism

Historically, when the world has needed great leaders, they have appeared. Perhaps they will again. Perhaps we are living through the darkest days now and there is hope for a better tomorrow.

If wars can be avoided (and they must), there is every reason to be optimistic for the future. The evil has already befallen us. Most of the destruction of economic and moral values has already taken place. We simply haven't been honest enough to acknowledge it. The future, though hard economically, should usher in some startingly new adaptations of more traditional values. After the shock period of increased violence and the riot points of hard times, stability of one sort or another will be restored. It always is. In this new environment there will be a search for new solutions. Another generation will have learned that you cannot print wealth, you must work for it. The old ideas of continual growth, impossible expectations, success without effort, glorification of materialism, and moral relativism will be seen to have been detours, not signposts on the road to real progress and human happiness. The age of permissiveness is almost dead. The persuading virtue of morality—either for a person or a nation—is simply that historically morality works and immorality doesn't. The American people will surprise even themselves with how quickly they will create a new idealism and sense of common purpose similar in kind (yet different in form) to that of the 1940s.

The inflationary alliance of the very rich and very poor can and will be broken by an angry and aroused middle class. There will be a new willingness to make an effort for one's employer as jobs become scarce, a new patriotism as our country is really threatened, a new evaluation of materialistic ideals as fortunes are lost, and a new spiritual rebirth among a people now suffering from too much information and not enough wisdom, too much doubt and cynicism and not enough faith and optimism.

Thus, difficult as future times may be, they will not be without their compensations, and as is true of most ages of chaotic upheaval, all that is most worthwhile shall be preserved.

A FOOTNOTE ON HOW YOU SHOULD SPEND YOUR MONEY

If and when fortune smiles on you and you achieve your goal of making a lot of money, you must take out the devil's due—the protection money for Uncle Sam—but then what do you do with the rest? This is not a frivolous question. One solution is to put it into something you can use and enjoy. If you are really rich, that would mean

- a nice car to drive (assuming there is gasoline)
- a nice house to live in
- furniture and rugs for its floors
- art for its walls
- jewelry for you and your spouse

These are not frivolous expenses. In fact, they are real investments. That which is rare and beautiful will always be coveted by the rich, and no matter what kind of government we have, the rich will always be with us. The most persuasive argument, however, is that things that give pleasure are always among life's best investments—an example of pleasure and profit happily coinciding.

If you have only achieved enough wealth to buy comfort and not luxuries, consider putting it into other people's future necessities that can be bartered for your comfortable retirement during a severe economic crisis. These include:

- medical supplies
- needles
- fish hooks
- tools
- coffee and tea
- guns and ammunition
- canned food (providing it is something that won't spoil)
- wine, liquor, and other commodities with long
  ascertainable shelf-lives.

Enough of these barterable goods might buy you a very comfortable, even relatively rich, retirement because they are items that are real, useful, and in great demand—things that might prove to be very shrewd investments in hard times.

What about stocks, commodities, financial futures, and currency speculation—all the vices you will have learned to love? If it's the real end of the 50-year credit boom party, it is also the end of funny money and everyone—even speculators—will have to go back to work again. At this point you want your investments where you can control, protect, and enjoy them because you might be too old to start over, maybe unable to go back to work. The reason what you will be able to do with your money at that time will be so narrowly circumscribed and basic is that the government in time of crisis will start changing all the rules and throwing new laws and regulations at you daily. Politicians will be so desperate they might do anything.

If they haven't already done so, it will be at this stage that the politicians will definitely change the money—issuing probably one new bill for every five, ten, hundred (or more?) old dollars. The government could enact laws and regulations that will limit your freedom in ways that none of us can now predict or even dream of in our worst nightmares. They probably will never take your car, home, art, oriental rugs, jewelry, or all the items you can secretly accumulate to barter for other's goods and services. Consulting history, these goods are the only property that governments respect as really belonging to *you*, undoubtedly because they don't seem to be worth very much.[1] Personal property can be secreted from crooks (including the government).[2]

SPECULATIVE POINT:
After the sequence of speculative opportunities plays itself out you must turn your wealth into real assets. After assuring a comfortable home to live in, personal property (rugs, jewelry, and art on one level and hoarded necessities on another) might be the ultimate investment—the only secure forms of real wealth to insure your retirement (or even survival).

---

1. In this they can be very much mistaken. Howard Hughes could have put his entire fortune in one small house, if it were in the form of jewels, precious metals, and art masterpieces.

2. In the case of the North Vietnamese, for example, one U.N.-appointed peacekeeper, sent before the U.S. involvement, witnessed the fact that the only wealth that survived the Communist takeover was art. All bank accounts in excess of $500 were confiscated.

Appendix

The appendix contains important information for investors. It includes:

1. How to project and predict interest rates. This section contains material that goes beyond the level of sophistication desired by the average reader. These abstract concepts and advanced ideas and techniques are extremely important to those who would make their own investment decisions and aspire some day to earn their living from speculations, especially trading financial futures.
2. Keeping a dynamic balance sheet—one that changes to reflect your real position at all times.
3. A glossary of terms used in the text.

HOW TO PROJECT AND PREDICT INTEREST RATES

We have already examined the mechanics of speculating in Treasury bills. But the ability to make a large amount of money trading them depends on more than just knowing they exist. In order to win big, you must first of all have a correct analysis of where we are in terms of an historical perspective. After that an understanding of the dynamics of inflation and a practical

225

working knowledge of how to use Treasury bonds and bills to profit from interest rate changes will give you the competitive advantage that a speculator needs to win.

We are now in a recession accompanied by a gradual decline in the inflation rate. After that, cynicism about politicians and a belief in their proclivity to do the wrong thing suggests a resumption of new and even more virulent price increases as deficits persist and the economy is restimulated to fight unemployment. But you will need more than generalities to trade successfully in financial futures. Not only are there the mechanics of trading T-bill and T-bond instruments to be mastered, you must understand interest rates and how and why they fluctuate so that you can pinpoint purchases and sales. This will be especially true as we move into the third or runaway stage of inflation when all the traditional thinking is likely to prove wrong. Remember, in 1923, the German interest rates on demand loans went above 10,000% on an annualized basis!

There are three factors that determine interest rates:

1. The *demand* for credit.
2. The *supply* of credit.
3. The *risk* to the lender in making the loan.

Basically, short-term rates are determined by demand, which is itself determined by business conditions. Long-term rates are principally influenced by supply, which is in turn determined by inflationary expectations. The interest rate, like price, is essentially a function of scarcity. Interest is the price of money. If there is a small amount of something, it will command a higher price. When the government prints a lot of money, you'd think that the increased supply would lower the price (interest rate). It's superficially true that lenders must compete for borrowers and, other things being equal, a greater supply of money available to lend should lower the interest rate. *But other things are not equal.* As inflation progresses, the government starts to print so much paper that everyone wants to borrow because the money is free (the rate of inflation exceeds the interest rate).

At this point something strange happens. As more money is

printed, instead of going down as you'd expect, interest rates go up because people need so much more money to operate their households or businesses. Since money is free (after taking inflation into consideration) everyone tries to borrow more and save less, so there never seems to be enough money, even though the system is awash with liquidity. In this stage of inflation conflicting analyses of the situation are voiced. Economists can't ever seem to reach a meaningful consensus because their heads are full of numbers not wisdom. But don't despair. It is just this diversity of opinion that will allow you to profit as a speculator.

One economist will point to the tremendous amount of money in the society and say there is a money surplus. Another will point to the tremendous amount of unfilled demand by worthy borrowers and say there is a *shortage*. In our Alice-in-Wonder-land world, both will be right.

Which one is more correct? It is really a pseudo-argument. When the Fed grinds out its favorite tune, "The Best Things in Life are Free," on its printing press organ what the easy money accompanists are really crooning is that there is a shortage of something that is free.

Seen in this light, there will always be a shortage of sea air, mountain streams, sunshine, fields full of wild flowers, moonlight, true love, and *free money.*

> AT A GIVEN TIME IN THE INFLATIONARY CYCLE, THE VERY CREATION OF MONEY (ADDING TO SUPPLY) SO INCREASES THE DEMAND THAT PRICE (INTEREST RATES) REACTS BY GOING UP, NOT DOWN.

We already know that all price changes in financial instruments depend on interest rate changes. Interest rates and prices are inversely related. If we knew future interest rates, we could make a fortune by buying or selling million-dollar Treasury bills in the commodities market, even if we had only a few thousand dollars to start with.

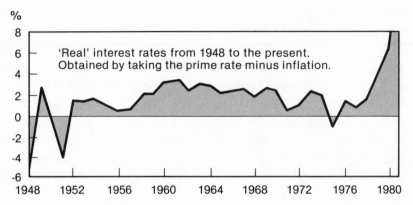

Figure 1. Real interest rates from 1948 to the present. You can see that historically this rate is around 3%.

The first thing to understand clearly is the distinction between real and nominal interest rates. Real interest is the coupon, or nominal, rate (what the bond pays) minus the inflation rate. A look at Figure 1 will show how the real cost of money is soaring to levels not seen since the early 1930s.

How high is up for interest rates in the future? The answer will always be determined by the amount of government competition for available funds, the extra interest that must be paid foreigners to induce them to continue to hold dollars, and the demand for money to replace and expand business plant and equipment. Add to this the natural upward pressure on interest rates caused by the anticipation of future inflation, and the equation we devised earlier correlating money supply figures minus 1% prevailing eighteen to twenty-four months ago and you have a working formula for a good part of the answer. To this, of course, must be added your intuition and flair.

The exact extent of such interest rate movements can only be ascertained after the fact, but there are some additional *clues* that you can use to help you make an educated guess about the future. First, there is the fact that historically each new cycle's low has exceeded the previous cycle's high. Starting from a very high base in 1982 suggests we might see extremely high interest rates in the coming cycle—especially near the next cycle's close. This could translate itself into very low T-bill and bond prices at that time. Over the intermediate term, we must look at the supply-and-demand curves for new loan funds likely to exist then. As usual, supply will come almost entirely from personal savings. What we call "demand" is made up of government and business borrowing needs. By studying the shape and consequences of government and corporate demand, we can see how that demand compares to what is available from personal savings and determine which way interest rates will tilt—up or down. As the national debt exceeds one trillion dollars, it will soon take about one hundred billion annually just to pay the interest on that debt. How much is a trillion? If a business like General Motors had begun losing a million dollars on the day of Christ's birth and had lost it every day to the present, it would still be able to lose at the same rate for another 800 more years before it would amount to a trillion dollars.

How much is the hundred billion necessary to service the debt every year? One hundred billion dollars is almost as much as all the *new* savings of all the combined savers of the country for a year.

On the supply side, we can project a figure of a little over $100 billion, a figure so low that government demand alone threatens to absorb all the available new supply of lendable funds. What about corporate demand? Planned capital expenditures in 1980 were about $20 billion higher than in 1979, higher still in 1981, and projected still higher in 1982, pointing to record borrowing demands. Since corporate liquidity is at a 30-year low, this means the money must be borrowed from somewhere. What would that mean? In 1979, there was a shortfall of a few billion in long-term funds available from personal savings, and what happened? The bond collapse of 1980 destroyed hundreds of billions in paper assets. This shortfall was the direct result of this relatively small deficit. The 1981 shortfall has continued to be translated into lower bond prices. In the future, even the forceful downward manipulation of short-term interest rates by the Federal Reserve Board still might not be able to do much to ameliorate the long-term deterioration in bond prices.

There has always been a multiplier effect at work. A shortfall in the supply of savings not only deprives current borrowers of needed capital but destroys the value of existing debt by a factor greater than the shortfall.

The optimistic thinking that interest rates can or will remain down for any protracted period of time thus seems highly unlikely. Nor does the bargain-basement price of bonds mean that they are now good long-term buys, as commonly assumed. The extraordinary lack of liquidity in the corporate sector should serve to keep long-term bond prices under pressure. The voracious appetite of the government for funds to finance its deficits completes the bleak outlook for both business and government to obtain the funds they need without credit rationing or a great increase in interest rates.

How low could bonds eventually go? In 1929, the stock market broke and commodity prices collapsed, but long-term bond prices didn't bottom out until 1932, three years later. If inflation continues, who knows how far is down? Certain perpetual British government obligations originally issued at 100 now sell under 20. This might provide a clue to future U.S. long-term bond prices. However, none of this precludes short-term rallies of substantial proportions as inflation periodically appears to have been brought under control.

In summary, interest is really the alignment of supply (savers) to demand (business and government's borrowing needs). If present trends persist, government will soon need all the nation's savings just to pay the interest on the national debt. Barring massive spending cuts, this point could be reached in a very short time.

The long-term consequences of this are enormous. The effect has already been felt by the real estate mortgage market. The next impact will be on business borrowers. During the next crunch, they will be hard put to get *any* money. Government will take it all. Because our economy could be heating up anyway, businessmen might be willing to pay extraordinary amounts for money that would drive interest rates to undreamed-of heights (and bonds to new lows). In the past, when interest rates soared, it was because the Federal Reserve Board was applying the brakes. In the next cycle, interest rates could go out of sight without any braking influence being exerted by the Federal Reserve Board. At this point the multiplier effect of capital shortfall explained earlier could decimate the bond market. All influences will be working toward higher interest rates and the Federal Reserve Board will find itself on the horns of a dilemma.

The traditional role of the Federal Reserve Board is to inflate early in the cycle to stimulate business and tighten up later to cool off the boom. But, given the extraordinary demand for money, interest rates could skyrocket without the Fed's help. The time will come when the Fed will be forced to print more money to bail out more banks and businesses as they are driven to the wall by tight money. But as more dollars are printed, inflation will become worse. The more money the Fed prints, the more everyone will want to borrow and the higher both inflation and interest rates could go. If the printing stops, there will be sudden collapse. If printing continues, there will be a bigger collapse later on.

The only apparent alternative is to ration credit, but this would cause more bankruptcies and be politically unpopular. If history is any guide, the Fed will hesitate, and he who hesitates is lost. *This is when you can make a great deal of money* by shorting Treasury bills and bonds. It won't take long. A few weeks of this and the monetary party will be over.

A technical consideration: In approaching an interest rate bottom or peak, how will you know when to move in on T-bills? If you smell a recession coming and you're contemplating buying, make your purchase as near as possible to the start of a downward move in interest rates because, as we've seen, the price of the bond or bill moves inversely to the interest rate.

Is there any clue as to when interest rates undergo cyclical declines? Yes, the interest rate rise turns down historically at the *onset* of recessions. See Figure 2. What about profiting from interest rate advances? If you see a crunch developing and con-

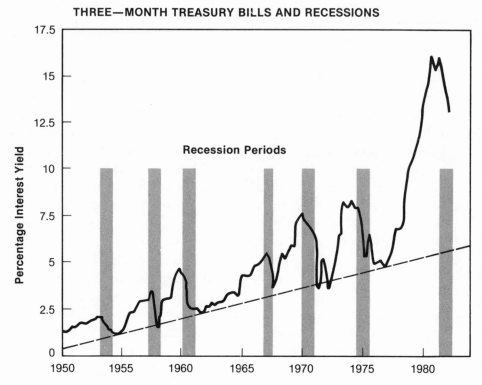

Figure 2. Shows how *interest rates rise until the onset of recession, then turn down sharply.* Buying T-Bills at each of the onsets of recession and selling them short after recovery would have produced substantial trading profits.

template selling short to capitalize on a decline in bond prices, you naturally want to do it as near the *start* of a substantial upward move in the interest rate as possible. These upward moves in the interest rates usually occur at the end of a recession, with the final blow-off occurring near stock market tops. See Figure 3.

1. Fed funds
2. T-bill rates
3. Prime rate
4. Discount rate.

So when you see Fed funds starting up, can T-Bill rates be far behind?

But what if the credit boom party isn't over and government props up borrowers and savers to have a whole complete cycle of rising and declining interest rates *after* the one we've been discussing? One fact that points to that possibility is that there are usually three false peaks of interest rates in every major inflationary cycle. Using severance of our last link with gold in 1971 as a logical starting point, we had one false peak coinciding with highs in the gold price in 1974 and a second in 1980. The third false peak could still be ahead of us. What would this do to your timing? Try not to follow dating as much as sequential events.

As a speculator, you naturally want as many cycles as possible and, by developing a feeling for the rotational characteristics of interest rates, you can live off the natural sequence of these cyclical phenomena. Remember, however, each cycle is likely to be bigger and shorter-lived than the previous one if we are, in fact, witnessing the end of the up-phase of a supercycle.

Short-term, the most we can reasonably expect is an end to the recession, lower interest rates and lower inflation. But as long as the mentality of greed persists in large segments of the population—masses of people who expect (and have become dependent on) a paternalistic Uncle Sam to provide for them—deficits will persist, and the only way to pay for this and an inefficient and growing military buildup will be by printing money. This means that sooner or later the Fed will play the whole sad inflationary song over again in double time because the melodic hum of the printing press sounds pretty good to large numbers of near-bankrupt businessmen, over-extended borrowers, welfare recipients, and Pentagon generals.

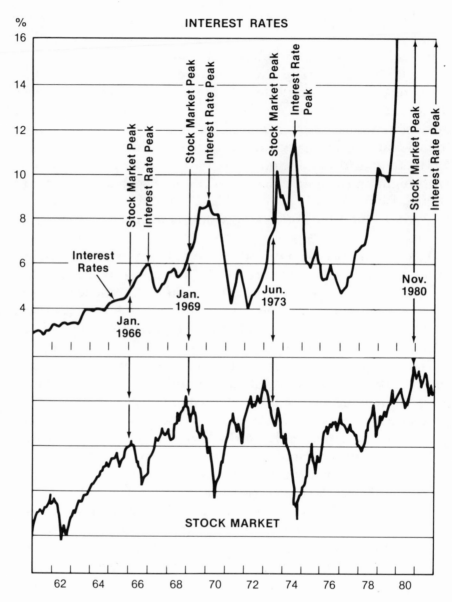

Figure 3. Market tops signal great interest rate rises in the offing. This again is a possible tool to use in determining when to sell short T-Bills.

KEEPING A BALANCE SHEET

A speculator must always know his (or her) position in order to know what future action is possible or indicated. What specifically can you do to keep up to date when the real inflation takes over?

You can begin now to learn a new way of calculating your income and measuring your assets, one that will keep you from forgetting what you have already learned about inflation. To do this, you can become familiar with and use a double system of accounting. This is not a second set of books to fool the government but a system that will enable you to correct for what printing press money is doing to your financial assets.

The first amounts are based on apparent, or nominal, amounts; in other words, the way you have always figured your balance sheet. So we will call these

BS DOLLARS.

The second set of figures indicates deflated dollars, or

DD DOLLARS.

When you count in DDs, you will be thinking in real terms, using real amounts instead of the numbers that are printed in green and black on your dollars (the BS amounts).

In order to distinguish real DD amounts from phony BS amounts, you will have to use a sliding scale based on the current annual rate of inflation as measured by the consumer price index. You have already learned that every year more money is printed by the Federal Reserve or created as checkbook money by the banks. This makes all money worth less and shows up as a percentage decline that is roughly equivalent to the percentage of price increase.

You may think we don't need to correct our figures for inflation when we see inflation decline to 8% or even 5%, but what we must realize is that someday it is coming back with a vengeance and only those that know the new "inflationary math" will survive.

Learning to count in real terms is easy.

All you have to do to get DD, or real, amounts is to subtract the yearly inflation rate from the BS amounts on your balance sheet. If you are going to make big money, starting right now, you are going to have to make and regularly keep a dynamic balance sheet. This sometimes will make you feel good, sometimes bad, but it will always tell you your current position to the dollar. It will also tell you when you are rich. Just get some notebook paper and on it write the key figures, preferably every month (but no less than every three months). If you don't have notebook paper, use anything that's handy. The important point is that you do it regularly.

To make it simpler, you can forget about converting each asset to DD Dollars and just reduce the total by the current annual rate of inflation (as things progress, you will probably be forced to use the current monthly rate of inflation) to get the correct Depreciated Dollar (DD) amount.

Assume you started in 1979 and wrote 1-1-79 on top somewhere, being careful to leave yourself a margin on the left-hand side. In this manner you listed assets in groups, starting with real property. Assume the fair market value of your home on that date was $100,000 and another lot you own had a value of $25,000. You entered $125,000 opposite real property.

Next you grouped your personal property. Try not to overstate it. You were probably surprised at how much it amounted to. Personal property usually loses a good deal of its value as soon as you purchase it. You must only put what quick cash value you could receive tomorrow if you sold it. Keeping a balance sheet automatically will make you aware of shifts from, say, cash to cars or sofas or clothes that will require 20%, 50%, or even 90% write-downs when you buy them. Assume, for example, you came up with $30,000 for personal property. You put the total (a rough calculation will do) opposite personal property.

Next, you calculated your stocks, if any. You did this by taking the number of shares and multiplying it by the price listed in the paper on the date of your balance sheet. Here, don't group them together. List each stock separately opposite its recognized ticker tape symbol as used on the stock exchange. For example, 100 shares of American Telephone would be entered as: 100 T; 50 IBM as 50 IBM; 200 U.S. Steel as 200 X.

Next you listed any bonds, mortgages, etc., and their fair market value. In the case of nonliquid assets like mortgages, reduce the value by the discount you would have to give to sell it tomorrow (or within a reasonably short time). This will prevent you from fooling yourself when you sell your house for $100,000, for example, and take back a ten-year mortgage for $50,000 at 10%. If conditions in the mortgage market are such that these mortgages are being discounted 20%, you can only enter (50,000–20% or) $40,000 under "Mortgages."

Remember, *don't fool yourself.* I assure you, if you start with the right figures it will give you great psychological pleasure to see them grow.

Lastly, you listed the most liquid of your assets: bank accounts, U.S. Treasury bills, etc. Use whatever abbreviations you are comfortable with.

When you have entered all the figures and made a total, this will constitute your gross assets and probably look something like the next page.

Most people are usually pleasantly surprised to see how much they are really worth, but we're not finished yet. Now you have to reduce the total by the amount of your indebtedness.

Say, for example, you owed $10,000 on your house and $2,000 to your credit union. You would group them as $12,000 under Debts. Now draw a line and subtract. The figure you get is your Net Nominal Assets (NNA) denominated in BS Dollars. The first time you calculate them, there is no reduction for inflation (which you will appreciate).

The government has been able to fool you up till now because they were making you think in a single-faceted (BS) way in what was really a multifaceted (DD) world. For a real dollar to become a BS Dollar, there has to be a *passage of time.* In order to show you how to calculate what happens over time, we are going to assume that you go to sleep for a year and wake up January 1, 1980. Naturally, the first thing you would want to

	1-1-79	1-1-80
RP	125,000	135,000
P/P	30,000	30,000
100 T	5,500	6,000
50 IBM	3,200	5,200
100 WLA	2,100	3,100
200 X	4,300	4,800
Bonds	10,000	10,000
SAV	5,000	5,000
CHK	1,210	1,210
S/L	2,500	2,500
NNA	188,810	202,810
DBTS	12,000	12,000
TOTAL	176,810	190,810
NET CHANGE in BS Dollars		+ 14,000
NET REAL CHANGE in DD dollars		− 10,805

Figure 3.

do would be to make your new Balance Sheet. It would look just like the old one (forgetting the reduction of loan balance and crediting of interest for a moment) except for one thing: Now you have to mark the value of certain of your assets up or down based on the market change.

You call your real estate broker and find that your house is worth $10,000 more than on January 1, 1979. Your stock broker tells you your stocks are worth $4,000 more. You feel $14,000 richer, but you must remember that it is all calculated in BS Dollars. Now the problem is to ascertain how busy the government and bankers have been creating money and credit while you slept and how much of your wealth is BS.

To do this, you pick up the paper and see that the Consumer Price Index has gone up 13% in a year, which means that the dollar will buy 13% less than it did a year earlier. This means that inflation has destroyed 13% of your total wealth. So to factor in the 13% inflation rate, you add your profit ($14,000) to 176,810 (your old total) and get 190,810, then multiply the new total by 13% to get the amount of BS there is in your balance sheet.

$$\frac{\begin{array}{r} 190,810 \\ .13 \end{array}}{24,805}$$

and when you subtract 24,805 from 190,810, you get the DD amount.

$$\frac{\begin{array}{r} 190,810 \\ -24,805 \end{array}}{166,005}$$

Then you calculate the change from the 1–1–79 (176,810) minus the corrected Depreciated Dollar amount:

$$\frac{\begin{array}{r} 176,810 \\ -166,005 \end{array}}{10,805}$$

which shows you that you really ended up losing 10,805 for the year and you feel pretty rotten when you see how your progress has only been in **BS** dollars. More importantly, you now know what really has been happening to you for years, and you feel good anyway because now that you are sophisticated, you realize that ignorance is not bliss, it's suicide.

Glossary

Basis Points Each percentage point of interest is divided into 100 basis points. For example, if interest rates on a bond rise from 10% to 10½%, the yield has gone up 50 basis points.

Big Winners Those who speculate successfully. In the 1930s, this meant selling short or profiting from declines. In the next crisis point it will mean those not only willing to sell short but those willing and able to buy various kinds of options so they may profit by holding in the ensuing run-up in prices.

Deflation Money being worth more.

Depression A severe economic drop caused by disequilibrium in the financial markets. Resulting as it does from financial excesses incurred over a period of time, depression does not lend itself to traditional means of restimulation.

Devaluation Decreasing the value of a currency; e.g., dollars, in terms of gold. It appears that gold has risen suddenly, but in reality paper money declined over a long period of time and gold is just catching up.

Discount Bond A bond issued when interest rates were lower whose price now reflects the higher current interest rate and hence sells lower than its original issuing price. Bonds don't go down to totally reflect the change in interest rates because they are redeemable at a future date at par (100). As that date approaches, the bonds close the gap. These bonds thus usually sell on a yield-to-maturity, not current-yield basis (the predictable increase in price toward 100 as maturity approaches being factored in).

Discount Rate The rate at which the Federal Reserve lends money to the private banks. The banks, in turn, will charge about three to five percentage points more as their prime rate to their best customers.

Disintermediation More money coming out of a financial institution than is going in. The reason for disintermediation is that higher rates for similar risks are available elsewhere.

Economic Cycles Manifestations of the law of action and reaction. Inherent in every action is a force that is set in motion to create an equal and predictable reaction in the opposite direction. This is one of the behavioral laws that accounts for cycles of all kinds throughout nature and guarantees, like the unseen law of gravity, that history revolve around a narrow axis and seemingly repeat itself in a three-dimensional spiraling fashion. If you don't understand this, don't worry. Nobody does.

Economists Complex people living in a simple world—their own.

Faith The act of believing beyond doubt or reason, against all odds.

Federal Reserve Board The governing arm of the Federal Reserve System, created in 1913 to set the monetary policy of the U.S. Actually it was created so all banks could inflate together and trouble in one spot of the balloon could be repaired before it spread to another. In practice it functions more like an Alice in Wonderland Club where old men meet to dream up new ways for banks to clobber consumers, the public, and potential competitors. When it isn't figuring out how many times its member bank deposits can be multiplied to create new credit, it is busy buying government obligations with money it will print to cover the purchase and creating money that way. What is most aggravating is the pompous attitude of intellectual excellence and great wisdom these charlatans assume while doing and saying the most devious and asinine things.

Fiat Money Money created by government edict or law which says that this piece of paper is legal tender or money. When governments have to tell you that it is money—it isn't.

Financial Asset An asset to the buyer (of a bond, for example). A liability to the issuer. Financial institutions—like banks— use a complicated system of accounting whereby their liabilities (to depositors) somehow become their assets (to create credit against).

Financial Net Worth Financial assets minus financial liabilities.

Flower Bonds Bonds selling at a discount that can be used at par (100) to pay off estate taxes, even if purchased shortly before death at a lower price (80 for example).

Fractional Reserve Banking The method used by banks to create money. The way it works? You deposit $1,000 in your bank account. The bank then loans $840 (under current reserve requirements) to a borrower. When the $840 is deposited by the borrower, the bank can loan $700 on it. When the $700 is deposited, the bank can loan another $588, and so on until about $6,000 has been created from your original deposit of $1,000. This happens because reserve requirements are a constant 16%, continuing to interact on a succession of money transfers within a closed system (The Federal Reserve Member banks).

Government Bailout Money extracted from all so that those with the political clout to be subsidized can continue to devote their energies and capital to produce a product that people don't want.

History Prior experience of others gained vicariously for oneself through study.

Hyperinflation An advanced or blow-out stage of a long continuing inflation. The severity cannot be set at any arbitrary
rate, but indicates a rate high enough to cause economic
chaos and suffering, especially when it creates interest rates
that exceed profit margins. This is what brings about a
collapse in the marginal efficiency of capital, bankrupts
businesses and causes unemployment.

Inflation Government producing money more rapidly than a
society can produce goods and services.

Interest Rate Inversion When short-term interest rates exceed
longer term rates.

Less Government What you need if you are to survive.

Leverage A way to increase your profit (or loss) by using borrowed funds. If you make a 50% profit by owning something
outright, you could have made 200% by borrowing half or
50%. You increase your profits, not to 100%, but 200%.

Liquid Asset Something that can be sold quickly without substantial loss.

Liquidity Crisis An economic event characterized by turmoil
in the financial markets precipitated by fear that businessmen and banks will not be able to refinance their short-
term loans as they become due. Such a crisis occurs when
interest rates are already high and sends them higher.

M¹, M², M³ All the various Ms are part of the economists mumbo
jumbo to make sure no one understands enough of what he
is talking about to challenge him. All M^1, M^2, etc., are only
clumsy ways of expressing all the weird kinds of money and
credit that have been invented in a hierarchy of debt. Some
debts are more liquid than others and cash is the most
liquid debt of all. That's all you need to know. Just to make
it clear that the Federal Reserve Board knows no more
about it than you do consider the opening statement of
Monetary Trends published by the FRB of St. Louis on
March 25, 1982: "The monetary aggregates have both increased and decreased markedly during the past nine
months."

Monetize To convert to money. If the U.S. Treasury printed enough money the tidy stack of new dollars can be used to pay its untidy old debt. The debt could then be said to have been monetized, that is, turned into money.

Monetizing the Debt The process whereby government debt is turned into money. Thus a dollar bill becomes an IOU once removed. If you can't figure out what that means, don't despair. What it really means is that after debt is monetized, no one owes anybody anything or has anything of value. This same strange phenomenon happens every year when the government prints money to cover the portion of its debt that it can't sell to others.

Money A call on all salable commodities, labor or things produced that took or will take time, thought and human effort to produce.

Money Supply The amount of money in circulation at a given time. There are several ways to measure it. The simplest is to add checking account funds plus currency held by the public.

Negative Yield Having less (after taxes and inflation) than when you started.

Nominal Rates people think they are receiving as wages or profits or paying as interest or price. Raw figures bandied about to make people feel good by hiding from them the real, or corrected, rate. See *Real Rates*.

Pain Index The rate of inflation added to the rate of unemployment. Used by politicians every four years in their speeches to discredit the incumbent administration.

Panic A sudden financial chaos characterized by a breakdown of the liquidity factor in the economy's credit structure. A panic is the result of long-standing abuses in expanding credit. It serves to puncture the balloons of bungling bankers and businessmen.

Principle of Acceleration Refers to the relationship between remote and near goods. It's based on the idea that a small increase in demand at the consumer level (a sewing machine, for example) gives rise to a much greater (and unsustainable) demand at the capital goods level (the machines necessary to produce the sewing machines).

Profits (Business) The value of production after material costs (including labor costs), taxes, inflation, regulation, depreciation, obsolescence, recession losses, and bankruptcy are subtracted. Historically, around 4% per year.

Profits (Individual) The real profits of business as set forth above minus more taxes, depreciation and living expenses. Historically, nothing.

Protection What you need if government is to survive.

Prudent-Man Rule Investing so carefully that even if the money is lost in an unbelievably stupid way, you won't be criticized.

Real Depreciation The price of replacing a depreciable or wasting asset based on replacement cost (not historical cost, as allowed by the Internal Revenue Code).

Real Rates Rates people are really receiving as wages or profits or paying as interest or price.

Recession A downturn in business—a slowing down to correct excess inventories or manufacturing capacity. The basic underlying consumer demand continues throughout.

Regulation Government agencies recruited by established businesses to protect them from competition to the detriment of the consumer.

Riot Point The point at which people become nasty and physically violent.

Short Selling Usually stocks are bought first and then sold later. When an investor sells short, the process is reversed. You sell first and buy later. Where does the stock come from that you sell in the first place? You borrow it from your broker and replace it (pay him back) when you buy later.

Speculation Buying and selling with a view to profiting from price changes.

Subsidies A way that individual businessmen with political clout use the power of the government to steal from other taxpayers by getting paid more than the market is willing to pay.

Tax-Free Bonds Bonds upon which you pay no federal (and usually no state tax if you are resident of the state where issued). The politicians promise not to steal your money twice to induce you to take even less interest.

Third Stage or Hyperinflation A short-lived third-stage runaway price inflation of the classic kind destroys wealth by transferring a part from those who possess bonds, savings accounts, securities, mortgages and other forms of paper to those who have debts or tangible property. The rest is destroyed completely and disappears through bankruptcy, etc.

Trade-Off The theory is that as inflation (money creation) increases unemployment declines. Conversely, lowering inflation (money contraction) raises unemployment. But in a later stage of inflation, the rise in interest rates caused by money creation itself causes business failures and this increases unemployment.

Wealth What you have that is real that you can use. Adam Smith logically proved that the real wealth of nations or individuals must be measured by the quantity of goods and services that they can command—not the means or monetary unit they use to command it.

Winners Investors who, thinking for themselves, sense that the boom is built on quicksand and sell out before it is too late.

Index

DISCLAIMER

This book is sold with the understanding that neither the author nor the publisher are, in its pages, engaged in rendering legal or investment services. Questions relevant to these areas should be addressed to a member of those professions, or the author should be consulted privately to evaluate your legal or investment problem on an individual basis.

Without such personal knowledge of your financial circumstances or background, it is impossible to offer intelligent advice to you as an individual. Consequently, the author and publisher disclaim any liability, loss, or risk, personal or otherwise, that is incurred as a consequence, directly or indirectly, of the use and application of any of the contents of this work on the reader's own initiative.

The author is available to consult with you on a personal basis, however, to bring his cumulative knowledge and experience gained as a licensed professional in the fields of law, real estate, and stock and commodity trading. The author is also a recognized expert in the field of art and collectibles. If you have further questions, address inquiries to William D. Montapert, P.O. Box 1294, Beverly Hills, California 90213.

ABOUT THE AUTHOR

Educated in Switzerland, Mexico, France, and the U.S., Mr. Montapert graduated magna cum laude and Phi Beta Kappa. After receiving his doctorate of law from the University of Southern California, he was a special postgraduate Fulbright Scholar in law and economics at the University of Paris.

Since 1954 he has been a practicing attorney specializing in real estate investments, tax planning, and money management for a select group of clients.

He is that rare combination of successful man with the highest academic credentials, a man who brings a new dimension of practicality to economic theory and academic excellence to financial writing.

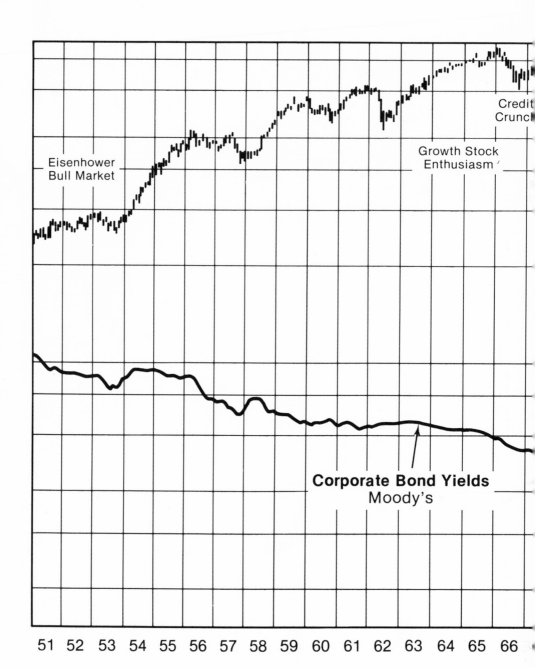

Eisenhower
Bull Market

Growth Stock
Enthusiasm

Credit
Crunch

Corporate Bond Yields
Moody's

51 52 53 54 55 56 57 58 59 60 61 62 63 64 65 66